THE WOUNDED JUNG

Effects

of Jung's

Relationships

on His Life

and Work

The Wounded *Jung*

ROBERT C. SMITH

NORTHWESTERN UNIVERSITY PRESS

Evanston, Illinois

Northwestern University Press
625 Colfax Street
Evanston, Illinois 60208-4210
Copyright © 1996 by Robert C. Smith
All rights reserved
Printed in the United States of America

ISBN 0-8101-1270-1

Library of Congress Cataloging-in-Publication Data
Smith, Robert C.
The wounded Jung : effects of Jung's relationships on his
life and work / Robert C. Smith.
p.   cm. — (Psychosocial issues)
Includes bibliographical references and index.
ISBN 0-8101-1270-1 (alk. paper)
1. Jung, C. G. (Carl Gustav), 1875–1961.
2. Psychoanalysts—Switzerland—Biography.   3. Parent
and child.   4. Freud, Sigmund, 1856–1939.   I. Title.
II. Series.
BF109.J8S65   1996
150.19′54′092—dc20
[B]   95-52247
                                                          CIP

CONTENTS

Jung is a complex personality who wrote in a style that is often esoteric and frequently obscure. Over the years I have found his life and writings a source of both inspiration and exasperation. Nonetheless, his writings repay careful study. Writing this book has been in some respects a humbling experience. It has made me confront the limitations not only of my own knowledge but also of my own discipline, the history and psychology of religion.

I view my efforts here as an attempt to integrate several recent studies on Jung and to begin the task of formulating an interpretive synthesis of his life and contribution. In what follows I will present and consider several issues that have been ignored by most of Jung's biographers. I will focus upon Jung's childhood conflicts and experiences and seek to show how these presaged topics that engaged him throughout his life: healing, creativity, and religious experience.

Robert Barton once stated that we are dwarfs who see further because we stand on the shoulders of giants. I believe Jung was one of the giants of our time, an intuitive genius who saw profoundly into the peculiar spiritual dilemmas of modern man.

A word of thanks is due to the many individuals and institutions who have assisted the research and writing of this book. Their help and encouragement as well as friendly criticisms have improved my efforts in both style and substance.

This study began in a National Endowment for the Humanities Seminar at the University of Chicago under the direction of Peter Homans. Professor Homans encouraged me to deepen and considerably expand what began as a paper for his summer seminar. Additionally, numerous release time grants and a sabbatical leave grant from the Committee on Faculty and Institutional Research at Trenton State College have aided my work. Assisted by an additional Travel to Collections Grant from the National Endowment for the Humanities, I was able to conduct research at the C. G. Jung Institute in Küsnacht during the summer of 1988. The institute invited me to serve as a visiting lecturer and thus offered access to materials that would have been impossible to secure elsewhere.

I also want to thank Dr. Richard J. Wolfe, curator of Rare Books and Manuscripts at the C. G. Jung Archive of the Francis A. Countway Library of Medicine in Boston, for the gracious assistance I received there. Dr. Wolfe and his staff gave me access to invaluable unpublished interview materials in the collection.

My special thanks goes to those who have read the manuscript and offered suggestions for its improvement. They are John Lounibos, Stanley Riukas, Peter Homans, Malcolm Diamond, Peter Hoffer, Kenneth Vos, Gene Thursby, Nelson Evans, Joseph Gorczynski, Daniel Noel, John Haule, Lee Harrod, and Elizabeth Johnson. I am, of course, responsible for the mistakes that remain.

Lastly, I want to thank my wife, Barbara, whose refreshing encouragement and unfailing optimism have been much in evidence throughout.

Grateful acknowledgment is made to the Francis A. Countway Library of Medicine, Boston, for permission to quote short passages from interviews conducted between 1969 and 1972 by Gene F. Nameche with Ruth Bailey, Susanne (Wolff) Trüb, Fowler McCormick, and John Layard, and for access to other unpublished materials in the library's collection.

Grateful acknowledgment is made to Stanley Riukas for permission to quote from his letter of September 18, 1990, to Robert C. Smith.

Grateful acknowledgment is made to the following for permission to reprint previously published material.

Chronology from *C. G. Jung: Word and Image*, edited by Aniela Jaffé. Copyright © 1979 by Princeton University Press. Reprinted by permission of Princeton University Press.

Excerpts from *Memories, Dreams, Reflections*, by C. G. Jung, edited by Aniela Jaffé. Translation copyright © 1961, 1962, 1963, renewed 1989, 1990, 1991 by Random House, Inc. Reprinted by permission of Random House, Inc., and HarperCollins Publishers, Ltd.

Excerpts from Daniel Noel, "Veiled Kabir: C. G. Jung's Phallic Self-Image," in *Spring* (1974): 224–42. Reprinted by permission of the author.

Acknowledgments

CHRONOLOGY OF JUNG'S LIFE *by Aniela Jaffé*

1875

Born July 26 to Johann Paul Achilles Jung (1842–96), then parson at Kesswil, Switzerland, and Emilie Preiswerk Jung (1848–1923).

1879

The family moves to Klein-Hüningen, near Basel.

1895–1900

Assistant physician under Bleuler at the Burghölzli, the mental hospital of Canton Zurich and psychiatric clinic of Zurich University.

1896

Death of father.

1902

M.D. dissertation, "On the Psychology and Pathology of So-called Occult Phenomena." Winter semester (1902–3) with Pierre Janet at the Salpetriere, in Paris, for the study of theoretical psychopathology.

1903

Marriage to Emma Rauschenbach.

1903–5

Experimental researches on word associations and complexes, later associated with archetypes. *Studies in Word Association.*

1905–9

Senior staff physician at the Burghölzli. Conducts policlinical courses on hypnotic therapy. Research on schizophrenia.

1905–13

Lecturer on medical faculty of Zurich University; lectures on psychoneuroses and psychology.

1906

Correspondence with Freud begins.

1907

First meeting with Freud, in Vienna.

1908

First International Psychoanalytic Congress.

1909

First visit to the United States, with Freud and Ferenczi; lectures on association experiment at Clark University, receives honorary LL.D. degree.

1909–13

Editor of *Jahrbuch für psychoanalytische und psychopathologische Forschungen.*

1910

Reading and lectures on mythology, leading to 1911–12 *Wandlungen und Symbole der Libido* (Psychology of the Unconscious, 1916), later revised as *Symbols of Transformation.*

1910–14

First president of the International Psychoanalytic Association.

1912

Another visit to the United States for a series of lectures at Fordham University on the Theory of Psychoanalysis. "New Paths in Psychology," later revised and expanded as "On the Psychology of the Unconscious."

1913

Break with Freud. Fourth International Psychoanalytic Congress, Munich. Jung designates his psychology as "analytical psychology." Resigns lectureship at Zurich University.

1913–19

Period of intense introversion and confrontation with the unconscious.

1916

Septem Sermones ad Mortuos (Seven Sermons to the Dead), text resulting from his encounter with the unconscious. First mandala painting. First description of active imagination in "The Transcendent Function." First use of terms *personal unconscious, collective unconscious, individuation, animus/anima,* and *persona,* in "The Structure of the Unconscious."

1918–19

Medical Corps doctor and commandant of camp for interned British soldiers in Switzerland. First use of the term *archetype* in "Instinct and the Unconscious."

1920

Journey to Algeria and Tunisia. First summer seminar in England, at Cornwall.

1921
   Psychological Types (published in English, 1923); first use of the term *self*.
1923
   First Tower built in Bollingen. Death of mother. Summer seminar at Polzeath, Cornwall, on Technique of Analysis.
1924–25
   Trip to United States; visits Pueblo Indians in New Mexico, also New Orleans and New York.
1925
   First English seminar at the Psychological Club, Zurich.
1925–26
   Trip to Kenya, Uganda, and the Nile; visits with the Elgonyi on Mount Elgon.
1928
   Beginning of encounter with alchemy. *Two Essays on Analytical Psychology*.
1928–30
   English seminars on Dream Analysis at the Psychological Club, Zurich.
1929
   Publication, with commentary, of *The Secret of the Golden Flower*, translated by Richard Wilhelm, an ancient Chinese text on yoga and alchemy.
1930
   Vice-president of General Medical Society for Psychotherapy, under Ernst Kretschmer as president.
1930–34
   English seminars on Interpretations of Visions at the Psychological Club, Zurich.
1932
   Awarded Literature Prize of the City of Zurich.
1933
   Publication of *Modern Man in Search of a Soul*, a widely read introduction to Jung's ideas. Beginning of annual Eranos conferences, where Jung lectured until 1951; first lecture, "A Study in the Process of Individuation."
1934
   Second lecture, "Archetypes of the Collective Unconscious."

1934–39

English seminars on Psychological Aspects of Nietzsche's "Thus Spoke Zarathustra" at the Psychological Club, Zurich. Edited *Zentralblatt für Psychotherapie und ihre Grenzgebiete* (Leipzig).

1935

Appointed titular professor at the Eidgenossiche Technische Hochschule (E.T.H.), Zurich. Presents Tavistock Lectures at the Institute of Medical Psychology, London.

1936

Receives honorary doctorate from Harvard University. Eranos lecture, "Ideas of Redemption in Alchemy," expanded as part 3 of *Psychology and Alchemy*. "Wotan."

1937

Presents Terry Lectures on Psychology and Religion at Yale University.

1938

Invitation to India on the twenty-fifth anniversary of the Indian Science Congress, Calcutta. Honorary doctorates from the Universities of Calcutta, Benares, and Allahabad. International Congress for Psychotherapy at Oxford, with Jung as president. Receives honorary doctorate from Oxford University; appointed Honorable Fellow of the Royal Society of Medicine, London. Eranos lecture, "Psychological Aspects of the Mother Archetype."

1941

With Karl Kerényi, published *Essays on a Science of Mythology*.

1943

Honorable member of the Swiss Academy of Sciences; appointed to the chair of Medical Psychology at Basel University.

1944

Resigns Basel chair on account of critical illness. *Psychology and Alchemy*.

1945

Honorary doctorate from University of Geneva on the occasion of his seventieth birthday. Eranos lecture, "The Psychology of the Spirit," expanded as "The Phenomenology of the Spirit in Fairy Tales."

1946

Eranos lecture, "The Spirit of Psychology." "The Psychology of Transference."

1948

Eranos lecture, "On the Self," expanded to chapter 4 of *Aion*. Inauguration of the C. G. Jung Institute, Zurich, the first training institute for Jungian analysis.

1951

Aion. Jung's last Eranos lecture, "On Synchronicity," expanded as "Synchronicity: An Acausal Connecting Principle."

1952

Symbols of Transformation, fourth revised edition of *Psychology of the Unconscious*. *Answer to Job*.

1953

Publication of the first volume of the American/British edition of the *Collected Works* (translated by R. F. C. Hull). *Psychology and Alchemy*.

1955

Honorary doctorate from the E.T.H., Zurich, on the occasion of his eightieth birthday. Death of his wife, Emma.

1955–56

Mysterium Coniunctionis, the final work on the psychological significance of alchemy.

1957

The Undiscovered Self. Starts work on *Memories, Dreams, Reflections*, with the collaboration of Aniela Jaffé (published 1961). BBC television interview.

1958

"Flying Saucers: A Modern Myth."

1960

Made Honorary Citizen of Küsnacht on the occasion of his eighty-fifth birthday.

1961

Finishes his last work ten days before his death: "Approaching the Unconscious," published in 1964 in *Man and His Symbols*. Dies after short illness on June 6 in his home at Küsnacht.

THE WOUNDED JUNG

The inward journeys of the
mythological hero . . .
are in principle the same.
—*Joseph Campbell,* Myths to Live By

Inasmuch as you attain to the numinous
experiences you are released from the curse
of pathology.
—*C. G. Jung,* Letters

Introduction

The Wounded Jung explores the life and writings of the
celebrated psychiatrist of Küsnacht, Switzerland, Carl Gustav Jung.
Jung is of central importance in the recovery of the spiritual quest for
healing and wholeness and in the formulation of an intimate connection between psychology and religion. This study shows that Jung
was an intuitive giant who profoundly saw into the peculiar spiritual
dilemmas of modern man. It demonstrates how Jung's interest in the
healing of the psyche was unmistakably rooted in the conflicts with a
troubled father and a mentally ill mother in his own childhood. Since
Jung himself was in many ways a divided self, his real life story illustrates the maxim "Physician, heal thyself."

This book presents Jung as a wounded healer who, because he confronted throughout his life the divided parts of his own psyche, was enabled to become a healer of others. It shows how Jung's own life experience led to his intense interest in confrontation with the unconscious, the creative exploration of religious images, myth and symbol, philosophy and literature, in the process of "soul making."

The central theme of this book, briefly stated, is that because of his "wounded" childhood, Jung was to embark, even as a child, on ways to integrate his life. As he candidly states in his autobiography, he possessed a dual personality, like his mother. Through a host of creative and imaginative means such as attention to dreams, fantasies, and later what he was to call active imagination, he was to find the key to effective utilization of his unconscious processes. That is to say, over a span of years Jung was to confront creatively and to a significant degree to overcome his personal pathology. Over time, amid numerous rationalizations and obscurities that can be found in his theoretical works, he acquired insight and, albeit through pain, became an integrated person. Only toward the end of his life, however, in *Answer to Job* and in his autobiography, did he effectively confront, still in a somewhat disguised and selective way, the effects of his childhood trauma. At long last Jung had achieved a measure of gnosis and, as D. W. Winnicott has put it, achieved exceptional "insight into the feelings of those who are inwardly split" (Winnicott review 450).

In *Memories, Dreams, Reflections*, Jung devotes several chapters to the importance of what he terms Personalities No. 1 and No. 2 in his formative experience. One of my hypotheses is that the dissonance in Jung's personality was a primary impetus in the innumerable new connections he made between psychology, mythology, and world religions. He had experienced a difficult childhood, and for this reason he was what Michael Whan has called a wounded healer (197). His intuitive insights, expressed in a rather abstract writing style, reflect the close touch he had with his unconscious. He focused upon the modes that effect the inner transformation of the individual. For instance, when his close friend Richard Wilhelm returned from China with firsthand material on Chinese alchemy, what interested Jung was the similarity between Chinese and Western archetypal modes of transformation.

According to Gerhard Adler, in Jung's therapy with patients he was more interested in fostering healing, bringing the person into contact with the numinous or the dimension of otherness, than he was in "curing" neuroses. Process more than effect held the fascination. Jung himself put this very succinctly in 1945 when he wrote to P. W. Martin: "The fact is that the approach to the numinous is the real therapy and inasmuch as you attain to the numinous experiences you are released from the curse of pathology" (Jung, *Letters* 1:377).

In the scholarly literature, interpreters still disagree whether Jung's father or his mother was for him the central figure. Some, like Murray Stein in his article "The Significance of Jung's Father in His Destiny as a Therapist of Christianity" and in his book *Jung's Treatment of Christianity*, have stressed the role of the father. My view is that Jung's mother played a more formative role in his childhood than did his father. Clearly, both parents had positive and negative effects upon Jung. From each the negative effects predominated and set an agenda that was to engage him thoughout his life. His mother in particular was an extremely flawed and divided personality. I will maintain that his mother's No. 1 and No. 2 Personalities are the underlying source of his own inner rift.

At least some of the time, Jung's mother was a figure of power for him in growing up. She was the more influential parental figure, and her presence or absence profoundly affected him. Jung experienced her absence from the home when he was three as abandonment. Unpublished materials at the Francis A. Countway Library of Medicine in Boston confirm the fact of his mother's mental illness. Her absence, for hospitalization, at a crucial time in his personal development became one of his most formative early experiences. His stress upon the dreaded anima stemmed from her. Jung himself said that his father was reliable but powerless (*Memories* 8). As I shall attempt to demonstrate in what follows, both of his parents were to play vital roles in shaping his life and work, with his mother being in several respects the more important figure.

Some interpreters, including several psychoanalysts, such as John Gedo, Harry Slochower, Leonard Shengold, Edwin Wallace, and Eli Marcovitz, have focused upon Jung's childhood conflicts and the trauma of a sexual assault by an older man whom Jung says he worshiped. Other interpreters, such as Anthony Storr, D. W. Winnicott, and Jeffrey Satinover, have stressed the central role of Jung's mother in his personality development. She, like Jung himself, possessed two personalities—a day personality and a night personality. One was grounded in everyday experience, and the other in the archaic wisdom of the centuries. Like Jung himself, she was interested in both the temporal and the eternal, the personal and the collective. I shall try to explore and extend the implications of this line of investigation, which I find to be especially productive.

Jung Scholarship

In recent years much new data have become available on the lives of Freud and Jung. In the case of Jung, we have his memoirs, *Memories, Dreams, Reflections*, *The Freud-Jung Letters*, and the letters from 1906 to 1961 to add to his voluminous *Collected Works*. Many other documents from Jung's life exist but are not available. For instance, only the tiniest fragments from his visionary diaries *The Red Book* and *The Black Book* have been made public. The full texts are still withheld from scholarly scrutiny by Jung's heirs, because of their "private nature," according to Aniela Jaffé ("Creative Phases" 174). Various letters and documents are also still confined to the Jung family safe. These include Jung's important letter to Sabina Spielrein, written at a time of his personal involvement with her. I hope these will one day be released. A raft of biographies has appeared in the past two decades, but in my view this fairly extensive literature is less than compelling in many respects. Several of the biographies contradict one another on crucial points of interpretation. Even the more sustainable interpretations are deficient on many details of Jung's life. Most interpreters agree that it will be at least another thirty years before the definitive biography of Jung can be written.

Jung's intense personal crises, his relationships with women (hardly mentioned in *Memories, Dreams, Reflections*), interpretations of his correspondence with Freud and a host of others, his visions and fantasies, and his stature as a psychotherapist, cult figure, and religious guru are all under scrutiny. The task of sorting out the material available is not helped by the fact that Jung himself offers us a strange mixture of refreshing candor and evasiveness to the point of presenting a stylized, if not distorted, image of himself.

The provisional state of information on Jung became apparent to me while reading transcripts of interviews with people familiar with the personal details of his life. From 1969 through 1972 Gene F. Nameche conducted 143 lengthy interviews, several of them multiple interviews, with a veritable who's who of persons who worked with and knew Jung intimately. These interviews are located at the C. G. Jung Oral History Archive at the Countway Library. All of the interviews conducted by Dr. Nameche were automatically restricted for ten years, even to qualified scholars. Twenty-one of these interviews are still restricted and will be for as much as another thirty years. Until these materials and those held by Jung's heirs are released and studied by scholars, it will not be possible to form definitive conclusions. We are reminded again that in *Memories* Jung revealed so much, yet so little!

For the time being we have nothing even approximating an authoritative biography of Jung. Members of Jung's family are said to like the volume by Gerhard Wehr, *Jung: A Biography*, but I believe it only perpetuates the romantic myth that Jung is a spiritual hero. Thomas W. Moore wrote in the *New York Times Book Review* that "it is comprehensive, well written and superbly translated. Unlike previous biographies, it avoids psychoanalytic partisanship, but when Mr. Wehr leaves the safe path of factual detail for interpretation, problems appear" (22).

In some ways it is impossible to assess Jung's career fully until more has been disclosed. Paradoxes abound. Jung's autobiography, *Memories, Dreams, Reflections*, is a remarkable book, reluctantly written as a capstone to his life's experience. It shows that he believed that his life was outwardly uneventful, though his accounts of his trips to distant places around the world, as to his beloved Bollingen, have enchanted the world. The heart of his life experience as he saw it consisted of inwardness, of dreams and visions.

The Task Begun in Memories

Memories, Dreams, Reflections is a painfully inward memoir and discloses Jung's inner feelings and images to the neglect of his interpersonal relations. For instance, his wife, Emma, is hardly mentioned, and there is no mention at all of Toni Wolff.[1] In several ways the book presents a stylized version of Jung's life. Paradoxically, it both reveals and conceals much at the same time. Jung was both a public and a very private man. As a youth he loved solitude and kept many secrets from parents, friends, and associates, so it is not surprising that the same tendency is followed in his autobiography, written very late in life when selective memory had become a factor. Much of what was disclosed in his 1961 autobiography came as a shock to those who knew him. From his erudite books one would never have been led to suspect what he revealed.

Jung once asked himself: What myth do you live by? He replied that he was no longer able to live by the traditional Christian myth and would seek for a myth true to his inner experience. To his credit, he possessed a nonconventional form of spirituality and embarked on a nonconventional quest for meanings in life. To a large degree, however, Jung himself has become a powerful myth for many persons. There is recognizable need for Jung's interpreters to embark upon a new quest for the historical rather than the mythical Jung. Some have so "spiritualized" Jung that they have made him into a cultural hero, mythologized beyond all recognition.

In *Memories* Jung clearly views himself as "the wise old man" (181). This Philemon image, which evolves out of an Elijah image, is for him an inner guide. It affords insight into the world of inner processes while devaluing those of the interpersonal realm. For the most part, however, the significant events evoking childhood feelings toward his parents are there for us to reflect upon. Some, such as the man-eater dream (*Memories* 12), had been kept as lifelong secrets. Apart from some reminiscences of his father, with whom he never formed a strong positive identification, and his recollections of Freud (a flawed father figure), he does not discuss important relationships with men. Eugen Bleuler, his former chief at the Burghölzli, is only mentioned once in passing and then in a late chapter on travels. Women, we know, were terribly important to Jung. He once stated that he wanted to be remembered as a man who was a great lover.[2] One would never guess this from reading his autobiography. Clearly, inner events were more important than external ones for him. But why must his reader be kept in the dark concerning so many of his relationships?

In a sense, Jung's life belongs to the public domain, for to a certain extent modern life reflects his vision of a person's quest for integration, the search for individuation, civilization in transition, and similar themes. In "The Spiritual Problem of Modern Man" he wrote: "Modern man is an entirely new phenomenon. . . . He is rather the man who stands upon a peak, or at the very edge of the world, the abyss of the future before him, above him the heavens, and below him the whole of mankind with a history that disappears in the primeval mists. The modern man—or, let us say again, the man of the immediate present—is rarely met with, for he must be conscious to a superlative degree. . . . He alone is modern who is fully conscious of the present" (*Collected Works* 10:74-75; hereinafter *CW*).

To the extent that Jung's vision was shaped by the events of his life, it is important, even crucial, that we understand the life forces that shaped those events. Perhaps by intention, the man and the myth that he and his followers presented are inextricably braided together. Both need to be seen and distinguished clearly. The question arises: Why did Jung reveal his inner feelings only to conceal the relationships that were so intimately related to those feelings? We cannot respond with certainty at this point, but it is important that eventually the full story be told. At present, the man and his myth are still so intimately intertwined that it is in everyone's interest that interpretations—partial portraits though they be—continue in the effort to correct one another.

The great man had a dark side, and that story too must be told. At times he was excessively aggressive to the point of abrasiveness. Sometimes he was angry, even enraged. At still other times he was known to be extremely competitive, especially in his relationship with Freud. My own correspondence with Jung in 1960 convinced me that far from being a plaster saint, he was, in Nietzsche's words, "human, all too human." At a time when Jung's life and works have been overly romanticized, there is a particular need to insist that the story of the actual man be revealed.

While working on my doctoral dissertation on Carl Jung and Martin Buber, I wrote to both men about their controversy over the eclipse of the divine, in the hope that some further clarification could be achieved concerning their disagreement in the German journal *Merkur*. Though both were advanced in years, they graciously answered my queries. However, when I asked Jung if he was a "modern gnostic," he took particular offense. I expected he would be objective and not take these issues personally. I was surprised to learn that in spite of outward appearances, he could be quite sensitive and excessively involved in defending what he had written. Only much later did I learn that the academic establishment had opposed his ideas throughout his life. In one of his letters to me, replying to my query asking whether he was a monologist, he likened himself in a rather strange way to John the Baptist, as one crying in the wilderness (Jung, *Letters* 2:571).

Theoretical interpretations from Freudian and Jungian perspectives still differ, and no doubt such differences will persist. Concerning Jung's personality structure and his basic conflicts and their resolution, however, the distance is beginning to narrow. One question that still exists is whether Jung was a dissident (Ernest Jones and Henri Ellenberger) or an originator from the start (the view of Marie-Louise von Franz). These are the orthodox extremes, and most investigators tend toward a middle view.

My own judgment is that errors exist on both sides of psychology's great chasm. Certainly Freud was incorrect when he perceived Jung to be a gentile Christian who would save psychoanalysis from its Jewish sectarianism. A pastor's son does not automatically proceed from the same psychic assumptions as did his father. Jung didn't. This is especially true when the father is unhappy and disillusioned with his vocation. It is by no means unusual for such a son to go to an opposite extreme in the search for his values. Jung himself frequently stated that it is the fate of children to live out the unlived and neglected side of their parents' lives. This truth pertaining to perceived and actual psychic deflation or inflation became a central issue in his therapeutic method, which sought to restore a sense of psychic balance he was to term the *coincidentia oppositorum*.

Preview

In my research for this book, my main task was to investigate the connection between Jung's inner conflicts begun in childhood that continued into his mature years and the psychological, religious, and creative themes of his life. Part I deals with Jung's formative and transformative life experiences. In the early chapters I will examine Jung's relationships with his mother and his father (chapters 1 and 2), reflect upon several recent interpretations of his life, and offer interpretations of my own.

Chapter 3 discusses the evidence of Jung's inner conflicts and creativity in his relationship with Freud. When Jung was amiable with Freud, Jung's own creativity was relatively quiescent. Its emergence toward the end of the relation, with his writing of *Symbols of Transfor-*

mation, made the split with Freud inevitable. Their relationship ended abruptly when each man's unconscious needs asserted themselves.

Chapter 4 explores Jung's descent into the unconscious. This period was initially devastating for Jung. Later he patiently worked through the emergence of disorienting forces. This creative encounter with the explosive forces of the unconscious was to enable Jung, over time, to recover his equilibrium and to produce some of his most original and creative work. Here data from Jung's 1925 Seminar Notes are considered. In these notes he mentions several items of importance that are omitted from his autobiography. Jung's use of visionary exploration through such means as journal keeping, sand and oil painting, and active imagination allowed him eventually to come to terms with his unconscious and to resume an active and productive life.

Chapter 5 focuses on Jung's personal relationships with women, a subject almost totally absent from his autobiography. His relationship with his wife, Emma, is considered, as well as his long and personally valuable relation with Toni Wolff. Following recent object relation theory, I will attempt to interpret the role of the feminine in his mature experience.

Part II will demonstrate Jung's lifelong exploration of a vision of life that largely reflected his own experience. His intellectual mentors—Goethe, Schopenhauer, and Nietzsche—were divided selves, in many ways like himself. In ways reminiscent of the shamans of archaic society, he perceived and experienced many of the mental upheavals of modern man in search of a soul. To his credit, he both perceived and responded to the profound shift in sensibilities in modern times. Thus, he was to explore the parameters of a vision of inner healing or transformation that became a mode of therapy both for himself and for others. Part II discusses the ways Jung's personal experience can be understood through his study of romantic literature and philosophy, his reassessment of religion as inner process as well as his fascination with gnosticism and alchemy, his reinterpretation of evil as a process to be integrated into human existence, and his attention to psychology as myth and the realization of selfhood.

Chapter 6 analyzes Jung's interest in and use of Goethe, Schopenhauer, and Nietzsche. Interestingly, these figures, to whom he was especially drawn, experienced the world much as he did. Intuitively his method fostered visionary insight and inner illumination. Jung wanted to find meaning in an individual life. More than almost any other psychiatrist or philosopher, he explored and exposited both philosophical and religious meaning throughout his writings. His was not a purely detached quest for knowledge but one based upon a life-long need to heal an inner rift.

Chapter 7 examines the factors that determined his views on religion. Religion was for Jung the intuitive psychotherapy of the ages. He was of two minds about religion. His investigations of the archaic dimensions of religion—shamanism, gnosticism, and the experience of the numinous—reflect a fruitful reliving and transforming of childhood trauma.

Chapter 8 deals with the importance of myth for Jung. Some might say that myth became a lifelong preoccupation for him. Here I argue that his views on this topic need to be related to his childhood experience. None of the many books on Jung do this satisfactorily. By nurturing the unconscious, I assert, he gained insight into the nature of inner division (now commonly known as splitting) and thereby eventually achieved self-integration. Thus, Jung's inner experiences were to determine the shape and direction of his creative explorations to a considerable degree.

Chapter 9 is a discussion of the ways in which Jung fostered a creative encounter with the forces of the unconscious. Freud's and Jung's conceptions of creativity are considered, as well as the difference between psychological and visionary creativity. Jung was a "wounded healer" who was able to tap the numinous dimension of human experience in ways that few pioneers of the psyche have been able to do. The process of symbolization became for Jung a means of creativity, inner healing, and integration.

A short postscript summarizes the book's findings and ties together several of the themes that run throughout the text. A glossary is appended to assist those who may be unfamiliar with some of the terms used by Jung and Jungian specialists.

Jung's life and work are inextricably bound up with the problems and crises of modern consciousness that are deservedly given so much attention by thoughtful persons today. He was a thoroughly modern man, but one who was concerned with those processes that further the therapeutic dimension of consciousness in an age in which the dark shadow of nihilism drew near for many.

PART ONE

Formative & Transformative Life Experiences

There are powerful forces in whose grip
mankind is helpless.
—E. R. Dodds, The Greeks and the Irrational

In the adult, there is hidden a child—an eternal child,
something that is always becoming, is never completed,
and that calls for unceasing care, attention, and fostering.
This is the part of the personality that wishes to develop
and complete itself. But the human being of our time is
as far from completion as heaven is from earth.
—C. G. Jung, Psychological Reflections

CHAPTER **I**

Mother No. 1 & Mother No. 2

Carl Jung was born in July 1875 in Kesswil, Switzerland. Kesswil is a small village near Romanshorn on Lake Constance in eastern Switzerland and part of Canton Thurgau. His parents had come from Basel; thus the members of Jung's family were known as Baslers. Six months after Jung's birth, his parents moved a short distance to Laufen in Canton Zurich. Later still they moved to the village of Klein-Hüningen, near Basel.

His father, Johann Paul Achilles Jung (1842–96), was a Protestant pastor. He had been trained as a philologist at the university but had been unable to secure an academic position. Hence he became the minister to a series of small country parishes. Living in drafty parsonages made an indelible mark on the younger Jung's life. When Jung was exploring the possibilities for a vocation, his father said, "Be anything you like except a theologian" (*Memories* 75). The senior Jung desired something better for his son than he had for himself.

Jung's mother, Emilie Preiswerk Jung (1848-1923), was born in Basel and came from a long and distinguished line of Protestant clergy. She was the youngest daughter of the famed antistes of Basel, Samuel Preiswerk (1799-1871). (In the Swiss Reformed Church the antistes functioned as an authoritative leader of the parish.) Her mother, Augusta Faber, was descended from French Protestants. Emilie's father was first a pastor in Muttenz and later taught Hebrew and Old Testament in a theological seminary. He was recognized as a celebrated scholar on biblical matters and authored a text on Hebrew grammar. Carl Jung's father met his future wife in the home of Samuel Preiswerk while pursuing his own interest in Hebrew grammar.

Aniela Jaffé recites an anecdote describing how Jung's grandfather Samuel Preiswerk reserved a special chair in his study for the ghost of his deceased first wife, Magdalene. Each week he would hold intimate conversations with the ghost of Magdalene, to the dismay and distress of his second wife, Augusta. Pastor Preiswerk, though he was a highly learned man, gifted in writing poetry, believed he was constantly surrounded by ghosts. Jung explained that his mother sat behind her father when he wrote his sermons, presumably to frighten away the ghosts. "He could not bear the thought of ghosts passing behind his back and disturbing him while he studied. If a living person sat behind him, he believed the ghosts were frightened away" (cited in Jaffé, "Details" 40). Samuel Preiswerk, then, was a visionary given to "conversations with spirits" (A. Oeri, cited in G. Wehr 17). Jung's maternal grandmother, Augusta, was also thought to be endowed with extrasensory perception. In fact, on both his mother's and his father's sides, Jung's family was steeped in beliefs concerning the power and influence of supernatural forces. Jung's mother especially, as we will see, continued in the visionary tradition of her forebears. Growing up, and even in later years, Jung himself was to take his own particular stance with regard to voices, visions, and the belief in spirit power that had been part of his family's perceptions for generations.

Recent scholarship has focused in a variety of ways upon what can be learned of Jung's childhood experience. The main source of in-

Formative & Transformative Life Experiences

formation on his life has been his autobiography, *Memories, Dreams, Reflections.* In many ways it is a remarkable book, for in the process of writing *Memories* Jung experienced "long-submerged images of childhood" (vi). It especially reflects his inner feelings and plays down his interpersonal relations, which in his view were hardly worth recounting.

Memories itself leaves much room for analysis and interpretation. Jung frequently expressed his distaste for exposing his life to public view, but in old age he reluctantly agreed to write his life story. Between 1957 and 1961 he wrote the early chapters and dictated the later chapters to his secretary, Aniela Jaffé. As in all autobiographies, selective memory affected Jung's narrative. That is to say, Jung emphasized precisely what fit into the image of his life he wanted to convey. In addition, the manuscript was further edited at the behest of family members who wanted certain elements toned down and others eliminated.

Jung was a solitary and unhappy youth given to periods of fitful introspection and private rituals that provided him with solace. His parents' marriage was an unhappy affair marked by prolonged separations and periodic mental illness. Clearly Jung's childhood was a critical period of intense inner conflict that persisted in some ways throughout his life. Several independent but convergent lines of investigation largely agree on the general picture of the conflicts that Jung encountered. My task will be to focus upon and draw out the main lines of Jung's primary relationships in the formative period of his life. I will argue that Jung was a "wounded healer" whose explorations into the psyche were part of his creative effort to find wholeness and integration.

Jung's Distrust of a Twofold Mother

In an abbreviated account of Jung's life, Anthony Storr has called attention to the way in which Jung was mother-oriented: "Jung's mother is described by him as problematical, and also inconsistent, in that she sometimes expressed conventional opinions which another, unconventional part of herself proceeded to contradict; so that the boy early recognized that she did not always say what she really meant, and thus was a divided person" (*C. G. Jung*, 2). Storr's point is that Jung developed an ambivalent attitude toward his mother. She embodied the images of woman as devourer and destroyer as well as protector. This internalized ambivalence provided the basis for a deep distrust of women in general. We shall see that in his youth Jung was greatly occupied with the task of extricating himself from the untoward influence of his own mother.

For Jung the central figure of his formative experience was indeed the mother. Jung himself says: "She always seemed to me the stronger of the two" (*Memories* 25). If his perception is accurate, we need to be very clear about what kind of mother Emilie was. In this respect *Memories* could not be clearer in its broad brush strokes. Jung presents the reader with several examples of his mother's twofold nature. He writes:

> There was an enormous difference between my mother's two personalities. That was why as a child I often had anxiety dreams about her. By day she was a loving mother, but at night she seemed uncanny. Then she was like one of those seers who is at the same time a strange animal, like a priestess in a bear's cave. Archaic and ruthless; ruthless as truth and nature. At such moments she was the embodiment of what I have called the "natural mind." I, too, have this archaic nature, and in me it is linked with the gift—not always pleasant—of seeing people and things as they are. (50)

Jung tells us that in many respects his mother was very good to him. She embodied a sense of charm and magnetism, was a marvelous cook, and provided an enjoyable ambience in the home. He describes her as a portly person in her mature years, both a good listener and an engaging conversationalist: "Her chatter was like the gay plashing of a fountain. . . . She held all the conventional opinions a person was obliged to have, but then her unconscious personality would suddenly put in an appearance. That personality was unexpectedly powerful: a somber, imposing figure possessed of unassailable authority—and no bones about it" (48). He continues: "I was sure that she consisted of two personalities, one innocuous and human, the other uncanny. The other emerged only now and then, but each time it was unexpected and frightening. She would then speak as if talking to herself, but what she said was aimed at me and usually struck to the core of my being, so that I was stunned into silence" (49).

Or again "there came moments when her second personality burst

Formative & Transformative Life Experiences

forth, and what she said on those occasions was so true and to the point that I trembled before it" (52). Jung's mother's personality was marked by a profound dichotomy. He recognized that she did not always say what she really meant and was a divided person. What Jung himself did not openly acknowledge or emphasize is that it was precisely this ambivalence and inner inconsistency that he himself came to internalize. Numerous interpreters of Jung, preoccupied with his esoteric symbolism, abstract archetypal formulations, and theoretical conjectures, have overlooked this most important point.

Jung tells us that his parents did not communicate very well with each other, and like many in a religious vocation they exhibited a public demeanor far different from the bad temper frequently shown at home. Jung writes: "My mother usually assumed I was mentally far beyond my age, and she would talk to me as a grown-up. It was plain to see that she was telling me everything she could not say to my father, for she early made me her confidant and confided her troubles to me" (51–52). Paul Stern has written: "The figure of the mother would undoubtedly have appeared less demonic to the boy if her energies, languishing in her marriage, had not focused too exclusively on him, her oldest surviving—and for nine years, her only—child" (25).

Maternal Absence Experienced as Abandonment

In *Memories* Jung refers to dim intimations of trouble in his parents' marriage that hovered around him (8). Difficulties in the marriage are only part of the matter. His mother's hospitalization for several months in 1878, when he was three years of age, was to affect him profoundly. He felt abandoned. This was also the beginning of an "anima" projection upon a dark-haired maid who cared for him during his mother's absence.

In the first draft of *Memories,* with its penciled and penned additions and deletions, Jung indicated some of the circumstances surrounding his mother's hospitalization in Basel. He explained that she was hysterical from disappointment with her husband, whose life took a turn for the worse after his final examinations at the University. In the original version of his autobiography, Jung had included even more details of his mother's mental aberrations, but other family members, fearing these would tarnish the family image, insisted that they be removed.[1] A crucial sentence that was omitted stated that his mother only recovered her health after his father passed away.[2] (By that time Jung was twenty-one years of age.)

During the period of his mother's absence he developed somatic problems, such as a case of generalized eczema. Jung writes: "My illness, in 1878, must have been connected with a temporary separation of my parents. My mother spent several months in a hospital in Basel. . . . An aunt of mine, who was a spinster and some twenty years older than my mother, took care of me. I was deeply troubled by my mother's being away. From then on, I always felt mistrustful when the word 'love' was spoken." (In a sentence edited out of the final version of *Memories*, Jung spoke of fearing still another separation from his mother.) Here we have a key to understanding his core personality: "The feeling I associated with 'woman' was for a long time that of innate unreliability. 'Father,' on the other hand, meant reliability but powerlessness" (*Memories* 8).

Jung candidly tells us that the play and counterplay between what he terms his own Personalities No. 1 and No. 2 ran throughout his entire lifetime (45). He insists that his experience of dual personalities has nothing to do with a split or dissociation in the ordinary medical sense. But is he to be taken seriously in this regard? Quite amazingly, he argues that this same phenomenon is played out in the life of every individual. This shows, I think, how conditioned he was by his own unique childhood experiences. He assumed that others shared his experiences.

Jung explains to the reader of *Memories* that his No. 1 Personality gave him a place in time, but that Personality No. 2 provided a sense of the imperishable, of peace and solitude, and was of supreme importance. In his view this latter personality is what related him to the eternal and archetypal dimension of existence. Jung confesses: "Somewhere deep in the background I always knew that I was two persons. One was the son of my parents, who went to school and was less intelligent, attentive, hardworking, decent and clean than many other boys. The other was grown up—old, in fact—skeptical, mistrustful, remote from the world of men but close to nature . . . and above all close to the night, to dreams, and to whatever 'God' worked directly in him" (44-45). Again we are made to understand that his No. 1 Personality was the schoolboy of 1890. "Besides his world there

Formative & Transformative Life Experiences

existed another realm" where lived the "Other," who knew the divine as a hidden, personal, and at the same time suprapersonal secret (45).

Much in Jung's account of his childhood reappears indirectly in his theories. His extreme loneliness surfaces as introversion. His early interest in secrets becomes a lifelong fascination with spirit power. His identification with his mother permits an unusual attention to archetypal dreams and the fantasy life. Many of these form the basis of his later teachings, almost unique in the history of psychology but quite pertinent to the study of mystical religious phenomena. For Jung, the reappropriation of the maternal was linked to the expression of the creative.

Achieving psychic security became a first priority for Jung as a youth, since he needed to deal with his mother's unreliability and changing moods. One of the ways he did this was through private rituals that he thought would effect magical results. These dramatic enactments certainly compensated for feelings of isolation and inadequacy. At times he would make a fire in the garden and establish a particular and unique relationship with it. For instance, in the interstices of the wall surrounding the family garden Jung would tend a little fire with the assistance of other children. Jung seems to have played a central role in the childhood ritual of fire building, directing his peers in their assigned roles. His fire was maintained by united efforts of wood gathering. But he insisted that he was the only one allowed to tend this particular fire. Others could tend other fires, but these were "profane," whereas his fire was sacred and living (*Memories* 20). His imagination led him to engage in a visionary experience with the fire so that it would "burn forever." Doubtless this ritual gave him enhanced social status among his peers, a sense of self-importance, and a sense of unity with nature.

Or again he would sit on a stone in the garden and wonder: "Am I the one who is sitting on the stone, or am I the stone on which *he* is sitting?" (*Memories* 20) These statements have parallels in the history of religious philosophy. For instance, there is Chuang-tzu's puzzlement about whether he was a man dreaming he was a butterfly or a butterfly dreaming he was a man. The curious ambivalence of what is Self and what is Other in Jung's childhood stems from the inner need for security in an alien and aloof environment.

It is significant that Jung himself relates these rituals to an inner split and mentions that cherishing his secret relationship with these objects offered him much security. Years later at his Bollingen retreat, Jung would, upon arising, customarily greet and talk with the utensils by which he cooked his meals over an open fire.[3] He referred to them as his "friends."

Winnicott's Interpretation of Jung's Childhood

One of the most discerning and provocative lines of analysis of Jung's childhood is to be found in D. W. Winnicott's brief review of *Memories* that appeared in the *International Journal of Psychoanalysis* in 1964. As a pediatrician turned psychoanalyst, Winnicott devotes himself entirely to the first 115 pages of *Memories*, which he asserts are genuine autobiography and should be required reading for all psychoanalysts. Winnicott states that

> Jung in describing himself, gives us a picture of childhood schizophrenia, and at the same time his personality displays a strength of a kind which enabled him to heal himself. *At cost he recovered, and part of the cost to him is what he paid out to us, if we can listen and hear, in terms of his exceptional insight. Insight into the feelings of those who are mentally split.* I must ask the reader at this stage to understand that I am not running down Jung by labeling him a "recovered case of infantile psychosis." (450; emphasis added)

Winnicott claims that Jung's psychic illness and the defenses that were to serve him so well were established by the age of four. From extensive experience as a psychoanalyst and from a close reading of *Memories*, he maps out Jung's childhood illness as follows: healthy potential but an infancy disturbed by maternal depression. This was counteracted by his father's motherliness. By the time Jung was four years of age, the main defensive organization of the personality was in place (452).

Winnicott indicates that Jung's personality defenses include the emergence of a secret True Self (termed by Jung Personality No. 2) and the False Self (according to Jung's usage, Personality No. 1). Finally, the forging of a lifework proceeds out of this defense organization, along with a permanent tendency to heal the split. Throughout his writings Winnicott uses the concept of a True and a False Self to refer to a split that originated in a failed relationship, in flawed bonding between mother and infant in the earliest stages.

Given a general formulation of psychoanalytic theory and the circumstances of Jung's childhood, several points emerge. To paraphrase and to some degree extend Winnicott's line of reasoning:

1) Jung spent his life looking for his own self, which he never really found, since he remained to some extent split (except insofar as this split was healed in his work on his autobiography). He spent his life looking for a place to keep his inner psychic reality, although the task was an impossible one. By the age of four he had incorporated into his psyche the sophisticated and frightening concept of the underground man-eater dream, closely associated in his case with the burial of the dead. In Winnicott's words, "He went down under and found subjective life" (453).

2) At the same time Jung became a withdrawn person. From this developed his exploration of the unconscious, and his concept of the collective unconscious was part of his attempt to deal with his lack of contact with what could now be called the unconscious according to Freud. This gives the idea of Jung's work being out of touch with instinct and object relations except in a subjective sense.

3) Jung's extroverted False Self (No. 1) gave him a place in the world and a rich family and professional life, but Jung makes no bones about his preference for his True Self (No. 2), which for him carried the sense of the real.

4) It is not possible to conceive of a repressed unconscious with a split mind; instead, what is found is dissociation. The only place for Jung's unconscious in the Freudian sense would be in his secret True Self.

5) Jung was threatened by an ego disintegration (a depersonalization), a reversal of the maturational processes settled down into a splitting of the personality, related on one level to the parental separation.

6) There is, according to Winnicott, evidence of maternal depression that affected Jung's infancy and provided the negative for the positive qualities that he projected onto the landscape, onto things, and onto the world.

7) For Jung there is no evidence of a direct clash with the father in extrovert living. Jung's father became the reliable but powerless mother figure in his life.

8) Whatever Freud was, he had a unitary personality. Jung was different. He knew truths that are unavailable to most men and women. Jung was especially concerned with intuitive and mystical ways of knowing that are inaccessible to many.

9) In old age he appears to have dropped his No. 1 Personality to a large extent and to have lived by his True Self. This observation is substantiated by Jung's autobiography, where in later years the persona is dropped. He gave thorough attention to issues of the second half of life, such as developing a religious attitude, meditation, solitude, and death. He especially enjoyed the solitude afforded by Bollingen, where he had the opportunity to think through so many of his creative ideas.

An increasing number of psychiatrists from differing perspectives seem to concur with the main thrust of Winnicott's analysis of Jung as a recovered split personality. These include Joseph Wheelwright, John W. Perry, Jeffrey Satinover, Michael Fordham, and John Gedo —all highly respected therapists. As Peter Homans puts it, "One might expect that on this point, more than any other, Freudians and Jungians would find ample reason to disagree; but such is not the case" (*Jung in Context* 87). For instance, Fordham, a British therapist, tells of Jung's asking him what he thought after he had read the first draft of the childhood chapters of the autobiography. Fordham replied that Jung had been "a schizophrenic child, with strong obsessional defenses, and that had he been brought to me I should have said the prognosis was good, but that I should have recommended analysis—He did not contest my blunt statement" ("Memories and Thoughts" 109).

As I am not a psychiatrist, my own concern is not that of identifying and diagnosing Jung's childhood psychopathology. Rather, I hope to achieve a clearer focus on Jung's primary parental relationships and their impact upon his writings in general. Winnicott's analysis seems to offer one such explanation that provides greater internal coherence to Jung's discussion of his own and his mother's No. 1 and No. 2 Personalities.

Winnicott does not directly address the extent to which Jung's prodigious creativity and creative imagination are related to his inner conflicts. He does, however, allude to Jung's insights into his own dissociation. Also, Winnicott does not explicitly say that he views them as a creative resolution of the conflict of opposites or dissonance. In my view, claiming the latter would seem to follow indirectly from Winnicott's analysis and to be a warranted conclusion.

Other Analyses

In a penetrating analysis entitled "Jung's Lost Contribution to the Dilemma of Narcissism," Jeffrey Satinover, past president of the C. G. Jung Foundation of New York, has expressed his general agreement with Winnicott's assessment of Jung's personality structure (416). Satinover has shown that Jung was primarily concerned with "the personality-like character of . . . split-off portions of the psyche, with their consequent will-like autonomy" (411). Using the work of Homans, Stern, and Winnicott and a large measure of originality to make his case, Satinover shows how Jung's theories can be "taken not as hypotheses but as symptoms" (415) and how mother images can come to "dominate fantasies of fragmentation" (423). He also shows how widespread the phenomenon of splitting is, calling attention, as does John Gedo, a Chicago psychoanalyst, to Jung's successful adaptation. A tacit but undeveloped connection with Jung's own visionary creativity would seem to be implied. That is to say, Jung's method of amplification of unconscious images through visual imagination was a mode of self-healing that was also successfully used with countless patients by him and others.

Satinover states that the content of psychotic, or near psychotic ideation may be understood as a depiction of the fragmenting self and of the psyche's attempt at restoration. In his view, "the symptoms of an 'illness' arise from an attempt at self cure" (423). Discussing the theories that Jung formulated following his self-cure, Satinover states: "As a consequence of the regression into a nurturant phase, mother imagos (split into the 'Great Mother' and the 'Terrible Mother') dominate fantasies of fragmentation. Jung focused many of his mythological researches on the stories of the dying and resurrecting hero-gods that figure prominently in primitive cultures and in Christianity. . . . These god figures are usually the sons of good and bad mother goddesses" (423).

In another article on the same issue, Satinover writes: "While Jung's pathology was probably within the psychotic spectrum, broadly conceived, it does not appear to have been nearly so severe as what today we would call childhood schizophrenia" ("At the Mercy of Another" 64). In this insightful article Satinover follows and expands on Winnicott's earlier review of *Memories* with the above clarification. Further, both Winnicott and Satinover agree that the psychotic symptoms are not the illness but the psyche's attempt to restore health.

Jung in Modern Perspective, edited by Renos K. Papadopoulos and Graham S. Saayman, also has a bearing on this topic. To this volume Papadopoulos contributes "Jung and the Concept of the Other." He calls attention to Jung's emphasis that "the play and counterplay between personalities No. 1 and No. 2" has "run throughout my whole life" and that their interrelationship and dialogue offered him his profoundest experiences, "on the one hand a bloody struggle, and on the other supreme ecstasy" (*Memories* 45, 48).

Early on, Jung established a second, an Other, personality within himself whose contribution he valued sincerely. Papadopoulos calls attention to Jung's experience of "disunion" with and alienation from himself: "The influence of this wider world, this world which contained others besides my parents, seemed to me dubious if not altogether suspect and, in some obscure way, hostile" (*Memories* 19). To alleviate the fear and insecurity that these states produced in the childhood world of imagination, Jung found ways of healing that "split" and reestablished his "inner security," which was threatened (*Memories* 19–23).

Papadopoulos offers an exceedingly comprehensive study of Personalities No. 1 and No. 2 throughout Jung's life. Rather strangely, he largely ignores the role of Jung's mother as one who shaped his personality, except to comment that "since that Other was now located within, Jung was no longer a lonely, frightened boy, but had the resources to heal his condition of 'disunity' and 'alienation'" (Papadopoulos and Saayman 59). In addition, he began observing similar divisions in other people. This made him aware of the complexities of human personality, and he ceased to see people in unidimensional, childish divisions of good and bad. As a first step, he distinguished his own mother's No. 2 Personality.

To some extent the review by Winnicott and the article by Papadopoulos complement one another, for Winnicott is concerned with Jung's early childhood experience while Papadopoulos specifically introduces the importance of Jung's secrets and traces the motif of the two personalities throughout Jung's life. In another sense, the two writings offer a contrast of interpretation. Papadopoulos seems to follow much more closely (and accept as true) Jung's own contention that all persons have a consciousness of a Personality No. 2 (a True Self). This contention differs markedly from Winnicott's notion of the unitary self versus the divided self.

According to Papadopoulos, it also gradually dawned on Jung that since Personality No. 2 was of an impersonal, timeless, cosmic nature, by implication all people had one. Then all people were in a sense connected through a transpersonal eternal realm. One can doubt Jung's assumption and ask: Do all persons have a No. 2 Personality as Jung's mother had and as he later had? Why does it necessarily follow that a No. 2 Personality is timeless, impersonal, and archetypal rather than finite, personal, and conditioned? A developmentally grounded analysis has no need to postulate a transpersonal eternal realm in its mode of explanation. The facts in the case provide reasons enough. Winnicott has expressed it well: "Generally the problems of life are not about the search for a self, but about the full and satisfying use of a self that is a unit and is well grounded" (review 455).

Jung's Mother and His Own No. 2 Personality

In growing up, Jung had two perceptions of his mother: First, she was unreliable in that she was hospitalized during at least one critical period of his youth. Second, she was unreliable in such a way that he could not take what she said at face value. He writes: "I was about eleven years old when she informed me of a matter that concerned my father and alarmed me greatly." He went to tell an influential person about the incident. When Jung called at the door of this man, he was told by the maid that the man was out. Upon his return home, his mother told him an altogether different version of the story. He tells us that thereupon his confidence in his mother came to be strictly limited: "I decided to divide everything my mother said by two" (*Memories* 52).

Jung's mother's No. 2 Personality was "possessed" by what may be called the features of "primitive" spirituality. I am struck by the way in which, in his youth, Jung over time internalized several of the features of his mother's No. 2 Personality. Her "night personality" in particular evoked in him numinous feelings of both terror and fascination. Some of the feelings we can note in Jung's mother are shamanic certainty connected with inner spiritual power ("That personality was unexpectedly powerful" [*Memories* 48]); pagan spirituality connected with the earth and the erotic ("She had a hearty animal warmth" [48]); and moments of religious ecstasy, mystic illumination, and visionary insight ("Deeply awed by my mother's excitement, I withdrew penitently . . . and began playing with my bricks" [49]). His mother's mystic feelings apparently alternated with other feelings of distress, pain, and agony. Finally, she was tactless. In particular, she at times spoke in a blunt manner without regard to consequence. "But then came the moments when her second personality would burst forth, and what she said on those occasions was so true and to the point that I trembled before it" (52).

On balance we can see that Jung's was a difficult, even terrifying mother, at times. Of the period after his mother's return to the home following her hospitalization, Jung speaks quite candidly of the anxiety she repeatedly caused him. "That is why as a child I often had anxiety dreams about her" (*Memories* 50). For Jung, anxiety was frequently mixed with depression: "Later my mother told me that in those days I was often depressed" (42). These and similar episodes resulted in psychosomatic illnesses, including generalized eczema, which impaired his functioning. Thus it would seem that Jung was more profoundly affected by his mother's behavior toward him than his autobiography would initially lead us to believe.

We can further observe that Jung's second "personality" was very much like his mother's No. 2 Personality. The No. 2 Personality in Jung and his mother related to the nocturnal, the realm of nature, and the esoteric as well as the numinous and uncanny aspects of experience. Of himself Jung writes: "The daimon of creativity has ruthlessly had its way with me" (*Memories* 358). It is quite possible that many of the features of his mother's split personality became incorporated into his own youthful perception of the world.

If we accept the main features of Winnicott's explanation of Jung's childhood development, it would seem to follow that Jung's mother was a divided self in much the same way that he was. Each in turn saw and experienced numinous realities that others did not. They both also possessed shamanic powers of influence and persuasion that were used with considerable effect upon others. Jung's sense of numinosity seems to emerge, at least to some extent, from the contact he had with his mother's No. 2 Personality. Jung refers to the times when her second personality would "burst forth" (*Memories* 52). There is no doubt that he found this side of her "both unexpected and frightening" (49) because of her inconsistent nature. Both Jung and his mother tended to personify aspects of the self. Frequently in his autobiography he refers to the ruthlessness of his mother's No. 2 Personality. But he too, as he acknowledges at the end of *Memories* (356), could be utterly ruthless at times.

Jungian analysts have used the term *mana personality* to refer to the extraordinary and compelling power that emanates from certain individuals. Andrew Samuels in *A Critical Dictionary of Jungian Analysis* points out that since Jung's death, studies of transitional states confirm that during liminal periods or borderline states, a person such as an initiate, novice, patient, or analysand is particularly susceptible to attraction by so-called mana personalities. The term *mana personality* refers to "the presence of an all-pervading vital force, a primal source of growth or magical healing that can be likened to a primitive concept of psychic energy" (Samuels, *Critical Dictionary* 89). As people often believe that such a figure has attained a higher state of consciousness, they are confident that they can make the needed transition in the person's presence.

Jung gives attention to being "grasped" by spirit power, being in the grip of the daimonic. "There was a daimon in me. . . . It overpowered me, and if I was at times ruthless it was because I was in the grip of the daimon" (*Memories* 356). Or again, "I had to obey an inner law which was imposed on me and left me no freedom of choice. Of course I did not always obey it. How can anyone live without inconsistency?" (357). An inconsistency occasioned by a change of perspective is one thing; one manifesting inner dissociation is quite another.

Given Jung's childhood deprivation, restoration of the maternal imago became a lifelong preoccupation. Jung pursued this in symbolic ways, through formulating theories such as anima/animus, by writing books on self-integration, and through his interpersonal relationships. The quest was most likely traced out in his relations with Emma, Toni Wolff, and Sabina Spielrein and in the maternal aspects of his theories.

Jung was to write extensively on both the mother complex and the psychological aspects of the mother archetype. Perhaps one reason for this focus was the pain his mother caused him in his growing up, as well as her lengthy absence from the home at an early and critical juncture of his childhood. It is clear that he distanced himself from his mother in a variety of ways. Because of difficulties in his parents' marriage and a lack of true communication between them, his mother frequently spoke to him as one would to an adult and lavished undue attention on him. In effect, more was demanded of Jung than could reasonably be expected given his age.

Ruth Bailey, Jung's housekeeper for many years, shared some of Jung's memories of his mother: "She used to have . . . mental aberrations, she would go shopping for one thing and come home with another. That used to amuse him very much but exasperate him at the same time because it was a waste of money. She would go [looking] for something like a dish cloth and come home with a netting to keep the birds off, something vaguely connected but quite the wrong thing."[4] Jung's theories repeatedly speak of the archetypal aspects of the Great Mother. The personal pain caused by his real mother was too close for him to speak of directly, even in later years.

We can suppose that many of the qualities Jung observed in a rather ambivalent fashion in his mother may have found their way into his unconscious, into his writings, and even into his interpersonal expectations. It should not seem too far-fetched to assume that he would seek at least some of these qualities in his relations with significant others. We will have occasion to explore this topic in greater detail in chapter 5.

New Directions in Jung Research

Some of the most promising research on Jung's life lies in journal articles that are relatively inaccessible to the general public. These offer reinterpretations of Jung's relationships with his parents.

Winnicott's object relations theory, expounded at length in his numerous writings, holds that the innate growth potential of a child is expressed in a variety of spontaneous manifestations. At the stage when fantasies are a necessary part of the growth process, an ordinary good mother responds to the child with gestures of trust and reassurance. Hence, bonding occurs. Thus the conformity between the child's experience and the mother's response gives to the former an omnipotent, creative quality. Repeated experiences of this kind establish in the infant a sense of wholeness, of conviction about the

Formative & Transformative Life Experiences

goodness of reality, and a belief in the world as a rewarding place. This core of feeling gives rise to a True Self because of its full maturational potential.

Although Winnicott does not elaborate on the connection between his general theory and Jung's experience, it is interesting to speculate how he might have done so. It appears that Jung's mother did not establish a relation of sufficient trust with her child, so that his fantasies became incorporated into his No. 2 Personality. While still struggling to deal with the outer world, he partly withdrew from it and became introverted, finding refuge in an internal fantasy world. This has been described by object relations theorists as a problem not of impulse control but rather of ego splitting. Hence Jung's flawed childhood relation with his mother led him into a quest for the realization of creativity as a mode of self-healing throughout the many decades of his life. While this point is impossible to verify with certainty, it would seem to be developmentally rooted.

Several object relations theorists have shown that confidence in one's mother is established through basic trust and permits the gradual giving up of feelings of omnipotence. This involves necessary disillusionment as well as mood swings between intense love and hate. Frustration beyond a certain level cannot be contained within the affective cohesion of the experiences of the True Self. Negative experience gradually becomes organized to form a False Self.

According to a study by Berta Rank and Dorothy MacNaughton, one of the impediments to a successful synthesis of the various components of the personality is the absence of a stable mother image. Arnold Modell makes the similar point that the child who has been separated from the mother may resort to magical thinking for the purpose of uniting with the lost love object. Feelings of omnipotence combined with strategies of magical thinking counteract feelings of helplessness. Early loss of a parent for a time is known to affect self-idealization patterns and give great impetus to ambitious and creative personality patterns. All of this would seem to apply to Jung's childhood.

Only a very few interpreters have commented on Jung's mother's split personality. Satinover, in an all-too-short article titled "Jung's Relation to the Mother," has remarked on the ways in which Jung's mother was "rarely soothing and caring, but instead was mostly intrusive and, more specifically, phallic. By 'phallic' I mean to convey everything that the term suggests with respect to personality, from what we mean when we speak vulgarly of someone as a 'prick' to what we mean when we compliment someone with 'a seminal mind.' . . . Jung speaks of his mother as having, like himself, a 'number one' and a 'number two' personality" (16). Further, Satinover makes the point that Jung's experience of his mother was later transformed into his experience and concept of the anima: "The anima as Jung described it was powerful (phallic) and potentially castrating (viz. Jung's Salome, whose beautiful namesake had the head of John the Baptist. . . .). Likewise Jung regarded the phallic aspect of women (the animus) with the same mixture of fascination, suspicion, and wariness with which he responded to his own mother" (17–18).

This is all to the point. Contrary to outward appearances of warm-heartedness and joviality, Jung's mother did not present him with the consistent image of a warm and nurturing person. Rather, her intrusive ways of acting produced an attitude of caution and suspicion on Jung's part. Dual feelings of fascination and wariness are exactly what Rudolf Otto meant when he described numinous feelings that contain the dual aspects of dread and ecstasy.

Brilliant as Satinover's discussion is in some respects, on the crucial issue he equivocates. Seemingly he wants to have it both ways, explaining in detail a developmental conception of Jung's mother while at the same time alluding to an archetypal understanding of "the mother." Moreover, what Satinover does not explain to us is how Jung's reenactment of his mother's split and her emotions (which we see replicated in Jung himself) are related to Jung's own view of religious and creative images. Throughout the pages that follow, I shall attempt to trace many of these connections. That is to say, already in Jung's childhood we have the primary data for his later notions of the healing functions of the numinous, the power of the daimon, and the sources of his spiritual journey into the self as attempts to heal the rifts within the inner man.

It is becoming increasingly clear that Jung's extraordinary creativity stemmed in large measure from his childhood conflicts, which until the publication of *Memories* were unrecognized. Even there the true nature of Jung's conflicts is disguised to a considerable degree. As Winnicott puts it, emotional illness "may not only give a person a lot of trouble but push that person on to exceptional attainment" (review 455). Creative work itself is an attempted resolution (never complete) of internalized inner conflict. The creative person is more conscious of an alien will beyond his or her comprehension. This is what has been termed by Jung an autonomous complex and is a detached portion of the psyche that leads an independent life. The reconciliation of opposites, a theme so often recited in Jung's work, would seem to embody the element of coming to terms with unconscious contents that need to be reunited into the larger frame of consciousness. Dissociation, for all its difficulties, has its positive value as a spur to creativity.

Be anything you like except a theologian.
—*Johann Paul Achilles Jung, quoted in C. G. Jung,*
Memories

*My memory of my father is of a sufferer stricken with
an Amfortas wound, a "fisher king" whose wound would
not heal.*
—*C. G. Jung,* Memories

CHAPTER 2

The Personal & Mythic Father

Jung's father was a man whose primary frustration was that Christian symbols no longer mediated psychic power. Jung found his father's concealed religious despair a source of frustration and consternation. His father had lost the innocence of childlike faith but nonetheless tenaciously held to Christian doctrine. Belief was for him a shallow anchor, not a rock or ground of sustenance or renewal.

Jung's father was trained as a linguist and took a doctorate in Oriental languages at Göttingen University. During his years as a pastor of small churches, he often smoked a pipe, as he had done in his university days. A possible interpretation of this action is that in fantasy he wished to return to his earlier years as a student. According to

Jung's account, "His days of glory had ended with his final examination. . . . As a country parson he lapsed into a sort of sentimental idealism and into reminiscences of his golden student days, continued to smoke a long student's pipe, and discovered that his marriage was not all he imagined it to be" (*Memories* 91). In important respects it is apparent that Jung's father failed to develop inwardly in new directions once he entered the parish ministry. His inner defenses seem to have precluded this. In fact, one might say that the rest of his life went downhill. As Murray Stein puts it: "Jung later held Christianity partly accountable for his father's plight, but held his father accountable as well" ("Significance" 24).

Toward his father Jung had feelings based on reliability and tenderness, for as a lad his father sang songs to soothe him. Because of his mother's absence at crucial points of his youth, it is understandable that his father adopted attitudes of motherliness toward him. His father would sing the comforting words: "Alles schweige, jeder neige" (*Memories* 8). This means something like "Everything is quiet and peaceful, each one bows low." Even in his later years Jung recalled his father's compassionate singing to him as a small child in the middle of the night.

At the same time, his father was filled with anger over being trapped in the role of upholder of church doctrines through the means of blind belief. The father is generally the source of ego and superego development. It would seem that Jung did not sufficiently identify with his father, whom he perceived as ineffectual. When the time came for him to consider a vocation, his father told him, "Be anything you like except a theologian" (*Memories* 75). Thus, his childhood ambition, like that of countless youngsters, was to surpass his father in a host of ways. He had no desire to emulate his father, for he was only too well aware of the ways that church and religion had become a straitjacket that had thwarted his father's inner development.

Early Childhood Myths

From his childhood days Jung fantasized about Jesus. He was torn between what he heard taught in church and in his home about Jesus' love and kindness and the frightening image of Jesus as a "crucified and bloody corpse" (*Memories* 13). Many other elements of organized religion also struck terror into his young heart, such as seeing the ministers with long black coats and the shiny black boots that were worn to funerals, and overhearing his father's account about an infamous Jesuit. These metaphors had multiple meanings for him that only served to reinforce the ambivalent view he had of religion, especially buttressing its negative side. Given what we have learned of the frightening side of his mother's No. 2 Personality, such experiences doubtless only increased his youthful anxiety.

From his youth onward Jung was concerned with the liberating and therapeutic dimensions of religious images and rituals. Throughout his long life he was to explore thoroughly the implications of an alternative vision to that which his father represented. The healing dimensions of a religious vision rather than the stultifying aspects of religious belief and doctrine were the central features of this vision.

Jung had many important visions in childhood, stemming from impressive experiences that exerted a powerful impact upon him. Toward the end of his life he disclosed many of these for the first time, in his autobiography. These include the so-called man-eater dream, which created the fear that he would be devoured, and later a vision of a cathedral being destroyed, the memory of which brought him a feeling of liberation and exuberance. The man-eater dream, with its core element of an erect phallus, would seem to evoke the memory of a frightening primal sexual experience. In one of his letters to Freud, Jung speaks of a sexual assault by an older man whom he had "worshipped." Quite possibly the man-eater dream is linked to this childhood experience. Jung kept the memory of the assault secret from all except Freud until old age. The account does not appear in his autobiography (see Freud and Jung 49J). The "cathedral destroying" vision is something else again. From the way this vision is presented in *Memories*, it would seem that Jung had the unacceptable heretical thought that God from the heavens was intent upon destroying his father's church. One can speculate that the young Carl may have reasoned that a church that honored blind belief and that had in effect destroyed his father's spirit and psyche needed itself to be destroyed.

Jung recounts: "God sits on His golden throne, high above the world—and from under the throne an enormous turd falls upon the sparkling new roof, shatters it, and breaks the walls of the cathedral asunder" (*Memories* 39). These are forbidden thoughts that Jung kept to himself and never once thought of sharing with his parents. How should they be interpreted? Clearly they reflect something of

Jung's childhood anger, together with destructive overtones. This vision seems to be directed at his father's church and indirectly at his father. To his great surprise, lifting this inner rage to the level of consciousness and expressing it in thought is therapeutic. With the intonation of a burden being lifted, he states: "So that was it. . . . Instead of the expected damnation, grace had come upon me and with it an unutterable bliss such as I had never known" (40).

His image of an enormous turd falling on the roof of a cathedral would seem to be destructive of conventional piety and to awaken negative impulses. These images of the underground phallus and the turd striking the cathedral, as Jung in other contexts has taught us in his writings, have multiple meanings. The careful reader can readily ascertain that the youthful Jung was very far from being a Christian in any ordinary sense. In fact, he was anything but.

Childhood Secrets and Private Ritual

For the first nine years of his life Carl Jung was an only child. From his youth astrological signs such as those of Virgo (the Virgin) and Taurus (the Bull) were to fascinate him. By his own account he spent long periods of isolation and suffered from illness during his early years. Jung's early childhood was filled with ominous and sinister events. He had several brushes with death, as when he nearly slipped through the rungs of a bridge.

We have already noted some of the ways Jung as a child developed private rituals. Most of these were disclosed to no one. For instance, he held imaginary conversations with a carved manikin associated with a yellow varnished pencil case of his early school years. At the end of his ruler he carved a little figure about two inches in length, and he included a frock coat, a top hat, and shiny black boots. This figure he blackened with ink, sawed off his ruler, and placed in his pencil case, where he even made "his friend" a little bed and an overcoat out of wool. In the pencil case he also placed a smooth black stone from the Rhine, which he said was "his stone." The carved manikin in his pencil case he carefully hid in a place known only to himself. At times when his father was irritable or his mother's illness was especially troublesome, he would think of his manikin friend. At these times he would secretly retire to the attic of the house to look at the manikin and his stone and to communicate his secrets in private.

Each time he would place into the case another little scroll of paper, which contained messages written during school hours in a "secret language of my own invention" (*Memories* 21).

In his autobiography Jung notes that the manikin was his attempt to give shape to the secret that he mentions in connection with "the dream of the phallus" (21). These private rituals made such an impression on him that in *Memories* he tells of other blackish painted stones and carved figures of wood that he had well into adulthood. These objects evoked echoes of early memories.

Years later, without consciously recalling his childhood experience, Jung was to carve out of wood two similar figures that he had reproduced in stone and supplied with the name Atmavictu, which means "breath of life." Significantly, he relates that it was a "further development of that fearful tree of my childhood dream which was now revealed as . . . the creative impulse" (23). Even later in life he was to note that a similar cloaked god, a "veiled kabir" of the ancient world, was located in the temples of Asclepius. Classicists have pointed out that the healing cult of Asclepius in ancient Greece and Rome had phallic associations with the god Telesphoros (Smith and Lounibos, chap. 2). Jung later became aware of these associations. In his autobiography he recalls his youthful experience with the little man in the pencil case (*Memories* 21). The phallic elements he came to view as archaic psychic components. Indirectly Jung acknowledges the phallic component but curiously does not directly connect it with his own experience of sexuality.

Daniel Noel has called attention to Karl Kerényi's "The Mysteries of the Kabeiroi," where Kerényi refers to "ghostlike phallic demons," and his work on Asclepius (and Telesphoros) as "possibly representations of the phallus" (Noel 241). On this point Noel has written:

> Along with all this phallicism it is important to recognize the central part played by hiddenness, secrecy, mystery, or invisibility. The clothing of Telesphoros—the hooded cloak, which goes back in Jung's remembered images to the clothes worn by pallbearers and the "disguised" Jesuit—has this meaning; but so does the coffin or kista in which the kabir is concealed and, by extension, the chamber which hides the phallus beneath the meadow. This is the "veiled" character of Telesphoros the kabir, the shape Jung gave to his childhood secret. (228)

Formative & Transformative Life Experiences

The youthful Jung's "veiled kabir" or preoccupation with the carved, hooded Telesphoros strikes me as unmistakably connected to his own autoeroticism. The name Telesphoros means "he who brings completeness," for it identifies a god of inner transformation. Clearly, from Jung's early childhood his private myths and rituals were a source of comfort to him, an isolated and lonely child.

Jung's childhood experience of Christianity, his confirmation, and his first experience of communion were all disappointments to him, as was his father. Much later his identification with Freud as a surrogate father made him euphoric for a time, as did his identification with the "holy cause" of psychoanalysis. (This topic will be addressed in the next chapter.) Having secrets became a matter of special import. The "man-eater dream" (*Memories* 12), not recounted until late in life, has been interpreted by various psychoanalytic writers as Jung's awakening to the frightening aspects of sexuality.

Jung's autobiography provides ample evidence that time and again the young Carl wanted to share his rich visionary life with his father but was put off. He feared, perhaps correctly, that his father would not understand his feelings. Profound doubts arose about virtually everything his father said. Late in his school years Jung complained: "I would have liked to lay my difficulties before him and ask him for advice, but did not do so because I knew in advance what he would be obliged to reply out of respect for his office. . . . My father personally gave me instruction for confirmation. It bored me to death." When the subject of the Trinity came up, his father confessed that it was a topic he had never understood. Here was a subject that truly fascinated the young Carl, precisely because it was a logical impossibility. "Here was something that challenged my interest: a oneness which was simultaneously a threeness." We can see that from an early age Jung was not primarily interested in distinct and separate rational ideas but rather ones that could be experienced. Intuitively the notion of the Trinity fascinated him because of its "incomprehensible" nature and its very "inner contradiction" (*Memories* 52–53).

Following Erik Erikson, many psychologists have shown the great importance of identity formation for later personality development. The reader of *Memories* may well be struck by the way that Jung was both unable and unwilling to accept his father's double vision of the world. On the conscious level Johann Paul Jung was an exponent of the Christian faith, but on a deeper level other feelings existed. One gets the feeling that for Jung's father, life became profoundly externalized. Feelings of depression and despondency were either denied or repressed. For the elder Jung, belief and faith were exalted, while religious experience was deprecated. At all costs he avoided an immersion in "despair and sacrilege which were necessary for an experience of divine grace" (*Memories* 55). In Jung's view his father had committed a *sacrificium intellectus* of which he himself was incapable. For his father, like Tertullian before him, even a faith that was absurd was not a cause for concern. In later years Carl Jung was to say that he was unable to believe anything that he did not understand. This was one of the reasons that religious gnosis was to have such great importance for him.

As Jung grew up he was acutely aware of the paradox that existed in his father's use of Christian doctrine, especially the church's teaching that Christ died for the salvation of the world. He was also aware of the painful reality that for him the church itself represented death and not life. Years later Jung recalled the disappointment he experienced after receiving his first communion. Of that experience he wrote: "Why, that is not religion at all. . . . It is an absence of God; the church is a place I should not go to. It is not life which is there, but death" (*Memories* 55). He wondered whether the failure of communion to have a positive effect upon him was his own fault. He had prepared for it diligently and had desired an experience of grace and illumination, but nothing had happened. This fact of his psychic experience was to make him feel "cut off from the Church and from my father's and everybody else's faith" (56).

Early Rejection of Traditional Religion

Jung's repudiation of traditional Christianity (or better still, his efforts to supersede it in certain respects where it produced pathology and not health) has several sources. One of the most important is connected with his failure to identify with his father. There is some evidence that as a child he held the church to be devoid of meaning, for his father and for himself also. His father, a traditionalist, saw his task as being the defender and guardian of Christian doctrine, even though he became despondent and despairing in the effort.

As Jung could not identify with his father or his ideas on religion, he was predisposed to look for answers to important questions elsewhere. The traditional ideas of God as an all-loving judge just did not work for him from his school days on. He was to reject once and for all his father's vision of religion. To his mind, it had only succeeded in making his father an unhappy, frustrated, and miserable man. Apparently Jung was to hold Christian institutionalism to some extent responsible for the fate that had befallen his father. Having to be the protector of Christian doctrine was for the elder Jung an onerous task. Johann Paul Jung lost hope and was frequently depressed, for he could not face his doubts, which remained largely unconscious. For this Carl was to blame the moribund and sterile nature of Christian religion as he had experienced it. Hence we have one of the reasons for his profound ambivalence toward Christianity throughout his life.

Recent Interpretations

Peter Homans in *Jung in Context* has argued that Jung's primary problem in growing up should be understood to be related to narcissism. Following Heinz Kohut, Homans argues that psychosexual development necessarily negotiates three stages: an undifferentiated one, that of narcissism proper, and the oedipal stage of object relations. Kohut has particularly focused upon the second stage of "idealizing transference" and "mirror transference." By calling attention to the way in which Jung developed a grandiose self and grandiose fantasies, Homans, I believe, has made a valuable contribution. We need to remember, however, that narcissism is but one explanatory strand in a chain of formative factors that all played a part in the development of this complex man.

Jung's primary conflict, in my view, concerns not his narcissism, as Homans holds. It should, I believe, be related primarily to the split between his Personalities No. 1 and No. 2. The narcissistic elements of his temperament, though, do seem to stem from his failure to identify with his father. As we will see in the next chapter, on his relation with Freud, this inspired his "desire to merge with a powerful source of self esteem" (Homans, *Jung in Context* 40).

Jung's own intense religious visions would seem to stem from the experience of his own inner dissonance. In an elaborate process of visionary or active imagination, an elaborate set of mythical connections was set in motion. In another way his rejection of traditional Christianity stemmed from his analysis of modern society and its unique spiritual problems. Murray Stein cites a variety of dark and ominous images to call attention to what he has termed Jung's Christianity complex. He argues that at the center of this complex, together with Jung's early suspicion of Jesus and his perception of God's dark side, stood Jung's own father. His father was caught, Stein says, in "Peter's net," by the task of having to be the guardian of Christian doctrine even though he became very unhappy in the process.

Stein has performed a useful service to all interpreters of Jung by emphasizing that one of Jung's lifelong psychic tasks was to overcome the legacy he received from his father. In Stein's book, *Jung's Treatment of Christianity*, he maintains that this was the reason that Jung was to become a therapist to the Christian tradition. From his own experience and later in his experiences with patients, Jung became convinced that Christian culture had become stultified. Hence Jung's basic concern was to address the integration of unconscious and archetypal images into the wider circle of consciousness. His own early remembrances of his father served to remind him, lest he forget, of the debilitating effect of his father's psychic woundedness. Even at an early age he intuitively knew that he must follow a different path, one more in keeping with his own inner reality.

Stein underscores the stunning impact of the elder Jung's tragic suffering upon his young son. Jung himself writes: "My memory of my father is of a sufferer stricken with an Amfortas wound, a 'fisher king' whose wound would not heal—that Christian suffering for which the alchemists sought the panacea. I as a 'dumb' Parsifal was witness of this sickness during the years of my boyhood, and, like Parsifal, speech failed me. I had only inklings" (*Memories*, 215). But frequently inklings suffice. People are rarely able to hide their true feelings from those who know them well. As Stein has so vividly expressed it, for Jung, his father was both representative and victim of an ailing religious tradition ("Significance" 24). Thus, one of Jung's lifelong tasks became to breathe new life into the dry bones of Christian imagery.

In responding to Stein's emphasis upon the stultifying impact that Jung's father had upon Jung's life, another analyst, Harry Wilmer, suggests that his father's woundedness may have been Carl's salvation: "Just as the wounded wounds himself, so the healer heals himself" (*Memories* 216). Jung experienced deep wounds in connection with both his parents. His explorations into the imagery of creativity were later to address this pain.

From what we can tell—and there is plenty of evidence on this point—Jung never identified with his father's view of life but very early was taken up with his own fantasies, images, and visions. As a lad when he walked to school from Klein-Hüningen, he had "the overwhelming impression of having just emerged from a dense cloud. I knew all at once: now I am myself! It was as if a wall of mist were at my back, and behind that wall there was not yet an 'I.' But at this moment I came upon myself" (*Memories* 32).

As we saw in the previous chapter, Jung developed a profound ambivalence toward his mother because of her divided personality. Because of her illness, his father came to assume a motherly role (part of Winnicott's interpretation). Yet his father was in his own way also a deeply divided individual. As we have seen, he was of two minds toward the Christian religion. Consciously, he was its champion, but unconsciously he obviously doubted its veracity.

Given his father's conflicts and the way his own development proceeded, it was absolutely necessary for Jung to pursue his own path. However, the matter seems to be even more complex. On still another level it would seem that just as Jung's father assumed the mother's role at certain early periods of Jung's life, so too Jung's primary ambivalence toward his mother was transferred to his father and on a deep level to his father's church. This could well be still another reason for his childhood fantasy of a turd from the heavens thundering down upon those powers and principalities (the Basel cathedral?) that were thwarting and so directly affecting his own life.

If Jung was inwardly split, as Winnicott and Satinover have strongly contended—and as I tried to show in the previous chapter—then doubtless maternal as well as paternal determinants were involved. Jung's various attempts to overcome his inner rift became the source of his most enduring and creative explorations. This is true with regard to his own psychic integration and his contributions toward alternate modes of realizing the spiritual quest.

We are lived by Powers we pretend to understand.
—*W. H. Auden, "In Memory of Ernst Toller"*

Jung & Freud: A Daimonic Tug of War

As never before, the childhoods of both Freud and Jung are the subjects of a great deal of scrutiny. It is now becoming apparent to most investigators that the classic features of the legendary Freud-Jung saga (1907–13) owe many of their most interesting features to the activities of the unconscious. This is true not only of the motivations that brought these great men together but also of an assortment of features of the relationship itself. It is no exaggeration to say that their lives and letters bear eloquent testimony to the activities of the unconscious that they propounded. It is my desire to illuminate the features of this relationship by exploring its largely unconscious motivations. Many questions can be posed: Aside from desired collaboration, wider recognition, respectability, and expediency, what factors drew the two men together in the first place? Which factors sustained the relationship? What were the virtually inevitable factors that led to the bitter dissolution of their collaboration and friendship?

Freud had discovered the psychoanalytic method, published *The Interpretation of Dreams* in 1900, and made his mark as a pioneer of a new approach to psychiatry. His major experience had been working with neurotics. His colleagues were nearly all Jewish physicians. Jung had built a reputation at the prestigious Burghölzli Mental Hospital in Zurich for his work with schizophrenics. Not inconsequential, of course, was the element of complementing one's worldview with the stimulation of a new perspective. Jung had a personal vitality and sense of presence that Freud found compelling. Jung, for his part, knew that Freud was on the cutting edge of a therapeutic technique that was just then coming into being.

The psychoanalytic camp has complained that Jung was a deviant. This is Ernest Jones's view. Both Freudian and Jungian commentators once agreed that Jung's theoretical development in the years during his psychoanalytic affiliation prompted his open split with Freud and the psychoanalytic movement. Careful review of Jung's early work by investigators like Paul Stephansky fails to substantiate this assumption. This scholarship indicates Jung's honest belief that "his limited appropriation of certain psychoanalytic mechanisms and attendant theoretical modifications constituted full-fledged loyalty to psychoanalysis as he understood it" (Stephansky 216). It now appears that from the beginning there were acknowledged differences of approach between Freud and Jung concerning the practice of psychoanalysis.

The Freud-Jung correspondence has been the subject of intensive reinterpretations by both Freudians and Jungians in recent years. These studies make it quite clear that the infatuation that characterized the relationship embodied several unconscious determinants. Much more than professional interests were at stake in this relationship. Early identity needs were involved, as was the feminine dimension of each man's personality structure, which Jung later was to term the anima.

Ernest Jones (2:141), without real evidence, insists that Jung was more deeply involved in the relationship than Freud, but a close reading of their correspondence does not substantiate this claim. Both men were committed to the relationship. Freud frequently initiated the exploration of new topics and complained that Jung did not reply soon enough. Yet for a long time the relationship was symbiotic and stimulating to each man. There is little doubt that the termination of the relationship was far more traumatic for Jung than for Freud, but this may merely reflect the fact that Freud had already been through similar experiences with Joseph Breuer and Wilhelm Fliess. A negative factor in Freud's temperament had a way of asserting itself time and again.

Even a biographer as sympathetic and protective of Freud's image as Ernest Jones claims that Freud suffered from a psychoneurosis. Jones maintains that it was in the years when Freud's neurosis was most intense (as during his relationship with Fliess) that Freud did his most original work (Jones cited in Brome, *Freud* 126). Vincent Brome has surmised that Freud's sublimated homosexual impulse redirected his libido to the highest creative purposes. This interpretation implies that Freud's experience was an original source for direct involvement in the development of his concept of sublimation.

A Father Complex with a Holy Cause

The father-son complex that emerged between Freud and Jung was a significant determining factor for the relationship, more than any other single element. It profoundly stirred and exhilarated both men from the start. In 1906 Freud's reputation was already secure. He was fifty years of age, whereas Jung was a relative neophyte of thirty-one. Their relationship expressed a numinous quality accompanied by dual feelings, tinged by a certain eroticism. It appears to have been characterized by a love-hate ambivalence in which temporarily one factor or the other was either overemphasized, projected, or repressed. On Jung's part, repressed anger toward "the father" was a significant element.

Very early on, a strong, almost magical attachment developed between the two men. Jung and Freud's first meeting, on Sunday, March 3, 1907, resulted in an animated discussion in a smoke-filled room from early afternoon until the early hours of the next morning—a thirteen-hour marathon. The bonding was instant, if flawed. Each man supplied something the other lacked. For Freud, Jung embodied youthfulness, vitality, the epitome of manly vigor, and a gentile constituency. By 1907 Freud had become the savant of psychoanalysis. *The Psychopathology of Everyday Life* and *The Interpretation of Dreams* were already behind him. He had received widespread recognition, if not permanent status, for his controversial theories on the etiology of neurosis, but he perceived that his movement had a narrow cultural, ethnic, and geographic base. Jung, though a relative neophyte working with schizophrenics, broadened the applicability of psychoanalysis and represented a wider gentile community. Jung's need for Freud is harder to identify, but it seems to lie in his desire to be perceived as a pioneer. By allying with his greatest contemporary in psychology, pioneer, Jung could enhance his own image and reputation.

In *Memories* Jung tells us he was displeased to discover that his association experiments agreed with Freud's theories. He was in fact tempted to publish the results of his experiments and conclusions without mentioning Freud. As he puts it: "After all, I had worked out my experiments long before I understood his work. But then I heard the voice of my second personality: 'If you do a thing like that, as if you had no knowledge of Freud, it would be a piece of trickery. You cannot build your life upon a lie.' With that, the question was settled. From then on I became an open partisan of Freud's and fought for him" (148). The fact that Jung's association experiments were in agreement with Freud's theories was hardly sufficient reason for Jung to attribute them as much to Freud as to himself. The attribution is curious, for in most situations Jung was not known for his self-deprecation. As the loyal ally of Freud, he would appear to have temporarily submerged his own sense of ego. Already one sees the intensity of Jung's need to align himself with a kind of holy cause, or, as he puts it, "warfare" against external foes. On one level the relation was bonding in quest of professional status. On a deeper level it may represent, as Homans indicates, "a psychic merger" (*Jung in Context* 40). Throughout his life Jung was not averse to espousing unpopular causes in both psychology and religion. In fact, he seemed to thrive on it.

At the start of the relationship with Freud, Jung was a brash, self-confident bon vivant who exuded optimism and was the very epitome of the ambitious, even self-serving young psychiatrist. His professional experience complemented that of Freud, for he was recognized for his work *The Psychology of Dementia Praecox*. "Jung . . . showed himself full of self-confidence and surrounded by the aura of success. He promised the marvelous" (Shengold 189). This mutual enchantment must have raised unrealistic expectations. We have here the hope of a mutual metamorphosis in the Faustian mode. Surely these men must have dimly glimpsed that the relationship awakened unconscious striving. In their correspondence, the notion of the devil or daimonic comes up with frequency and is a metaphorical pseudonym for instinctual drives.

A primary source for the Freud-Jung correspondence is *The Freud-Jung Letters*, published in 1974 and edited by William McGuire. There we can see that from the start, Jung's view of psychoanalytic inquiry is considerably different from Freud's. Jung seeks Freud's approval, but it comes with strings attached. In an early letter Freud says, "I am delighted with your promise to trust me" (8F). One suspects that Freud planned to allow some modest measure of independence to Jung, with the idea that Jung would come around in due time. The words *sacrifice, deviate,* and *abandon* are repeatedly used by Freud, with appropriate symbolic meaning. Jung is admonished to hold true to Freud's doctrine.

In another early letter Freud writes: "Don't sacrifice anything essential for the sake of pedagogic tact and affability and don't deviate so far from me when you are really so close to me for if you do we may one day be played off against one another" (11F). Freud's request is ridiculous when closely analyzed. Nonetheless Jung "dutifully" complies. In a follow-up letter Jung says, "I shall never abandon any portion of your theory that is essential to me, as I am far too committed to it" (12J). I am struck by Jung's phrase "essential to me," which suggests his adherence only to those of Freud's ideas he found useful to himself. This indicates that even at this early phase of their relationship, Jung's compliance may not have been as complete as it would seem at first glance. Again we can see that key words like *trust, sacrifice, deviation,* and *commitment* indicate that Freud expects Jung to be a "true believer" (to employ Eric Hoffer's phrase) and that Jung willingly obliges.

In the initial phase of their correspondence, Freud especially seems to need the letters and chides Jung for his lapses in writing and for letting the opponents of psychoanalysis affect his writing (11F). Freud was not always one to let the chips fall where they would. One senses mutual admiration in the letters; flattery exists on both sides. Jung commends Freud on an "excellent analysis" (19J) and signs, as it were, a bond of mutual allegiance. There are, of course, attempts to deny this development. In one place Jung writes: "I only fear that you overestimate me and my powers" (19J).

In 1907, when Jung was discussing delusional persecutory ideas on paranoia with Freud, he wrote: "The delusional ideas are as a rule a crazy mixture of wish-fulfillment and the fear of being injured. The following analogy has always struck me as enlightening: the religious ecstatic who longs for God is one day vouchsafed a vision of God. But the conflict with reality also creates the opposite for him: certainty turns into doubt, God into the devil, and the sublimated joy of the *unio mystica* into sexual anxiety with all its historical specters" (24J).

Rapidly in their friendship Freud and Jung formed a close link against the challenges of the outside world. In the euphoria of positive transference, they were "warriors together" against the foes of the new movement, and they often used the language of battle. In one place Freud writes: "Thank you very much for the two bombshells from the enemy camp" (27F).

For a long time there was much psychic stroking in the letters. Both men performed idealized imaging for the other. They were also "priestly confessors" to one another, offering absolution without the need for undue acts of contrition. Freud says, "What you call the hysterical element in your personality, your need to impress and influence people, the very quality that so eminently equips you to be a teacher and guide, will come into its own even if you make no concessions to the current fashions in opinion" (38F). In a follow-up letter Jung agrees that his ambition provokes his fits of despair (39J).

Religious Allusions

At one point Jung voluntarily took a vow of submission and subservience to Freud, somewhat like a disciple or initiate to an omniscient master. Seemingly Jung preferred the subservient role; apparently he feared too great an emotional involvement with Freud. Typical were statements like "I shall naturally confine myself to your theory" (19J) and "I have boundless admiration for you both as a man and as a researcher" (49J). Jung's excessive veneration shows how strong was his need to be liked and accepted by the older man, but

I suspect that it was unconsciously encouraged by Freud. The adulation suppressed the element of self-conscious determination and competition that existed between the two men.

The question arises as to whether Jung even wanted a relationship of mutual autonomy with Freud. Early on, he clearly did not. There is more emotional security in a formalized relation. Throughout their correspondence and collaboration, Freud was the one who took the initiative and who sometimes bitterly complained that Jung had not written for a considerable time. One could also interpret this as a resistance on Jung's part toward even deeper psychic involvement with Freud. In due time Jung's reverence turned into resentment and rage.

The early allusions to the eventual falling-out, even if tongue-in-cheek, are striking. Early in the relationship Jung indicated he lived "from the crumbs that fall from the rich man's table" (29J). Later, in an unpublished letter of Freud to Jung of February 28, 1908, Freud said that "Jung was to be the Joshua destined to explore the promised land of psychiatry which Freud, like Moses, was only permitted to view from afar" (Jones 2:37). Later still, Freud expanded on the Moses/Joshua metaphor and said: "If I am Moses, then you are Joshua and will take possession of the promised land of psychiatry" (Freud and Jung 125F).

In an article entitled "Freud's Father Conflict," Edwin Wallace indicates that Moses played many different roles in Freud's unconscious life. He writes: "There is a bewildering array of identifications. Freud is alternately Moses the glorious father, Moses the victimized father, Moses the conquering son and parricide, Jesus the redeemer, Ikhenaton the father, Joseph the victim. Freud's father, Jung, and others are variously represented by these roles as well" (52). There are other pseudo-religious allusions in the correspondence. One is Freud's reference to Jung's trip to Amsterdam as an "apostolic journey," in that it was aimed at proselytizing for the Freudian cause. Another is when Freud approved of one of Jung's confessions: "What you say of your inner developments sounds reassuring; a transference on the religious basis would strike me as most disastrous; it could only end in apostasy" (Freud and Jung 52F). Still another biblical allusion can be seen in the letter from Jung to Freud in which Jung proclaims: "Anyone who knows your science has veritably eaten of the tree of paradise and become clairvoyant" (28J). Jones translates the passage as "whoever had acquired a knowledge of psycho-analysis had eaten of the tree of Paradise and attained vision" (2:32). Conversion to the cause, discernment, and proselytizing, on the one hand, and apostasy and spreading heresy, on the other, form the opposite sides of a secularized doctrine seemingly rooted in the conflicts of childhood and allowing little room for unorthodox deviance.

Jung confessed to Freud a traumatic event of his childhood: "I was the victim of a sexual assault of a man I once worshipped" (Freud and Jung 49J). Shengold has said the " 'man [he] once worshipped,' whoever he was, must have had the significance for the boy of his pastor father and of the Christian God with whom Jung was so ambivalently obsessed in his youth" (193). Shengold is only partially correct. The effects of that childhood trauma affected Jung throughout his life and clearly came into play with his relation to Freud. Jung did not become obsessed with the Christian God, as Shengold contends. Rather, his ambivalence toward his father, the church, and the traditional deity initiated his quest for a heterodox deity. Indeed, we may well have here one of the primary reasons that Jung's notion of God was so idiosyncratic. For instance, a tenet to which he steadfastly clung was that deity was as much characterized by evil as by good.

Sexuality and the Response to Godlike Power

In *Memories* Jung goes to considerable lengths to point out that for Freud sexuality is a numinosum (150). His contention is that in effect it is a "sacred datum" for Freud in its determining power and unquestioned ability to explain. Reading this, one might get the impression that Jung is contending that Freud was unconsciously religious. Another possibility is that Freud was influenced by his unconscious in much the same way a believer would be influenced by God. That is, he was motivated by an unconscious daimon. From his standpoint, Jung only slightly overstates his case when he insists: "At bottom, however, the *numinosity* that is the psychological qualities of the two rationally incommensurable opposites—Yahweh and sexuality—remained the same" (151). Yahweh and sexuality may in some ways be similar, but they are not identical.

When Jung writes to Freud, "I fear your confidence" (Freud and Jung 49J), one suspects that he both feared and desired it. Given Jung's ambivalent relation with his father, it would seem that numinosity (comprising both attraction and repulsion) also characterized the tone of his relation with Freud. As Vincent Brome has put it in *Freud and his Early Circle*, "Freud would have recoiled in horror, and rightly so, from Jung's attempt to invest his propositions with religious meaning. . . . Jung develops a series of mystical attacks on Freud which use an ill-defined farrago of terms totally alien to the vocabulary of Freud" (112–13). Brome's point is that like many attempts to describe mystical experience, Jung's remarks extend the meaning of terms like *numinosum* and thus blur rather than clarify the meaning intended.

Jung's childhood sexual trauma, reluctantly confessed to Freud, deeply motivated his behavior during this period. He writes: "This feeling, which I still have not quite got rid of, hampers me considerably. Another manifestation of it is that I find psychological insight makes relations with colleagues who have a strong transference to me downright disgusting. I therefore fear your confidence" (Freud and Jung 49J). Jung's emotional scar, carried so long in secret, resulted from the actions of an admired and respected father figure. The effects of this painful memory are in turn projected onto Freud and are evident in the "religious crush" that develops. Because of Jung's earlier trauma, with understandable ambivalence he both fears and desires the relationship with Freud.

In a follow-up letter Jung explores a dream he had when he visited Freud in Vienna. He dreamed that Freud walked beside him and was an extremely frail old man. Doubtless the dream is a form of undoing. As Jung says, it set his mind at ease about Freud's dangerousness. In the following letter Jung confesses: "My old religiosity had secretly found in you a compensating factor which I had to come to terms with eventually" (51J). Jung leaves the matter of a connection between his religiosity and his feelings toward Freud somewhat oblique; it is not clear what is being compensated for. I sense that just as Jung claims that for Freud sexuality is a numinosum, for both Freud and Jung residual feelings of unconscious energy are tinged with overtones of sexual feelings.

Paul Roazen has called attention to the passage in *The Interpretation of Dreams* where Freud states: "My emotional life has always insisted that I should have an intimate friend and a hated enemy. I have always been able to provide myself afresh with both, and it has not infrequently been so completely reproduced that friend and enemy have come together in a single individual" (cited in Roazen, *Freud and*

His Followers 31). Under certain circumstances friend became enemy. Clearly, the inner dynamics of both Freud and Jung were such as to make this possible.

At the same time that Freud was carrying on a correspondence with Jung, he was also corresponding with Karl Abraham. Abraham first worked at the Burghölzli under Jung and Bleuler and later in Berlin. The Freud-Abraham correspondence helps us to understand more clearly one of the reasons for Freud's attraction to Jung: expediency. Simply stated, Jung was a gentile and possessed a persuasive manner. He could serve as an apostle to the bourgeois Swiss and others of the wider gentile world in a period when a rapid expansion of psychoanalytic teaching was to be desired.

At the Salzburg Congress in April 1908, which Freud attended, both Jung and Abraham had made presentations on dementia praecox. Jung had argued that a toxin acting as a pathogenic agent was responsible for the disease, a position he had stated elsewhere. In his paper Abraham failed to cite the previous work of Bleuler and Jung. In a letter to Freud, Abraham wrote: "They turn aside from the theory of sexuality, therefore I shall not cite them in connection with this" (Freud and Abraham 36, dated May 5, 1908). Jung was irate at the slight and wrote to Freud: "The chief obstacle is my pupils. . . . To get ahead at my expense, while I stand still. . . . I beg you to have patience with me, and confidence in what I have done up till now. I always have a little more to do than be just a faithful follower. You have no lack of those anyway. But they do not advance the cause, for by faith alone nothing prospers in the long run" (Freud and Jung 86J).

Freud then tried to mediate between Jung and Abraham. He needed them both, but on the issue at hand he was to agree more with Abraham than with Jung. He wrote to Jung, advising him to be helpful if Abraham consulted with him about the publication of his dementia paper and to "accept the fact that this time he took the more direct path, whereas you hesitated" (Freud and Jung 87F). As Robert Steele has put it, "Abraham's orthodoxy was highlighting Jung's deviancy" (209). In a letter to the young Abraham in Zurich on May 8, 1908, Freud wrote:

> Please be tolerant and do not forget that it is really easier for you than it is for Jung to follow my ideas, for in the first place you are

completely independent, and then you are closer to my intellectual constitution because of racial kinship, while he as a Christian and a pastor's son finds his way to me only against great inner resistances. His association with us is the more valuable for that. I nearly said that it was only by his appearance on the scene that psycho-analysis escaped the danger of becoming a Jewish national affair. (Freud and Abraham 34)

Freud had no way of knowing that Jung had come to differ profoundly with the views of his father. Jung, at that phase of his life, completely rejected institutional religion. Freud wanted a gentile connection to give the fledgling movement of psychoanalysis respectability, and Jung was the first gentile to give the movement status.

In a letter to Freud in July of that year, Abraham reported: "Jung seems to be reverting to his former spiritualistic inclinations. But please keep this between ourselves. However, if Jung gives up for this reason and for the sake of his career, then we can no longer count on the Burghölzli" (Freud and Abraham 44, July 16, 1908). Two letters later Freud mentioned to Abraham his suspicion that the suppressed anti-Semitism of the Swiss that he was spared himself "is deflected in reinforced form upon you" (46, July 23, 1908).

Strong rivalries developed between Abraham and Jung, which Freud tried to mediate for the good of the cause. To Abraham, Freud wrote: "You see . . . how important it is to me that in these matters in which each of you forms an opinion of the other both of you should turn out to be wrong and I to be right. I cannot tolerate that 'two such fellows' both of whom are close to me should not be able to get on with each other." Later in the same letter Freud confessed: "Our Aryan comrades are really completely indispensable to us, otherwise psychoanalysis would succumb to anti-Semitism" (Freud and Abraham 63–64, Dec. 26, 1908). In Freud's overall scheme for the dissemination of his teaching and the expansion of his movement, Jung had a purpose to serve.

Abraham was to replace Jung in Freud's affections, just as Jung had replaced Fliess. After the schism was an irrevocable reality, Freud wrote to Abraham: "So we are at last rid of them, the brutal, sanctimonious Jung and his disciples" (Shengold 230). Interestingly, Shengold points out that Freud had used this very word *brutal* to characterize Fliess. Freud had described Fliess's pamphlet on bisexuality as the result of "the overbearing presumption of a brutal personality" (cited in Shengold 230n).

We may ask how a relationship that had begun so propitiously, albeit with certain elements of unrealistic projection, should founder upon the rocks of bitter animosity. From the start each man was of two minds toward the other. Residual childhood experiences were to undermine what had been a productive relation of cooperation. For a time this anger was projected onto their enemies. When intense stress in the relationship emerged, however, long repressed childhood anger exploded. This anger was frequently expressed in proportions quite inappropriate to the actual situation. Rage on each man's part was eventually to erode the relationship.

Symbols of Transformation

On the surface, in *Symbols of Transformation* Jung's deviance from Freud on the question of a sexual or symbolic interpretation of libido is at stake.[1] Yet there is much more to it. In this volume Jung deals with the fantasies of a Miss Frank Miller, a pseudonym for a New York woman.[2] He exposits at great length upon the impersonal nature of the psyche, which he later was to term the collective unconscious. As he wrote this volume, he was speculating on the meaning of a wide range of mythological material and labored under intense feelings of inferiority (Freud and Jung 215J). In his foreword to the revised edition of *Symbols of Transformation* Jung wrote: "This book was written in 1911, in my thirty-sixth year. The time is a critical one, for it marks the beginning of the second half of life, when a metanoia, a mental transformation, not infrequently occurs. I was acutely conscious then of the loss of friendly relations with Freud and of the lost comradeship of our work together" (*cw* 5:26).

A central tenet of *Symbols of Transformation* is that everything has both lower and higher meanings. Hence we encounter a plethora of symbolic meanings. As Steele has shown, "Jung made almost no attempt to speculate on Miller's past or her childhood difficulties. . . . there is hardly any psychoanalytic interpretation. . . . it was to show that a modern young woman was a myth-maker and that in our fantasies and dreams we are still making myths" (237).

Even after their break, Freud readily acknowledged that Jung was the first to draw explicit attention to the striking similarity between the disordered fantasies of dementia praecox and the myths of primitive peoples (*Collected Papers* 5:129). Both men became interested in exploring the features of these myths. Their correspondence focused for a time on the details of the ancient Iranian religion called Mithraism and on its sacrifice of the divine bull as well as the self-castration of the priests. For example, Jung pointed out to Freud that the Mithras myth had undergone an adaptation to the calendar, in that the crab that pinches the bull's testicles is the scorpion of the autumnal equinox, who deprives the bull of his fruitfulness (Freud and Jung F199a, 200J).

It is by no means easy to determine how the myths of primitives are linked to individual psychic experience. Many of the connections that Jung makes are exceedingly tenuous, to say the least. Homans asserts that what Jung offers us is a record of his own fantasies, not an interpretation of the myths and symbols of the past (*Jung in Context* 66). It is an understatement to say, as Ellenberger does (696), that Jung's work does not make easy reading. The problem lies deeper. At times Jung makes so many connections that through all the discursions his argument is virtually lost. His citations range across classic works such as the Gilgamesh epic, the Bible, and the Upanishads, to hosts of writers, ethnologists, philosophers, playwrights, and poets—Creuzer, Steinthal, Goethe, Nietzsche, Longfellow, Emerson, Shakespeare, and Samuel Johnson, to name a few. He even includes a quote from his own grandfather, Samuel Preiswerk. It is not so much Jung's examples but his procedural method that is questionable and leaves much to be desired.

Let us consider the example Homans cites from *Symbols of Transformation:*

In the midst of one of her reveries (234f.) Miss Miller imagined a "city of dreams." This provoked Jung to a discourse on cities in ancient cultures and mythologies. . . . then he noted that cities and women are also related to land; this led him to reflect on the movement of the sun over "maternal" waters; which reminded him of Frobenius's concept of the night-sea journey; that stimulated Jung to think of Noah's journey, but he then added, journeys are an expression of the wish for rebirth; this prompted a discussion of the Book of Revelation; and so on. Not until page 263 did Jung return to the next phrase in Miss Miller's brief report. (Homans, *Jung in Context* 66)

Homans has put his finger on what is so troubling throughout Jung's entire corpus. It is one thing to draw legitimate parallels between psychic experience and the world of the mythopoetic, and quite another to engage in free-floating flights of visionary imagination. Through it all, there is the distinct impression of "overkill," for one senses that Jung attempts to overwhelm the reader with carefully and not-so-carefully chosen parallels.

Jung wrote *Symbols of Transformation* at top speed at a time of a growing rift with Freud and at a time when he was becoming preoccupied with myth. With such a profusion of images, the thread of Jung's argument becomes exceedingly difficult if not impossible to ascertain. In a letter to Freud, Jung indicated his belief that "it may very well be that, thanks to your discoveries, we are on the threshold of something really sensational, which I scarcely know how to describe except with the Gnostic concept of Sophia (inner wisdom) which is particularly suited to the reincarnation of ancient wisdom in the shape of psychoanalysis. . . . I . . . would counsel you [to let my "Transformations and Symbols of Libido"] unleash your associations and/or fantasies: I am sure you will hit upon strange things if you do" (Freud and Jung 269J). Jung's strategy here is to appeal to Freud's vanity while persuading him to engage in gnostic fantasies, as he himself was already doing. Freud's more analytic temperament would obviously not go along with Jung's enthusiastic suggestion.

Jung had begun the study of mythology when he still idealized Freud. Why did mythology assume such importance for Jung? Why did it come to eat him "alive"? (cited in Homans, *Jung in Context* 57). His language suggests the devouring nature of cannibalism.

In connection with his illuminating study of Jung's narcissism, Homans shows that *Symbols of Transformation* is not a detached study in the psychology of ancient mythologies but "an incredibly grandiose effort to compress the complexity, richness, diversity, and contradictoriness of ancient symbolism into the mold of the simplistic libido theory. Its manner of execution is, furthermore, easily as grandiose as its method and conclusions" (*Jung in Context* 66). Homans has convincingly demonstrated that Jung produced a record of his own fantasies rather than an interpretation of myths and symbols of the past. It is hardly sufficient to say that Jung was engaging in a mythopoetic mode of thinking. I am impressed, as is Homans, by the exceedingly tenuous links between one image and the next. An interesting question follows from this line of interpretation: If Jung had such a vested interest in his studies of mythology and was trying to deal with his own inner conflicts, does his method yield any clues about the nature of his struggles?

One clue lies in the importance accorded to the myth of the hero. This topic had already been considered by Otto Rank in a different way in 1909 (Progoff, *Death and Rebirth* 191), and now Jung deals with the mythological battle for deliverance from the mother and with his struggle with a monstrous beast. I strongly suspect that mythological deliverance is a disguise of a more basic inner conflict.

Several themes important to Jung are interconnected. These are the claim that the unconscious represents an impersonal or collective (even universal) substratum; the idea that the anima represents the unconscious feminine dimension, which arouses fear and ambivalence; the motif that these themes are archetypal or of universal significance; and the desire for union of the dissociated fragments of the personality. The importance of dissociation in Jung's own consciousness is reflected in his frank admission of a lifelong interplay of Personalities No. 1 and No. 2. Jung was investigating the effects of dissociation in a split personality and concluded that in such cases especially, Freud's explanations overstated the sexual motif. He found it quite impossible to transfer Freud's theory of libido to dementia praecox. On the contrary, he explained that "this illness produces a loss of reality which cannot be explained by the deficiency of the libido defined in this narrow sense" (*Symbols* 143). Jung insisted that it was paranoia, closely related to dementia praecox, that compelled Freud to enlarge the earlier limits of the conception (142).

Winnicott's review of Jung's autobiography is important in this connection. A late chapter in *The Symbols of Transformation*, "The Dual Mother Role," is also pertinent. As we have seen, Jung's mother caused him much psychic distress because of the unpredictability of her vacillating moods. Perhaps his fascination with the dual mother in a mythological mode reflects a form of safe distancing, combined with his need to relive in a more adequate way the pain he experienced in relation to his actual mother. If this is the case, then his attention to myth is a mode of therapeutic reworking of his own early painful experiences. Still another topic related to Jung's excursus into mythology is that of psychic merger. The motif of the *hieros gamos* (sacred marriage) or mystical unity came up in Jung's ideas repeatedly. It appears to be closely linked to Jung's attempts to achieve unification through the process of symbolic enactment.

By all this Freud was not impressed. Jung had shown that Miss Miller's sexual attraction to a man was sublimated in fantasies. In at least one respect Freud must have been pleased. To both men, at that point in their lives, religion throughout the ages represented a form of compensation for erotic desire. Jung's evolving method sought to show how this compensated desire found in spirituality could be employed in the basis of a therapeutic method.

The theme of incest also hovers in the wings of this discussion. Jung was of the opinion that actual cases of incest were quite rare, whereas what he called "spiritual incest" is constantly seen in the writings of mythology. These were not reinterpretations that Freud could welcome. In fact, Jung's writings on the topic were to prove costly. This is precisely why he hesitated for several months before committing these ideas to writing. Jones reports that Freud knew the exact page where Jung went wrong. It was page 174 of the *Jahrbuch für psychoanalytische und psychopathologische Forschungen* (Jones 2:143).

The last chapter in *Symbols of Transformation* is entitled "The Sacrifice." In *Memories* Jung states: "I knew in advance that its publication would cost me my friendship with Freud" (167). In *Symbols* he indicated his own understanding of incest, libido, and still other topics on which he and Freud differed. Intuitively he knew, but did not want to recognize, that the sacrifice needed to be made. In hindsight, what happened between the two men seems only too obvious. In a certain sense Jung became the burnt offering.

Jung was in a double bind. For his own ideas to come forward, he had to sever, however harshly, his dependence upon Freud. It is possible that he displaced his intensely personal feelings toward Freud on the impersonal archaic images of mythology, later termed archetypes, to assuage the pain. Much attention has been focused on Jung's use of mythology. Very few attempts have been made to account for his reasons for embracing it. As soon as Jung completed *Symbols of Transformation*, he was struck by "what it means to live with a myth and what it means to live without one" (*CW* 5:xxiv).

Hogenson, in a study of the differences between the two men, has written: "Freud is haunted by the image of the Egyptian Moses, and Jung turns to the Gnostics" (164). Hogenson further asserts that repression assumes primacy for Freud, just as projection does for Jung. Following Jung's line of reasoning, Hogenson then points out that Freud's objective in setting forth his Oedipus complex was to establish not simply one successful system of interpretation, but the true interpretation (165). For this reason, Jung in his later writings insists that his own approach is but a subjective confession, implying that it is not universally valid. To a large degree, each man's conception of the world is dependent upon and limited by his own experience and place in it. Freud's view of a monotheistic patriarchalism in secularized form and Jung's heterodox religiosity in quest of inner certainty reflect their originators to an uncommon degree.

Psychoanalysis and analytical psychology have made very different assumptions about the world. One method assumes that behind the chaos, an underlying intelligibility exists. The other assumes that the world is essentially mysterious and in need of mythmaking. Hence, psychoanalysis has sought to *analyze* unconscious motivation. Analytical psychology from its inception sought to *amplify* symbolic meanings. For example, for Jung, a topic like incest becomes symbolized, whereas for Freud it remains a matter of psychic history.

Intimate Friend Becomes Hated Enemy

In time, Jung had served his purpose for the cause of psychoanalysis. New disciples took his place, and his value for Freud diminished dramatically. In a letter to Abraham when the break was virtually assured, Freud wrote: "Jung is crazy, but I don't really want a split; I should prefer him to leave of his own accord. Perhaps my Totem work will hasten the break against my will" (Freud and Abraham 141, June 1, 1913).

Contrary to what Freud wrote to Abraham, there is evidence that Freud wanted a split with Jung, as Jung did with Freud. Of this Freud may not have been fully conscious. On several occasions he called Jung's unconscious slips to his attention, which infuriated Jung. Further, toward the end of their association he began to pursue topics in the psychology of religion, notably in *Totem and Taboo*, which previously had been Jung's exclusive province. Whether intended or not,

Formative & Transformative Life Experiences

this heightened the competition between adopted son and surrogate father. Also, Jung played his part in bringing about the break, especially by referring to Freud's neurosis. Freud had a hard time determining how to respond to this challenge to his authority. In the end there was something of a conspiracy among Freud and his loyal associates to maneuver Jung out of his position as president of the International Psychoanalytic Association. To this development Jung put up surprisingly little resistance.

Jones cites three episodes that played a part in the final dissolution of the relationship. First, Freud went at Whitsun to see Ludwig Binswanger at Kreuzlingen. This produced a misunderstanding on Jung's part, which "completely puzzled Freud" and about which Freud made sarcastic remarks. Second, in Jung's New York lectures, he sought to make psychoanalysis more acceptable to his American audience by leaving out sexual themes. On this development Freud commented, "All one had to do was leave out still more and it would become still more acceptable." Finally, Jung sent the wrong date to Jones for the Munich meeting, and as a result Freud commented to Jones that one should not do such things even unconsciously (Jones 2:143).

Other factors leading to the dissolution of the relationship were Jung's dream of skulls in the basement of a house and Freud's fainting episode. The latter has been interpreted as a response to Jung's death wishes with regard to Freud. At the time and later in his autobiography, Jung vigorously rejected this assessment (*Memories* 157). The final blow came when Freud called an unconscious slip to Jung's attention (Freud and Jung 337F). Jung had started out to write "Even Adler's cronies do not regard me as one of theirs" but made a slip, changing "theirs" to "yours" (335J). Freud's observation triggered the rage that had been building in Jung for years, and he replied with an intemperate and incensed letter, in which he referred to Freud's neurosis. He accused Freud of sniffing out the symptomatic actions in his vicinity, reducing others to the level of sons and daughters while he remained "on the top as the father, sitting pretty" (338J). The picture of Freud in a superior position would seem to evoke a childhood memory. We can see quite clearly Jung's ambivalence toward his own father, a weak and vacillating man. His anger over what he perceives to be Freud's superior position in their relationship reflects to some degree the dependence of his childhood.

Jung continued: "You see, my dear Professor, so long as you hand out this stuff I don't give a damn for my symptomatic actions; they shrink to nothing in comparison with the formidable beam in my brother Freud's eye." This is obviously a strange twist to the biblical metaphor. "I am not in the least neurotic—touch wood! I have submitted . . . to analysis and am much the better for it. You know, of course, how far a patient gets with self-analysis: not out of his neurosis—just like you." Jung's inner frustration came bursting forth, an indication that he was unable to tolerate any criticism from Freud at that tenuous juncture in their relationship. He said, "Your technique of treating your pupils like patients is a blunder. In that way you produce either slavish sons or impudent puppies." He continued, "If ever you should rid yourself entirely of your complexes and stop playing the father to your sons and instead of aiming continually at their weak spots take a good look at your own for a change, then I will mend my ways and at one stroke uproot the vice of being *in two minds* about you" (338J; emphasis added).

Like his relations with his father and mother, Jung's relation with Freud was characterized by profound ambivalence. It would seem that Jung's childhood conflicts have relevance here. He saw his relationship with Freud as requiring from him either servile obedience or righteous indignation and anger. Thus the relationship based on unrealistic expectations came to an end.

After their falling-out Freud described Jung as "a person who was incapable of tolerating the authority of another but who was still less capable of wielding it himself and whose energies were relentlessly devoted to the furtherance of his own interests" (*On the History* 43). At this point Freud's interest in maintaining authority and Jung's conflict with authoritarianism were antithetical. Among recent interpreters, Homans has noted Jung's injured self-esteem, narcissistic injury, fear of abandonment, and narcissistic rage (as in childhood when his mother was hospitalized for several months). In the end Freud's and Jung's narcissistic investments clashed, as one might have expected.

Freud's investment in maintaining control of the relationship and preventing any deviation from his orthodox doctrine is evident. In the polemic he wrote against Alfred Adler and Jung in 1914, Freud noted that he could be "as abusive and enraged as anyone" (*On the History* 39). Freud's bitterness over this challenge to his authority

Formative & Transformative Life Experiences

never disappeared. Binswanger later asked Freud how it had come about that his oldest and most talented disciples, Jung and Adler, had broken with him. Freud gave the illuminating reply: "Precisely because they too wanted to be popes" (cited in Roazen, *Freud and His Followers* 244).

The ultimate break had been presaged for some time. Freud's correspondence with Emma Jung is of interest given the two men's psychologies. She tactfully broached with Freud the issue of his father complex. On November 6, 1911, she wrote to him: "You should rejoice and drink to the full the happiness of victory after having struggled for so long. And do not think of Carl with a father's feeling: 'He will grow, but I must dwindle,' but rather as one human being thinks of another, who like you has his own law to fulfill" (Freud and Jung 279EJ). History has shown that each man was possessed by his own inner daimon and was unable to accept or creatively respond to that of the other.

The breakup of the relationship was far more devastating for Jung than for Freud. There are doubtless several reasons for this. Freud's reputation as the father of psychoanalysis was already secure, and his circle of associates was wide, even though the young movement had to win its way. Jung, on the other hand, was very much isolated by the break, as most of his former associates sided with Freud. In the short run the break was to take a heavy toll on Jung. The subsequent illness Jung suffered, however, was to provide the insights that were to become the foundations of his best theories.

After the parting of the ways with Freud, a period of inner
uncertainty began for me. It would be no exaggeration to call
it a state of disorientation. I felt totally suspended in mid-air.
—C. G. *Jung*, Memories

CHAPTER 4

Creative Illness:
Jung's Relation to the Unconscious

After his break with Freud in 1913, Jung entered upon
a prolonged period of extreme introversion, which has come to be
known by many of his interpreters as his creative illness. This period
of Jung's life is known for the intensity of lively visions and images
that were so extreme and strong that he withdrew from many outside
activities. For a long period of time he neither wrote nor lectured.
Besides giving up the presidency of the International Psychoanalytic
Society, he gave up his position of lecturer at Zurich University.
However, he did continue meeting with his patients.

The background of Jung's creative illness can be summarized as a convergence of his traumatic break with Freud and their mutually narcissistic and unrealistic projections, the disjunction of two separate and distinct sides to his personality structure, a crisis in midlife of unusually severe intellectual and emotional intensity, and the need for a more satisfying myth of his place in the world. As James Heisig has expressed it, "Like the empty spaces in Chinese painting, the time when nothing happens is often of the deepest significance" (*Imago Dei* 29). The period was for Jung one of intense activation of the unconscious and, hence, a period of profound inner creativity that produced the seed ideas of most of his later theories, which were to unfold over many years. As Jung wrote in the closing paragraph of "Confrontation with the Unconscious": "The years when I was pursuing my inner images were the most important of my life—in them everything essential was decided. It all began then; the later details are only supplements . . . and at first swamped me. It was the *prima materia* for a lifetime's work" (*Memories* 199).

We can, of course, ask why the break with Freud was so much more traumatic for Jung than for Freud. Interpreters are by no means agreed on this point. On the surface of things, Jung was now cut off from many of his former associates in the psychoanalytic movement. Most of these people sided with Freud in the either/or of one of psychiatry's great schisms. Jung's parting with this group produced in him feelings of isolation and abandonment from colleagues and was doubtless a profound trauma. There was much more to the break than the reasons thus far cited, however. On a deeper level Jung had lost his surrogate father—Freud—and thus a childhood identification problem was reactivated. This was of great significance to Jung, as he had never been able to identify with his pastor-father. The elder Jung held dogmatic religious beliefs that contradicted his actual feelings. By contrast, Jung, even in his troubled youth, was in touch with his inner images. These images provided him with considerable solace and comfort. Jung's later solution for healing involved identifying and using images that emerged from the unconscious.

There is an apparent connection between Jung's dream of skulls in the basement and the impending break with Freud. This dream was interpreted by Freud as an unconscious death wish on Jung's part before their break. After the break in 1913, it is also to be seen in the dream Jung had of the death of Siegfried. As Jung put it, "The dream showed that the attitude embodied by Siegfried, the hero, no longer suited me. Therefore it had to be killed" (*Memories* 180).[1] Nearly all psychoanalytic interpreters have drawn a direct and explicit connection between SIGmund Freud and the SIeGfried of Jung's dream.

In one of several reinterpretations of Jung's life to appear in recent years, the psychoanalyst Eli Marcovitz argues that the break with Freud in effect echoes an underlying anger that Jung felt toward his father. As Marcovitz writes, "It certainly seems as if Jung's hostile feelings toward his father were transferred to Freud, and that Freud's fainting in Jung's presence was precipitated by his unconscious recognition of Jung's death-wishes against him" (63). If, indeed, the feelings were death wishes (as Freud asserted and Jung denied), there is the question of the source from which they arose. Death wishes are frequently, but not always, based on anger. Marcovitz's contention would seem to be supported by something else. Toward the end of the Freud-Jung relationship, unrealistic anger came into evidence on each man's part. This anger was based on their unconscious projections. Jung's memorable letter of rage toward Freud clearly points to a deep source of his anger, very likely rooted in his childhood.

In contrast, Papadopoulos writes: "By leaving Freud, Jung did not only leave the security of a friendship; he also let loose his hopeful grip on the psychoanalytic framework. Without any framework within which to render comprehensible even his own drifting away Jung found himself alone and unprotected on the seas of his unconscious" (Papadopoulos and Saayman 76). Jung noted the painful untenability of his position: "The dialogue with myself became uncomfortable and I stopped thinking. I had reached a dead end" (*Memories* 171).

In his early years Jung had found the Christian myth unacceptable. Upon his break with Freud, the psychoanalytic myth also became untenable, so that for a time his psyche was without an explanatory paradigm of meaning, a situation not unique to himself. It was this situation he was later to describe as characteristic of the present age, namely, "modern man in search of a soul." In many of his later works, Jung makes psychic connections between the unconscious and the mythopoetic imagination. These are the sources of religious visions of wholeness and integration in virtually all cultures.

As we have seen, Jung's book *Symbols of Transformation* marks a turning point in his relationship with Freud. He hesitated for months before committing his thoughts to paper. When he did so, he analyzed the dreams and visions of the schizophrenic under the pseudonym of Miss Miller. Jung broke with Freud's use of Oedipus theory. In this difficult volume he offers a solution to the incest problem different from Freud's. As Jung sees it, incest is a symbolic theme in virtually all primitive and archaic cultures. In fact, Jung here prefigures his later stress upon the visionary imagination and mythic themes such as Osiris's night journey to the sea and Babylonian, Egyptian, and biblical motifs of deliverance and rebirth.

Jung's pivotal book is replete with digressions and questionable connections, in which one idea sends Jung into a process of free association, often making tenuous connections between the topics covered. It concludes with the chapter titled "The Sacrifice," which is filled with quotes from Hölderlin, Nietzsche, Chiwantopel, Goethe, Frobenius, Vishvakarman, Mithra, Rubens, and others. The term *sacrifice* generally refers to an offering or obligation made to a deity, a concept that has mythical reverberations. Jung rationalized that his friendship with Freud needed to be "sacrificed" in the cause of truth. One has the feeling, however, that in this matter he had little choice.

Jung's mental state in this period was such that he found himself "at the edge of a cosmic abyss. It was like a voyage to the moon, or a descent into empty space" (*Memories* 181). Amid the flotsam and jetsam of his life, he was tossed to and fro like a cork on an angry sea. Images came upon him suddenly and with great intensity. He was transported into space and back again. As a result of his extensive work with schizophrenics, Jung recognized the seriousness of his own condition. Over a period of months and years, his unconscious became activated, and he recognized that he was in danger of being overcome by unconscious forces similar to those that drove Nietzsche and Hölderlin mad: "I did my best not to lose my head but to find some way to understand these strange things. I stood helpless before an alien world; everything in it seemed difficult and incomprehensible. I was living in a constant state of tension; often I felt as if gigantic blocks of stone were tumbling down upon me. One thunderstorm followed another" (176–77).

In the past decade or so scholars have begun to reassess not only the events of Jung's life but also his theoretical contributions. Part of this has emanated from a thoughtful reappraisal of Jung's own words. He wrote: "After the parting of the ways with Freud, a period of inner uncertainty began for me. It would be no exaggeration to call it a state of disorientation. I felt totally suspended in mid-air, for I had not yet found my own footing" (*Memories* 170). Nor was he to find it for some years to come.

As Storr points out, "Jung regarded creative persons, including himself, both as being 'ahead of their time' and as being in touch with a source of superior wisdom which might be variously referred to as the 'collective unconscious' or later, quite openly as God" (*C. G. Jung* 14). For this reason his references to "God" should not be equated with traditional religious images of the divine, or if they are, the correspondence should be asserted only with the greatest of caution. To Jung's mind they represent only "the existence of an archetypal God-image. . . . But it is a very important and influential archetype. . . . And since experience of this archetype has the quality of numinosity, often . . . it comes into the category of religious experiences" (*Psychology and Religion: West and East*; *CW* 11:59).

During this period Jung had both auditory and visual hallucinations and was bothered by the intense activation of unconscious forces. Freudians have devoted much attention to his correspondence with Freud but strangely have virtually ignored this fascinating period of his life's journey. Jungians have tended to be rather prosaic about this extremely difficult period in Jung's life, using terms like "shamanic descent" and "night-sea journey" to describe it.

Jung's Confrontation with Madness

In December 1913 strange things began happening to Jung. He began what he came to call his descent into the unconscious. This descent conjured up the image of falling to the depths, as it were, through a hole in the surface of the earth. He had visions of a primal cave or fissure, which he had experienced earlier at a traumatic period of his childhood. Jung's world of the unconscious bears remarkable similarities to the unruly world of shamans, mystics, and prophets. His descent has been viewed by himself and many in the Jungian tradition as a "sacrifice" to the task of death and rebirth for the collective good. More important, it is valorized as a mythical journey by many of his interpreters. Joan Halifax, in *Shamanic Voices*, has written, "Shamanic initiation demands a rending of the individual from all that constitutes his or her past" (13). In a sense Jung descended to the "womb of primordial life" (Eliade's term) to enter into the mystical or religious side of his existence.

Following Jung's lead, this way of explaining his descent into the unconscious was common to the literature before 1970. Formerly Jungians played down the severity of Jung's illness, perceiving it to be a rite of initiation in midlife (see Henderson). Typically such crises are characterized by depression, whereas Jung's initial reaction was more like panic and fright born of terror. He was beset by vivid recurrent visions of a most disturbing nature, an unusual activation of his unconscious processes.

Newer interpretations by nearly all investigators have proceeded on the assumption that Jung's very sanity, and not just an interesting experiment in insight and introspection, was at stake. For example, Barbara Hannah italicizes Jung's sentence "*Therefore my first obligation was to probe the depths of my own psyche.* . . . This work took precedence over everything else" (*Memories* 176, cited in Hannah 113). Can it be that the "myth of shamanic descent" is a gloss on the agony of Jung's actual suffering? There would seem to be considerable evidence for this hypothesis.

A related side issue concerns whether Jung's disturbed visions of world destruction represent his reputed ability to see future events. Some interpreters have credited Jung with outright clairvoyance and the ability to foresee war. For instance, it has been held that he had premonitions of World War I in anticipation of the carnage of actual events. In *Memories* Jung states that the idea of war did not occur to him, but the British classicist E. R. Dodds, in *Pagan and Christian in an Age of Anxiety*, credits Jung with just such psychic precognition. That is, of course, one way that his visions of world destruction can be read. In a later period of his life, but before *Memories*, Jung was to recall that "there was already a faint smell of burning in the air" (*Essays on Contemporary Events*, cited in Dodds, *Pagan and Christian* 4n1).

Jung had a recurrent vision of a monstrous, world-destroying flood and consequent cosmic destruction that included floodwaters covering all the northern and low-lying lands between the North Sea and the Alps. When the flood came toward Switzerland, he saw the mountains grow higher to protect the country. The floating rubble of civilization and drowned bodies of uncounted thousands were followed by a paroxysm of a sea turned to blood. Of this vision of cosmic and potential personal annihilation, Jung said, "The vision lasted about one hour. I was perplexed and nauseated and ashamed of my weakness" (*Memories* 175). Then the vision of world destruction took on new imagery, for repeatedly he dreamed of the descent of an Arctic cold wave that killed all living beings. A third dream sequence involved a frightful cold wave transformed into a leaf-bearing tree. Because of his extensive experience with schizophrenia, Jung was aware that such visions of death and cosmic destruction frequently herald psychotic episodes. He says: "I was menaced by a psychosis" (176), implying that he had an experience similar in symptoms, a kind of near miss. Homans contends that Jung had temporary psychoticlike, but not in fact psychotic, mental episodes (*Jung in Context* 87).

It would seem that at this point in his life Jung was expressing something far more serious than a resurgence of the mythopoetic imagination characteristic of the age of archaic religions and long defunct in a rationalistic age. I hope to show that given the severity of these experiences, Jung's mode of dealing with them showed remarkable ingenuity and successfully activated precisely those aspects of the unconscious that were producing his disorientation. He tells us that to some extent he translated "emotions into images" but is less clear about the nature of the emotions themselves. Intense anxiety was undoubtedly present. Jung interpreted the process thus: "Had I left those images hidden in the emotions, I might have been torn to pieces by them. There is a chance that I might have succeeded in splitting them off; but in that case I would inexorably have fallen into a neurosis and so been ultimately destroyed by them anyhow" (*Memories* 177). Given the intensity of the images emerging from his psyche and the gravity of his situation, Jung's method of facing the situation head-on was remarkably creative and doubtless prevented a total psychic breakdown.

Storr has argued that though Jung's experiences were of psychotic intensity, his ego was strong enough to fend off a schizophrenic break. Also, he argues that Jung was able to use his creativity as a defense against breakdown in the way in which some other creative people, for example August Strindberg, have also been able to do (Storr, *Dynamics* 209–10). Storr argues that Jung's creative ways of dealing with his dissociation were, in fact, a source of his inner healing. In expanding on this point in a letter to Brome, Storr writes:

"I think his psychosis or near psychosis was of . . . the nature of a schizophrenic episode" (Nov. 10, 1975, cited in Brome, *Jung*). In an otherwise well-written study, without offering evidence to substantiate his claim, Brome in *Jung: Man and Myth* maintains that Jung was a manic-depressive.

We can also note that Jung's dream of a frightful world-destroying cold is followed by the vision of a leaf-bearing tree without fruit. This would seem to be a compensatory vision, which closely follows the earlier vision of terror and destruction. Jung tells us that the leaf-bearing tree without fruit represents his own life at that frightening moment of his existence. Suddenly the leaves on the tree without fruit are "transformed by the effects of the frost into sweet grapes full of healing juices. I plucked the grapes and gave them to a large, waiting crowd" (*Memories* 176). John Gedo, a Chicago psychoanalyst, has commented upon Jung's references to the tree of life and the transformation of the grapes into healing juices, which he plucks and distributes to the crowd. On slim evidence Gedo maintains that Jung himself had now become "the soothsaying God of the vine" whose prophet he had wanted Freud to be. Gedo even maintains that Jung views himself as a reincarnated messianic savior. He writes, "Jung saw himself as the reincarnated Christ, freed from the undesirable encrustations through which His divine message had been distorted by Christianity. From such a perspective, a Jewish precursor, Sigmund Freud, would take on the significance of John the Baptist" (Gedo, "Magna" 76).

Gedo's one-sided interpretation strikes me as unwarranted and judgmental. It represents an exceedingly facile explanation of a disturbed period of Jung's life. In one sense Jung does have a vision of himself as a messianic savior at the very time when, as if by irony, fruit is banished from the tree of his own life. In my view, his vision is not to be taken at face value as something for which he should be held accountable. On the contrary, the compensatory nature of his visionary experience over time was to enable him to work through his near psychosis.

Most of the dreams of this troubled period reflect death (falling through a hole in the earth) and rebirth or transformation. Falling is a recurring theme for Jung and may represent a reenactment of nearly falling through the rungs of a bridge as a child. Clearly, an individualistic religious motif combining death and consequent rebirth is a central part of his experience. Put another way, his experience of personal misery (i.e., inner dissociation) is closely linked with his perception of psychic mystery, coming into contact with the archetypal dimension of existence.

Again, the most disturbing images beset him. He stands helpless before an alien world. He feels as if gigantic blocks of stone are tumbling down upon him, as he had seen happen to Nietzsche and Hölderlin. He is crushed under their collective weight. The imagery is reminiscent of an earthquake, with large fissures in the earth appearing and the immense weight of huge stone blocks annihilating free action and routes of escape. This flood of disturbing visions is partially offset by what Jung calls the brute strength that was in him that insisted he find the meaning he was experiencing in these fantasies. The conviction comes upon him that he was "obeying a higher will" by so doing (*Memories* 177).

Around Christmas 1912 Jung dreamed that he was on an Italian balcony, that is, a loggia with pillars, marble floor, and balustrade. He is seated on a gold Renaissance chair in front of a table made of beautiful green stone resembling emerald. Surrounded by his children, he looks out into the distance, for the loggia is located high in the tower of a castle (*Memories* 171). One is struck by the precise visual imagery and the translucent numinous quality of this dream. It has something of the translucent quality of the visions of John's revelations on the isle of Patmos, where he describes a new heaven and a new earth. The street of the city is pure gold, transparent as glass (Revelation 21:21). Late in life, in *Answer to Job*, Jung returns to these very apocalyptic images: "I have seen nothing that even remotely resembles the brutal impact with which the opposites collide in John's visions, except in the case of severe psychosis" (*cw* 11:450).

Jung's dream reveals the intensity of color and form. A messenger dove descends and is quickly transformed into a little girl with golden hair, who runs off to play with other children. The vision may represent one of Jung's daughters who was of that age or else recall his childhood. The small girl returns to place her arms tenderly around his neck. She vanishes, and the dove returns and speaks in a human voice: "Only in the first hours of the night can I transform myself into a human being while the male dove is busy with the twelve dead" (*Memories* 172).[2] She flies into the blue air, and Jung awakens. One is struck by the multiple selves that emerge, somehow struggling for expression.

Jung was especially puzzled by what the business of the male dove with the twelve dead meant. He considered the twelve apostles, the months of the year, and the signs of the Zodiac but could find no acceptable solution. Was his unconscious wrestling with the twelve who had become dead for him? Assuredly this is no version of a traditional Christian myth, in which one man dies for the redemption of all. It is a myth in which opposites are magically transformed into a new synthesis. It marked the beginning of Jung's interest in the alchemical legend of Hermes of Trismegistus, which occurred so repetitively throughout his writings.

In *Faces in a Cloud*, Stolorow and Atwood have demonstrated quite conclusively that Jung's principle of the balance of opposites is grounded in his own psychic experience. According to these theorists, the balancing of opposite tendencies is required to avert the threat of self-fragmentation or of "being torn asunder into pairs of opposites" (Jung, *Two Essays* 83, cited in Stolorow and Atwood 84).

Again Jung dreamed of a region like the Alyscamps near Arles, where a lane of sarcophagi date back to Merovingian times. He stood before a row of tombs that reminded him of old burial vaults, where armored knights lay outstretched. These dead were not stone, though, but mummified corpses. Jung looked at the first one, a man of the 1830s, and the man came to life and moved his hands. Jung walked down the row, looking at each one in turn—going back in time, from the nineteenth century to twelfth—and each moved his hands when Jung viewed him. The last figure was a crusader, dressed in chain mail. Jung interprets: "Of course I had originally held to Freud's view that vestiges of old experiences exist in the unconscious. But dreams like this . . . taught me that such contents are not dead, outmoded forms, but belong to our living being. My work had confirmed this assumption and in the course of years there developed from it the theory of archetypes" (*Memories* 173).

In the context of Jung's traumatic break with Freud, the twelfth-century Christian crusader may represent an aspect of himself protected by chain mail (his persona) who in the struggle with Siegfried of the mountains is "dead yet not so dead" (Jung, *Analytical Psychology Notes*, lecture 5, p. 39). Further, at that period Jung had consciously abandoned the Christian myth, only to find a heterodox version of it located in the archaic or, as he soon formulated it, the collective unconscious, freed from the reductive onslaughts of his adversary Freud.

Plunge through the Earth

During Advent 1913 Jung was sitting at his desk when suddenly he had the experience of letting himself drop through the earth. "The ground literally gave way beneath my feet and I plunged down into dark depths. I could not fend off a feeling of panic." He found himself in a dark cave in which there also stood a dwarf with leathery skin. He waded through the icy water at one end of the cave, where he perceived a glowing red crystal. "There was running water. In it a corpse floated by, a youth with blonde hair and a wound in the head. He was followed by a gigantic black scarab and then by a red, new born sun, rushing up out of the depths of the water. Dazzled by the light I wanted to replace the stone upon the opening but then a fluid welled up. It was blood. A thick jet of it leaped up, and I felt nauseated. It seemed to me that the blood continued to spurt for an unendurably long time. At last it ceased and the vision came to an end" (*Memories* 179).

This vision, confused and bizarre as it appears in *Memories*, nonetheless reads like a profoundly expurgated version that Jung himself presented in lecture 6 of his 1925 Seminar. There he includes details such as "a cave full of insects, bat-like in form and making a strange noise." Or to cite another example: "Then there came floating past a big black something nearly as big as the body of a man and coming after him with moving legs. This was a scarab, and after it came a ball that was like a luminous sun, glowing dark red in the waters like a sun rise before a storm. When it was in the middle of the field of vision, hundreds of thousands of snakes threw themselves on the sun and obscured it" (*Analytical Psychology Notes*, lecture 6, pp. 47, 48). If Hollywood had discovered these materials, surely a movie would have already been made of them. *The Lost Weekend* and Spielberg's *Raiders of the Lost Ark* appear pale beside the vividness, detail, and sheer terror of the visionary intensity of Jung's psyche during this period.

In *Memories* Jung interprets this powerful and deeply troubled vision as a hero and solar myth, a drama of death and renewal (179).

In Egyptian mythology the scarab symbolized rebirth. He does acknowledge that the "intolerable" outpouring of blood was an abnormal phenomenon. The history of mythology may have provided examples of caves full of insects and bats and hundreds of thousands of snakes throwing themselves on the sun, but he does not supply them! Psychoanalysts have written voluminously about the break between Freud and Jung but have done little close analysis of this interesting material.

Homans, in *Jung in Context*, following a Kohutian analysis, has used recent studies in the psychology of narcissism to understand Jung. One can agree that Jung's psychic organization was narcissistic and preoedipal. The psychology of narcissism, with its concepts of narcissistic injury and vulnerability, may in some ways provide a richer and more complex view of certain neglected aspects of Jung's complex personality. Yet it fails to account for the severity of his breakdown and more particularly for the connection between his numinosity and his creativity, which over time provided the impetus for his inner healing, recovery of perspective, and later creative contributions.

Elijah, Salome, and Philemon

Jung also had a dream of Elijah and Salome. He likened his vision to a voyage to the moon. In this land of the dead he comes upon a crater. It is there that he perceives an old man with a white beard and a beautiful young girl, who is blind. Approaching the couple as though they were real, he listens as the old man explains that he is Elijah and the blind girl that she is Salome. In the vision Jung is assured that this strange couple had belonged together from all eternity. Additionally, the third figure in the story is a large black serpent (*Memories* 181–82). Here we see the contrast in Jung's unconscious mind of the older man (himself) and the younger woman (Toni Wolff). Wolff was thirteen years younger than Jung. Among other things, in 1914 Jung was going through what today commonly is called a midlife crisis—surely a time when the attraction of the younger woman, especially one who "understands" troublesome unconscious needs, is often a factor in male psychology.

Many years later in an important essay, "Stages of Life," Jung was one of the first persons to write perceptively about this problem.

Though not precisely linking Jung and Wolff with the Elijah and Salome of Jung's dream, Barbara Hannah comments: "This pair— the young girl with the old man—was destined to have a far-reaching effect on Jung's fate, for—at much the same time as the fantasy— he made the extraordinary discovery that of all his friends and ac- quaintances only one girl was able to accompany him intrepidly on his Nekyia to the underworld" (117).

To a considerable extent Jung's theories of anima/animus are de- rived from these images. His own interpretation of the dream is that "Salome is an anima figure. She is blind because she does not see the meaning of things. Elijah is the figure of the wise old prophet and represents the factor of intelligence; Salome the erotic element. One might say the two figures are personifications of Logos and Eros" (*Memories* 182).[3] Overlooking the obvious connections, he rational- izes the matter into impersonal principles of explanation.

If the interpretation linking Jung and Wolff with Elijah and Salome has any merit, then there would seem to be a reversal taking place in the dream mechanism, for at this period of Jung's life it was he who was blind, not Wolff. Wolff enabled him intuitively "to see" or "know" the depths of the unconscious. Jung projects onto Wolff his need for a companion to accompany him on the perilous mythi- cal journey through the psychic underworld. The diffuseness of the symbol "blind" can also be considered in the context of the world's spiritual traditions. There blindness frequently refers not merely to a physical affliction but also to the spiritual condition of being in a state of ignorance. It would seem to follow that in Jung's unconscious vision, at this troubled juncture of his life, Toni was not a qualified guide to his netherworld of deepened shadows. Possibly at the time, he was looking for a spiritual guide, a need that he later transferred and projected onto the figure of Elijah/Philemon. The unconscious mind modified through the dream censor would seem to have pro- duced a reversal of consciousness in this case.

The dream censor tends to disguise the latent dream content be- cause of its unacceptable nature. Hence in Freud's view of dreams the manifest dream content would be altered considerably, in a sense cleaned up, to pass muster. Jung, by contrast, held that at least some dreams offered a prospective view of things rather than a retrospec- tive view. Free association, according to Jung, was not necessary, for the dream was regarded as a natural production and not a disguise.

Formative & Transformative Life Experiences

In *Memories* Jung tells us that his family allowed him to keep his footing at times of inner upheaval. Yet at the same time he believed that conventional morality should be transcended so that self-realization could be achieved. One may surmise that such self-realization was achieved at the expense of an element of unconscious guilt with regard to his relationship with Wolff.

Martin Buber, in his William Alanson White Memorial Lectures, once distinguished between guilt and guilt feelings. Buber noted that some psychologists concern themselves solely with the removal of guilt feelings without addressing the more basic question of the genesis of the guilt. He was referring to those who justify their narcissistic concerns at the expense of others. Buber clarified his concern by writing: "Jung does not recognize at all any relationship between the individual soul and another existing being which oversteps the limits of the psychic. . . . In fact, in the whole great work of Jung's we learn nothing of guilt as a reality in the relation between the human person and the world entrusted to him in his life" (*Knowledge of Man* 124–25). Buber's observation would seem to point up a basic and significant difference between Jung's intrapsychic outlook and Buber's interhuman perspective.

In Jung's dreams the image of Elijah is subsequently taken over by that of Philemon, a winged guru with a lame foot whose wisdom Jung takes as an image of the idealized self. With Philemon, Jung has various long conversations. Of these Jung says: "He said things which I had not consciously thought. For I observed clearly that it was he who spoke, not I." From Philemon Jung learned what he came to call "psychic objectivity" or the autonomous "reality of the psyche" (*Memories* 183). As a result, he came to hold that psychic images have an independent existence of their own, like animals in the forest, people in a room, or birds in the air.

At this period of his life Jung aspired to be like Philemon, who represented superior insight. Jung likened him to an invisible guru. Jung had found yet a new father figure to "cleanse the horrible darkness of our minds" (*Memories* 184), as the alchemical treatise *Aurora Consurgens* states. In some respects Philemon is very much like the "wounded healer" that Jung himself embodied. Consequently, Philemon became an important guide for Jung to follow in meeting the challenges of the second phase of the life cycle.

To balance matters, Jung's fantasies soon focused upon a more earthly figure, Ka. "In ancient Egypt the 'king's ka' was his earthly form, the embodied soul" (*Memories* 184). In Jung's fantasy, however, the ka-soul came from the earth out of a deep shaft—reminiscent of the childhood man-eater dream and the later tunnel in the recurrent "descent into the depths of the earth" dream. In his studies of alchemy Jung sees various parallels to these figures in the visions of Zosimos of Panapolis and Mercurius. In time he says he was able to integrate both figures through the study of alchemy.

The Notebooks, Red and Black

During the years of troubled visions Jung wrote very little of a theoretical nature, and sometimes he read very little. This was a remarkable change in the life of such an avid student of every form of literature. Much of his time was spent in confronting and recording his often bizarre inner images, which filled 1,330 pages written and illustrated by his own hand. His handwriting at this time changed to a style used in the fourteenth century; his paintings were rendered with pigments that he himself prepared, after the manner of artists of previous ages. He had some of the most beautiful paintings and inscriptions bound in red leather, and they became known as *The Red Book*. It is said that the writings of this period fall into categories: some are bright and angelic, whereas others are dark and daimonic in form and content, reflecting the archetypal occult regions of Jung's own psyche. Once again we see the theme of the balance of opposites.

James Heisig has written that "the after-shock of his break with Freud brought an unusually polemical tone to his publications, overshadowing their once predominantly creative quality. . . . In Jung's case . . . these outwardly fallow years masked a spell of intense inner turmoil, bordering at one point on schizophrenia. Jung was experimenting on himself, with the truth of his theories of the unconscious" (*Imago Dei* 29). It was during this period that first *The Black Book* and then *The Red Book* were composed. These Jung regarded as conversations with his anima. Growing out of earlier notebooks, *The Red Book* came to comprise six hundred typewritten pages together with various mandala paintings, some of which have been reproduced in *Word and Image*, edited by Aniela Jaffé. Jung refers to *The Red Book* in *Memories*, but only a few paragraphs of it have been made available by Jaffé.

One of the few quotes available from *The Red Book* asserts a dichotomy between the "spirit of the times" and the "spirit of the depths." Jung writes, "Filled with human pride and blinded by the presumptuous spirit of the times, I long sought to hold that other spirit away from me. But I did not pause to consider that the spirit of the depths from time immemorial and for all time to come possessed a greater power than the spirit of the times, who changes with the generations and withers with the flowers of summer" (cited in Jaffé, "Creative Phases" 175). This emotive utterance took place after his break with Freud and during his troublesome midlife crisis. In this contest the emphasis upon life's transience and the certainty of a spirit visitation (even possession) is more readily understandable. It would seem that Jung was referring in other terms to the aspects of his inner split that earlier he had called Personality No. 1 (the bearer of light) and Personality No. 2 (the bearer of shadow) (*Memories* 88). By the same token, No. 1 was the bearer of time and No. 2 the bearer of timelessness, infinity, the " 'old man' who belonged to centuries" and eternity (68f.).

The second chapter of *The Red Book*, entitled "The Rediscovery of the Soul," states: "There is no other way. All other ways are false paths. I found the right way, it led me to you, to my soul. I return, tempered and purified" (cited in Jaffé, "Creative Phases" 174). The psychic gnostic stress upon intuitive inner certainty is evident.

Septem Sermones ad Mortuos

In 1916 Jung wrote *Septem Sermones ad Mortuos* (Seven Sermons to the Dead), later published privately as a booklet, which he gave to friends. It was also published as an appendix to Jung's autobiography, with his approval given most reluctantly. The language is regarded as being more or less in the style of *The Red Book*, resulting from conversations with personifications arising from the unconscious. These sermons are written in the first person, and Jung's unconscious speaks through Basilides of Alexandria, in an oblique reference to a famous Gnostic teacher of the second century. Heisig informs us: "The sermons are written in the first person, Basilides-Jung addressing himself as a kind of second Messiah to the dead Christians who return from Jerusalem in search of wisdom. The tract has all the marks of a heroic journey into the underworld" (*Imago Dei* 208). In expounding on the similarities between *The Red Book* and *Septem Sermones ad Mortuos*, Heisig refers to a "sort of inversion of values, wherein science is overcome by art, only in order that something new and higher may emerge from the ensuing dialectic" (ibid., 207).[4]

In this period of his life Jung is indeed retreating from the world of outer reality, reversing himself on science, so that inversion can be read as regression. Parenthetically, one can note that throughout Jung's life and in his writings the distinction between inner and outer reality or between personal vision and external objects is frequently blurred. Clearly the world of images is given priority. Heisig remarks that the style of *Septem Sermones* is "totally unlike anything else that Jung has ever published, and is similar to that of *The Red Book* except that the whole is more structured" (*Imago Dei* 208). It is true that the style of *Septem Sermones* differs from that of much of Jung's collected works. Yet the delight with esoteric hidden knowledge and irrational paradox can be found throughout Jung's corpus.

Sermon IV expands on the theme of Abraxas, the god-devil. In it Jung refers to the two images of the "Growing One" and the "Burning One." Both represent the conjunction of good and evil: the Burning One (or Eros) brings light while it consumes; the Growing One (or tree of life) buds and grows while it engulfs the living stuff around it. Together they form the burning tree, symbolizing God as the union of life and love (ibid., 212). By making this hypothesis is Jung not thereby positing a parallel to Freud's life instinct (eros) and the death instinct (thanatos)?

The enigmatic text of *Septem Sermones* is resplendent with paradox. Jung writes: "Nothingness is the same as fullness. In infinity full is no better than empty. Nothingness is both empty and full. . . . A thing that is infinite and eternal hath no qualities, since it hath all qualities. This nothingness or fullness we name the PLEROMA. . . . In the pleroma there is nothing and everything" (*Memories*, appendix 5, p. 379).

More than nearly any other thinker, Jung has inspired the further exploration of connections between inner psychic images and the world's great spiritual traditions. He was drawn to the experiential expressions of many if not most of these traditions. Not only are the passages in *Septem Sermones* like living gnosticism, but the parallel with esoteric writings in Taoism, Zen, and Tibetan Buddhism is unmistakable. In many ways Jung was on the same wavelength with

Eastern thought, which fascinated him greatly. Indeed, he was to compose a series of forewords for the works of writers like Heinrich Zimmer, Sri Ramakrishna, Ananda K. Coomaraswamy, D. T. Suzuki, and W. Y. Evans-Wentz. He believed that Eastern thought afforded evidence for the universality of archetypes. Whether that is the case or not is still a matter for speculation, but the paradoxical formulations of the East provided a mirror to his own experience.

It is well known that Eastern thought glories in deliberate paradoxes, frequently expressed as reversals of common speech. One example is the familiar "The more you clean it, the dirtier it becomes" (Waley 161). In Taoism ultimate reality is "heavy as a stone, light as a feather" (ibid., 50). In still another instance, the *Tao Te Ching* states, "Tao is eternally without action, and yet there is nothing that it does not do. Rather, the non-doing of all beings helps it do what it does" (Schoeps 198). Richard Wilhelm's translation of *The Secret of the Golden Flower*, shared by Wilhelm with Jung upon his return from China, also provides numerous examples of similar paradoxical expressions.

Today, Jung's unspoken promise to unite the opposites of science and spirituality is attracting the attention not only of many Christians but also of modern theosophy, with its fascination with spirit power and the occult. This is clearly shown by Stephan Hoeller's book *The Gnostic Jung and the Seven Sermons to the Dead*. Hoeller's book is itself cryptic, but it deeply reverberates to this dimension of Jung's experience and illustrates the diversity of spirituality in whose service his thought can find expression.

The alchemical tree of life became a prime subject in Jung's later theoretical speculations (*CW* 13:253f.). There, tree symbolism is presented as a universal archetype of the collective unconscious. Another of Jung's concepts, the *coincidentia oppositorum*, in which evil is taken into good even in the image of the divine, was already manifest in the imagery of his troubled period. It developed in greater detail in Jung's later writings such as *The Undiscovered Self*, *Aion*, and *Answer to Job*.

In time Jung's self-healing, marking a new upsurge of creative energy, appears to have taken place spontaneously, ushering in one of his most independent, original, and creative periods, which culminated in *Psychological Types* (c. 1921). Of this whole episode in Jung's life we can ask: What is the connection between Jung's unusually rich life of inward images, which shares the imagery of mental illness, and the search for integration? The connection would seem to be obvious. Images from the unconscious constitute the matrix from which the mythical vision is derived.

In an aside, while commenting on the phenomenon of Jung's "creative illness," Ellenberger has remarked that Freudian patients have Freudian dreams and Jungians archetypal ones, with notions of the anima, and so on. Was it not Freud's dictum that "genius is the capacity to engender one's own progeny?" Ellenberger comments: "Freud, who worked with neurotic [patients], and had not much experience of psychoses, came upon the unconscious of repressed drives and memories; Jung, who worked for nine years with severe schizophrenics, was bound to find the collective unconscious and the archetypes" (891).

Jung's encounter with the unconscious is viewed in *Memories* as a creative sojourn in which superior new insights are made manifest. Hence illness is transformed into creative exploration. Yet there was evidently much more pain, agony, anguish, and inner suffering than he recounted in old age. In the life experience of many people, misery and the longing for mystery are connected. For Jung, inner suffering and mystical consolations were transformed into psychological archetypes.

The creative person is more conscious than other people of an alien will or intention beyond his or her control or comprehension. Jung termed this an autonomous complex. It is a detached portion of the psyche that leads an independent life because its psychic energy is outside conscious control. Such split-off forms of consciousness require reincorporation into the wider frame of consciousness. Jung applied the autonomous complex theory to himself, and over time he healed himself by his creative encounter with the unconscious. It was to be for him a lifelong task.

If Jung had not had the childhood problems he faced and the difficulties in his mature years after the break with Freud, it is doubtful that he would have proposed so many of the creative bridging syntheses that are his hallmark. That is to say, he sought and found connections between vivid, often painful inner images (many of which took a religious form) and features that constituted the ethos of his creative dynamic.

The couples are coming out of the Tower
Love has its license, the darkmans its power,
Linking their arms as they pass up the hill
Notion their own though not what they will.
—*W. H. Auden, Ode IV of* The Orators

CHAPTER *5*

The Lost Feminine:
Jung's Relationships with Women

Anthony Storr has called attention, as few other biographers have, to Jung's deep distrust of women in general and to his ambivalent attitude toward his own mother in particular. Because of Jung's troubled childhood, his relations with women and his views on women are of great importance. We would, of course, like to know a great deal more about these relationships. I believe that what we now know, however, forms more of a constellation of meaning than has been generally recognized.

Earlier we considered several of the reasons for Jung's deep distrust of his mother. We shall now trace some of the ways in which his inner ambivalence toward women manifested itself in specific instances. As we have noted, this ambivalence seems to have stemmed primarily from his mother's absence from the home in his early years and from inconsistencies and a split in her personality. These we have linked to the split in his own personality. During Jung's school years, his mother believed that he was intellectually mature for his age. She confided her difficulties to him, relating things that she was unable to communicate to her husband. Having to deal with problems appropriate only to adults put an undue burden on him at an early age. Now we will examine the ways in which Jung sought to integrate the split-off elements of his personality through his unconventional relationships with women.

Gerhard Wehr says that "the central theme in the work of C. G. Jung is that of individuation, the self-development of the human being through the process of unifying the opposites" (86). He expands further by explaining that a woman can come to carry the projection of a man's own unconscious inner femininity. This was the case at several times in Jung's life, notably with Sabina Spielrein and, later, resulting in a more positive outcome for Jung, with Toni Wolff.

As we saw in chapter 1, from Jung's early childhood *woman* meant "innate unreliability" (*Memories* 8). By transferring allegiance from his disappointing mother to a maid in his home, he began a pattern that was to continue. The pattern of projection that he was to repeat with so many other women in his life, such as his cousin, Hélène Preiswerk, and Sabina Spielrein, takes on new significance in this light. As Jung himself states: "This type of girl later became a component in my anima" (ibid.).

In 1902, at the age of twenty-seven, Jung was engaged to Emma Rauschenbach. They were married on February 14, 1903. Emma was well educated and came from a wealthy Swiss-German family. When Carl first proposed, she turned him down. Later, when he was a psychiatrist at the Burghölzli Mental Hospital, she accepted. In many ways the relation between Carl and Emma was a happy one. She gave Jung a place in the world and fulfilled the needs of his No. 1 Personality.

During the period when Jung was a neophyte psychiatrist at the Burghölzli, he became Sabina Spielrein's psychiatrist. Spielrein, a Russian who studied medicine in Zurich in 1905, was in therapy with Jung from 1906—when she was twenty years old—until 1909. Jung diagnosed her illness to Freud as "psychotic hysteria." Spielrein experienced depression and suicidal thoughts, alternating with uncontrollable bouts of laughing, weeping, and screaming (Fisher 475). In recent years Spielrein's diary of forty-one pages, the twelve letters she wrote to Jung, the two letters she wrote to Freud, and the twenty letters from Freud to her have come to light and been translated, edited, and commented upon by Aldo Carotenuto, a Jungian psychologist in Rome. The data available on Jung and Spielrein's relationship are still far from complete, as the Jung estate has refused to authorize publication of the forty-six letters that Jung wrote to Sabina.

It is clear, though, that in therapy Spielrein fell madly in love with Jung, fantasized that he would impregnate her, and had a recurrent fantasy of bearing his son. She named her "unborn son" Siegfried and further fantasized that "Siegfried would be the visible sign of the Jung-Spielrein union, the living symbol unifying the Aryan and Jewish souls" (Fisher 479). Jung, for his part, got caught up in what is now termed countertransference fantasies of his own, and over time he had an affair with Spielrein. In a discussion of Jung and Spielrein, Gerhard Wehr mentions that despite Jung's self-analysis it was only "through the Sabina Spielrein affair that he first discovered his 'polygamous components'" (142).

Spielrein's mother corresponded with Jung about the matter. In responding, Jung defended his actions, offering as an explanation the fact that he had not taken money to treat her. Thereby he was not under the same obligation as a therapist who had received remuneration. Much discussion in the psychotherapeutic community has ensued about Jung's behavior, which he himself later stated was foolish and unjustified. Even Jung described himself as a scoundrel and a knave (Fisher 476). Freud's interpretation of this episode in the Freud-Jung correspondence was initially quite understanding and tolerant of Jung's situation. In a letter of June 6, 1909, Freud stated: "Such experiences, although painful, are necessary and hard to avoid. Only with them does one really know life and the thing he has got hold of. I myself have never actually been taken in quite so badly but I have been very close several times and had a narrow escape" (Freud and Jung 145F).

David Fisher's review of Aldo Carotenuto's *A Secret Symmetry: Sabina Spielrein between Jung and Freud* states: "Spielrein's diary and letters reveal that the Jung/Spielrein connection exceeded the boundary and propriety of the patient-physician relationship. All the available evidence suggests a passionate love affair, almost certainly one that was consummated sexually. Jung was Sabina's first love. He came to represent not only that indispensable person who had 'cured' her, but also her savior, rescuer, and personal charismatic hero" (476). Fisher points out that Freud reacted more negatively to the Siegfried fantasy than Jung. After Spielrein's marriage, Freud maintained that Spielrein remained pathologically attached to Jung, suggesting self-hatred on her part. Also, Fisher mentions that Spielrein, being Jewish, was upset by Jung's admonition and acceptance of the adage that the Jews were responsible for the murder of Christ, and he suggests that this implies "a masochistic identification with her anti-semitic aggressor" (479).

These interpretations are most revealing and doubtless contain more than a grain of truth. They present the perspective of an exploited victim, a psychotic and delusional young woman. Jung's treatment of Sabina Spielrein has been referred to by a health professional as "a case of colossal medical malpractice."[1] At the time Jung was, after all, a respected and trusted psychiatrist who was treating a delusional patient. Need it be said that more is expected of those who hold positions of trust than Jung was able to supply? For her part, Spielrein went on to become a brilliant and distinguished psychiatrist in her own right.

After his break with Freud, Jung was, as he said himself, menaced by a psychosis. At that time Jung experienced a variety of ominous dreams and visions. Toni Wolff was there to assist him, as she had been for some years. Wolff was twenty-three when she came to Jung for therapy in 1911. She had been exceedingly withdrawn and depressed. Under his tutelage she had blossomed. In a letter to Freud Jung called Wolff "a new discovery . . . a remarkable intellect with excellent feelings for philosophy and religion" (cited in G. Wehr 94). Later she became a gifted therapist herself. And so Jung and Wolff were to be close friends and collaborators over several decades.

Jung wrote a great deal about the male projecting the anima, which is related to extrication from the devouring mother. Jung could project his inner split onto Wolff, and at the same time she became for him a creative muse. I suspect that the dark-haired Toni had more than a few of the qualities of Carl's mother's No. 2 Personality. At the

Formative & Transformative Life Experiences

time of his illness, he shared his dark visions from the unconscious with her. Doubtless she performed an important role at this time.

In *Memories* Jung does not mention Wolff, much less her crucial role in his confrontation with his psychic underworld. Given Wolff's central role in Jung's quest for psychic wholeness, his failure to speak of her in his autobiography represents a serious omission. Further, it distorts the correct picture of his complex life. After all, their relationship lasted more than forty years, from 1911 until 1953, when Toni Wolff died. Jung has made it extremely difficult for biographers to trace the main features or tone of the relationship. After Wolff's death, on her instructions, her middle sister, Erna Naeff-Wolff, returned to Jung the letters he had written to Wolff. Jung then destroyed those letters, together with the ones she had written to him (G. Wehr 143). Jung's biographers agree that Wolff played an important role in his confrontation with the unconscious. They disagree on numerous details and on most of the crucial interpretations. Jung's relationship with Wolff has been well documented in the biographies by Hannah, Brome, and Stern, despite all their differences of interpreted meaning. It is further supported by extended unpublished testimony of many who knew Jung well, stored at the C. G. Jung Oral History Archive at the Countway Library.

Emma Jung and Toni Wolff had varying attitudes toward each other and toward Jung as Jung's relationship with each continued. Attitudes ranged from painful rivalry between the women in the early period, when Toni wanted Carl to marry her. They proceeded to Emma's partial acceptance of the other relationship's inevitability, and later she even openly acknowledged Toni's important role during Jung's night-sea journey. Jung's attitude toward the women also changed over time. It was in the early decades that Jung's relation to Wolff was most intense and meaningful. However, there was also pain, anguish, and suffering. Emma Jung conceded that Wolff was able to do things for her husband at this difficult period that she would never have been able to do. Hannah describes Wolff as an intuitive personality who was Jung's feminine inspiration. Her importance to Jung at the time of his creative illness should not be underestimated. Fowler McCormick, who knew Jung well during this period, has called attention to the connection between Wolff and the realization of Jung's creative impulses: "Creative persons are a law unto themselves. . . . [Above all] Jung was faithful to the creative instinct in him."[2]

Emma Jung is universally described by those who knew her as a model homemaker, mother, and therapist. By any standard Emma was both a tactful and insightful woman. In later years she took an interest in providing Jungian-oriented interpretations of the grail legend and writing a study that amplified Jung's notion of animus and anima. When Jung was having difficulties with Freud, she attempted, unsuccessfully, to play the role of mediator between the two men. She wrote to Freud that she was tormented by the idea that "your relation to my husband is not altogether as it should be, and since it definitely ought not to be like this I want to try to do whatever is in my power" (Freud and Jung 277EJ). In a later letter she indicated to Freud that he should not "think of Carl with a father's feeling . . . but rather as one human being thinks of another, who like you has his own law to fulfill" (279EJ).

We know that the relation among Carl, Toni, and Emma was a kind of threefold arrangement that after a fashion met Jung's needs. For years Jung saw Wolff every Wednesday afternoon. In addition, on frequent weekends he brought her home to share meals with his family—to the evident distress of some family members. According to Susanne Trüb, Toni Wolff's youngest sister, in the early years of their relationship "every Sunday Toni went to Jung's house. And that was the only day when the children had their father; otherwise they didn't see much of him." Trüb also notes that "in the summer months Toni regularly spent a certain period of time with Jung at the Tower," his Bollingen retreat.[3]

Jung's Need for Two Women

An important question arises, one that has rarely been addressed by Jung's biographers: Why did Jung need two women so intensely? This haunting question has been virtually ignored, but it is crucial to an understanding of Jung.

Without referring specifically to Jung, Melanie Klein has written that when a child has been profoundly disappointed by "abandonment" by the mother, the child develops an attitude of mistrust. In turn, the child builds many other relationships, in effect to compensate for the one that has been lost. The research of Klein and others

Formative & Transformative Life Experiences

of the object relations school of psychoanalysis, like Margaret W. Mahler, W. R. D. Fairbairn, and D. W. Winnicott, indicates that the feelings of a man toward a woman are always heavily influenced by his early attachments to his mother. Such attachments are largely unconscious and disguised in their manifestation. Klein shows that a man may choose as a love partner a woman who has some characteristics of an entirely opposite kind to those of his mother. "Perhaps the loved woman's appearance is quite different, but her voice or some characteristics of her personality are in accordance with his early impressions of his mother and have a special attraction" (Klein and Riviere 86).

The sources of Jung's creativity were his attraction to the esoteric (largely maternal) and his restiveness with conventionality (in spite of his need for it), balanced by his need to be deeply rooted in the mundane world. It was exactly this sense of security, of being rooted and grounded, that was lacking in his childhood. It is a fact that Jung was genuinely attracted to both Emma and Toni, but for very different reasons. One could speculate that Emma was like his mother's No. 1 Personality, in that she gave him a home and family (a security he lacked in childhood). The firm footing provided by his wife and children was one thing that helped him preserve a vestige of sanity at a difficult time. He wrote: "My family and my profession always remained a joyful reality and a guarantee that I also had a normal existence" (*Memories* 189).

Wolff, on the other hand, possessed an intuitive sense that helped her to serve as a guide when Jung's inner journey needed realization. She countered, in effect, the residual daimon of his mother's troubling No. 2 side. Wolff was uniquely qualified to accompany Jung on his descent into his unconscious when he was speaking and even writing journal entries to various parts of his split-off self. Hannah tells us that Wolff "had an extraordinary genius for accompanying men—and some women too in a different way—whose destiny it was to enter the unconscious" (118—19).

Hannah has been remarkably candid about the role played by Toni Wolff during Jung's "night-sea journey" (125-31). According to this interpretation, Wolff was an intuitive type and was therefore able to facilitate Jung's projections upon herself and to further his experiment in self-understanding. According to Hannah, Toni Wolff was "most fitted to carry the projection" of Jung's anima (118). Also,

Hannah indicates, Wolff had no formal training in the procedures of active imagination, even in her later years.

But biographers disagree. Hannah and Brome, for example, interpret Toni Wolff's role quite differently. For instance, Hannah writes, "It seems hard that just at the time he was tried to the uttermost by his 'confrontation with the unconscious,' Jung also had to deal with perhaps the most difficult problem a married man ever has to face: the fact that he can love his wife and another woman simultaneously" (118). This interpretation assumes the existence of the anima in Jung and posits that Wolff, an introverted, intuitive type, was most fitted to carry the projection of this figure. Without denying the role of Wolff in Jung's life at this juncture, Brome offers a very different explanation. As he sees it, "Simultaneously the sheet anchor of his family had shifted under the stress of his affair with Toni Wolff, the moral principles by which he lived were severely tested, and his struggle to plumb the deepest caverns of his own psyche threatened to tear him apart" (*Jung* 161). This interpretation implies that Jung's illness was in part triggered by his break with Freud and that his affair with Wolff was part of the problem rather than part of the solution. It emphasizes Jung's moral dilemma without trying to understand the psychic reasons for it.

Hannah romanticizes the affair with Toni Wolff, while Brome moralizes it. Neither interpreter relates it to Jung's early childhood difficulties with a split mother. Each sees part of the situation. Jung projected onto Toni "the whole numinous quality of the unconscious—yes, she even has the fascination of a goddess" (Hannah 118). Clearly Hannah is right that Wolff brought alive numinous aspects of the unconscious that in Jung's eyes endowed her with the qualities of a goddess. One can sense that Jung was enchanted with her because of the unusual nature of their relationship.

Throughout his life Jung was known repeatedly to declare a man's right to infidelity, as interviews at the C. G. Jung Oral History Archive attest. Evidently Jung held this conviction deeply. Yet the very intensity of his declaration makes one curious. For him, on an unconscious level, infidelity may have represented retaliation against his mother.

Another important theme in Jung's own psychology was the dreaded anima. At the time of his "confrontation with the unconscious," Jung wrote that he was greatly intrigued by the fact that "a woman should interfere with me from within." He concluded that this must be the "'soul' in the primitive sense" and that it had an archetypal basis, which he was from then on to term the anima (*Memories* 186).

Klein writes that the child "is proving to himself over and over again that his one greatly loved object, his mother, is not after all indispensable since he can always find another woman. . . . By deserting and rejecting some women he unconsciously turns away from his mother, saves her from his dangerous desires and frees himself from his painful dependence on her, and by turning to other women and giving them pleasure and love, he is in his unconscious mind retaining the loved mother or recreating her" (Klein and Riviere 86). It seems to follow from this interpretation that throughout much of his life Jung was, in effect, unconsciously getting back at his mother for the grief she caused him at an early age. By the same token, his psyche, seeking integrative wholeness, was trying to join the opposites of Personalities No. 1 and No. 2. Jungians, of course, have explained essentially the same phenomenon by reference to the dependence produced by the anima problem. In this interpretation, however, generally the retaliatory aspect has not been emphasized.

Klein's observations, based on numerous case studies, seem to apply directly to Jung's situation. By turning toward Toni, in a certain sense Jung was rejecting Emma (to the extent that she was unconsciously his mother). At the same time, though, he did not give her up completely, which would have meant divorce. His turning toward Wolff can be understood as an inner ritual of reenactment and potential resolution of his primary childhood trauma. By turning toward Wolff for a response to some of his needs, he was, in effect, reenacting the freeing of himself from the painful experiences of a difficult mother, who had made him the object of her concern because of her own unhappy marriage as well as her split personality.

Klein's hypothesis on the mechanism of psychic retaliation would seem to extend the analysis of Winnicott with regard to the childhood trauma Jung experienced as a result of his mother's illness. Also, it helps to account for the unusual dual relationship he had with Emma and Toni in his mature years. Conventional morality apart, his answer to the issue of the split feminine was certainly ingenious.

Ironically, Jung's view of women, in spite of some profound insights, was flawed in ways that are somewhat reminiscent of Freud's views. Recent discussions between feminists and Jungian analysts in the journal *Anima* have investigated assumptions about men being characterized by logos (thinking) and women by eros (feeling). These discussions have considered the adequacy of Jung's formulation: "Woman is compensated by a masculine element. . . . The animus corresponds to the paternal Logos just as the anima corresponds to the maternal Eros" (*CW* 9, pt. 2, par. 29, p. 14).

Perpetuations of the Lost Feminine

It is well known that Jung paid much attention to the effects of the anima and animus upon a person. These terms refer respectively to "the inner figure of a woman held by a man and the figure of man at work in a woman's psyche. Though unlike in the ways in which they manifest themselves, anima and animus have certain characteristics in common" (Samuels 23). Likewise, Jung called attention to the ways in which male and female elements of the personality are held in balance. This he referred to as the phenomenon of the androgynous self. In Jung's original formulation, *anima* referred to the hidden feminine side of the man and *animus* to the hidden masculine side of the woman. Now most interpreters have come to believe that his notion and theory of anima/animus is seriously flawed by being too one-sided. Several attempts have been made by James Hillman, Edward Whitmont, Verena Kast, Naomi Goldenberg, and others to modify and reformulate the theoretical construct. A number of these attempts that retain the concepts of anima and animus broaden the conceptual formulation by making both of them applicable to men and women.

To a large extent, Jung's theories on the animus and the anima originate from his own experience. In his 1925 Seminar, for example, he stated: "I was much interested in the fact that a woman should interfere with me from within. My conclusion was that it must be the soul in the primitive sense, and I began to speculate on the reasons that the name anima was given to the soul. Why was it thought of as feminine? What she said to me I found to be full of deep cunning" (*Analytical Psychology Notes*, lecture 6, p. 44).

Several times when describing his dreams and visions, Jung referred to conversations that he had with his unconscious anima (*Memories* 185). He recognized it as the voice of a talented psychopath who had a strong transference to him. Aldo Carotenuto has speculated that this voice was Sabina Spielrein (Jung, *Analytical Psychology Notes* 42n9). In my view Carotenuto is correct. The voice then said to him that what he wrote in a notebook was art. Thereupon Jung became obsessed over the question of whether what he wrote was art or science—a rather strange question, since it probably was neither. Finally, he says that it took him a long time to adapt to something in himself that was not himself, namely the anima (ibid., lecture 6, p. 45). Then he goes on to say: "I was in effect writing letters to my anima, that is to a part of myself with a different viewpoint from my own. I got remarks from a new character—I was in analysis with a ghost and a woman" (46).

Following this discussion, he raises the question of whether a woman has a soul. He states: "I decided she could not possibly have an anima, because then there would be no check on the woman from within. Then I came to the idea that woman must have an animus, but it was not till much later that I was able to develop this further because the animus is much harder to catch at work" (ibid.). The highly subjective and questionable nature of these claims is obvious. To hold that a woman could not have an anima because she would then have no check from within makes very little sense. This comment quite probably stems from Jung's childhood feelings of intense anxiety over not being able to control or adequately deal with his mother's No. 2 Personality.

It would therefore seem most likely that Jung's references to the anima in the 1925 Seminar Notes stem directly from his own incorporation of features of his mother's split feminine personality structure. Repeatedly he projected the split feminine upon the women of his life and in a secondary sense upon several of his theoretical formulations. Stolorow and Atwood, in *Faces in a Cloud*, have reached similar conclusions based primarily on an analysis of Jung's *Two Essays on Analytical Psychology*. They have analyzed many of the ways in which Jung regarded abstract ideas as if they had concrete or material existence. Thereby he reified his own unique problems into a variety of theoretical considerations.

Jung and Feminism

In recent decades feminist spirituality has flourished and has produced much scholarly research. These scholars have raised a host of questions about the origin of patriarchy: How and why did it come about? In what ways can it and must it be reversed in an egalitarian society? The questioning became part of the social criticism of the past two decades when political activists challenged many traditional assumptions about societal roles, including beliefs about the relationships between men and women, women and religion, women and nature, and religion and society. At present many persons are questioning the age-old patriarchal assumption that men are head (thinking) people and that women are body (feeling) people and turning Jung studies upside down. That assumption goes back to Aristotle and remained uncriticized by Jung.

Jung has been a key figure in the transformation of religion taking place in our time. For instance, Anne Carson, in the annotated bibliography *Goddesses and Wise Women*, lists no fewer than 739 books and articles, most of which acknowledge the impact of Jung upon feminist spirituality. The authors of these publications run a wide gamut, all the way from feminist theologians who are seeking to revitalize religious experience in the church to people who seek to express spirituality outside the boundaries of religious institutionalism. Some express such themes as the widespread appeal of goddess religion and the revival of witchcraft in our society.

One of the more influential of the feminist reexaminations of traditional thought is Naomi Goldenberg's analysis in *Changing of the Gods, The End of God*, and *Returning Words to Flesh*. Goldenberg writes of the challenge feminism represents to patriarchal religion and of the new visions women are creating of a wide range of images of spirituality. In her view, feminist thought is being utilized as a new kind of psychology that finds expression in many scholarly disciplines, creative arts, and woman-centered political activities. It is based in part on Jungian principles and upon respect for myth and symbol. Goldenberg has written: "Many feminists are in the same position as Jung and his patients. We are irrevocably estranged from traditional religion. We cannot go home again. Because of this we must seek religions elsewhere—if religion is what we want. Cursed by estrangement, we are also blessed with opportunity to build new forms to replace inadequate older ones. Jung can help us, but before feminists use him, a thorough critique is necessary, for Jungian psychology has become a form of patriarchal religion itself" ("Feminism and Jungian Theory" 15).

In particular, there has been considerable discussion of Jung's one-sided presentation in his writings on the issue of anima/animus. More and more feminists have found Jung's discussion of this topic too constricted, and several writers have revised Jung's ideas to make them applicable to both sexes. For instance, Goldenberg has severely criticized Jung's assumptions, as expressed in his volume *Aion*, that men are thinkers, whereas women are feelers. She holds that, for Jung, "the animus corresponds to the paternal Logos just as the anima corresponds to the maternal Eros" (Jung, *cw* 9, cited in Goldenberg, *End of God* 67). Goldenberg is doubtless right that there is a certain duplicity about Jung's attitude toward women. In my view, the reason for this is that Jung had a divided or split image of the feminine operating within his psyche. As we have seen, Jung's deep-seated ambivalence toward the feminine was rooted in his own experience of a dual mother.

For a variety of reasons, many feminists are of two minds with regard to Jung. Among leading feminists, Rosemary Ruether has been highly critical of Jung, claiming that his theories are more deceptively sexist than Freud's. She believes that Jung has attempted to translate the romantic view of women into psychological doctrine (Reuther 28, 152). Mary Daly in her early writings was somewhat less critical, at the time appreciating Jung's comments on the Catholic dogma of the Assumption. She noted that "the insight of Jung . . . is acknowledgment of the destructiveness caused by the degradation of women in the religious imagination" (*Beyond God the Father* 88). In her later writings, Daly has referred to Jung's theories as pernicious traps (*Gyn/Ecology* 253). Significantly, she quotes Jung's, where he writes: "I attribute to the personal mother only a limited etiological significance. That is to say, all those influences which the literature describes as being exerted on the children do not come from the mother herself, but rather from the archetype projected upon her, which gives her a mythological background and invests her with authority and numinosity" (*Psychological Aspects* 334–35). This interesting and revealing statement further confirms Jung's own need and desire to distance himself from his actual mother. On the same topic, Goldenberg has written: "Jung's concept of 'the feminine' is restrictive and probably unproductive for feminists who are interested in moving away from gender-identified stereotypes. The main value of Jung for feminists in Religious Studies is more likely to lie in his insights into religious innovation" (*End of God* 40).

Likewise, Jung's description of Mary has been criticized as a way "to freeze feminine images" (ibid., 64). In connection with this, Goldenberg has offered the following observation: "It is important to realize that Jung's view of 'Mary' typifies his view of 'woman.' In *Answer to Job*, he criticizes the Old Testament Yahweh for forgetting His relation to the feminine Sophia and for making woman less perfect than man. Yet [he] does exactly the same thing" (65).

Jung was enamored of the ways that the feminine could be and was being incorporated into the divine. For instance, he considered the Roman Catholic doctrine of the Assumption of Mary into heaven to be of great importance. While feminists criticize Jung as a defender of patriarchy and sexism, at the same time many find him to be an innovator struggling against the psychic oppression represented by the strict adherence to traditional parental and societal images. They are, in my view, rightly critical of Jung's preoccupation with the anima and his one-sided view of the animus. The latter is clearly not appropriate to the liberation of women's experience at present. Given Jung's own experience of a split mother, he made use of a variety of creative strategies to extricate himself from his difficulties. In this respect there may be an analogy for feminine experience.

Several writers have analyzed with considerable thoroughness Jung's interest in incorporating the feminine dimension of the divine into a reinterpretation of religious images. For instance, Jung's use of Sophia, in *Answer to Job* and several of his other writings, inspired the biblical scholar Joan Engelsman's book *The Feminine Dimension of the Divine*. In this study, Engelsman considers the expression and repression of the Sophia motif in religious history. It is now becoming increasingly clear that the wisdom tradition of Scripture and the apocryphal tradition were both suppressed and repressed in Western religious history. In our own time there is considerable evidence that those traditions are being revitalized.

Many feminists are interested in religion but strongly feel that Western Christianity is perhaps irretrievably bogged down in patriarchalism. Using an analysis of patriarchy and matriarchy based on authors like Jung, Erich Neumann, and Johann Jakob Bachofen, they have spawned a movement of enormous proportions. While Jung rarely quoted Bachofen, whose book *Myth, Religion, and Mother Right* has been quite influential, he was certainly aware of Bachofen's analysis. Like Jung, Bachofen offerred an analysis of symbols and myths. His thesis that matriarchy preceded patriarchy, now well known, is not without its critics. Yet if society were not so patriarchal in its basic biases, we would not be witnessing such widespread attempts to become liberated from this behemoth.

The topic of an archetypal understanding of human experience as considered by Neumann in *The Great Mother* and in *The Origins and History of Consciousness* has also engaged feminist attention. Neumann's contribution to psychological theory is the concept of centroversion, a synthesis of extraversion and introversion. Following Jung's concept of the archetype, Neumann in *The Great Mother* presents an analysis of the archetypal feminine, considering both its positive and negative features. His classic, groundbreaking study has been regarded by historians of religion as a sourcebook for the vast range of feminine symbols that occurred in antiquity and in the matriarchal societies of Egypt, Greece, India, China, and South America. More than Jung himself, Neumann follows Bachofen closely, but not uncritically, by emphasizing the way in which an age of matriarchy preceded an age of patriarchy.[4] In his view, however, the archetypal image is a psychic reality for the individual and the group, for both men and women. As he states, "When . . . we say that the matriarchal world precedes the patriarchal world, we are not referring to a sequence of sociological structure, such as that set up by Bachofen" (*Great Mother* 91). Neumann is critical of Bachofen precisely for his Christian patriarchal bias, which in Neumann's view prevented Bachofen from arriving at a full understanding of the matriarchal spirit, which Bachofen devalued as material and lunar (54n).

Feminists have been of two minds toward Neumann, just as they have been toward Jung. Indicating that archetypes are "vague/vaporous," Daly cites Neumann's litany of a negative series of symbols, including Deadly Mother, Great Whore of Babylon, Witch, Dragon,

Moloch, Sophia, Lilith, and Mary, to name a few. She indicates these as instances of "sado-sublime projection" (*Pure Lust* 81). Writers like Daly have sought to show that the phenomenon of the Great Mother in her negative aspect represents "patriarchal reversals." Neumann wrote: "In the patriarchal world, she is dethroned. . . . But she always retains her archetypal effectiveness" (*Origins and History* 133). Daly indicates that she is mystified as to which meaning of *archetypal* the Great Mother retains (*Pure Lust* 81).

The theme of religious polytheism, as discussed by Jungians like James Hillman and David Miller, is pertinent to those feminists who are thoroughly disenchanted with the rigidities of monotheistic patriarchalism. Several have shown particular interest in the phenomenon of the reemergence of the goddess as a motif expressive of our time.

In my view, characterizing the unconscious as feminine does not work for all women, as several leading feminists have testified. Likewise, one could object that for men (like Jung) who have had a bad childhood experience of a dual mother, such an explanation is misleading. These men need to work patiently through the negative aspects of the "split mother" in ways that will allow them to cope with their negative feelings constructively. A similar objection could, I believe, be formulated in the case of a given woman's experience.

We return to the fact that Jung's deep-seated ambivalence toward the feminine was rooted in his own experience of a dual mother. The current exploration and reexamination of these topics is a healthy sign, an expression of consciousness-raising. It is fair to say that feminist writers perceive the need for Jungian views of human psychology to be cleansed of stereotypes and sexism. In time the strengths and weaknesses of Jung's perspective will be understood more clearly. One thing is sure: the future will doubtless see even more discussions along a similar line.

PART TWO

Jung as Modern
Man in Search of
a Soul

It was about this time that my mother, or rather, her No. 2 personality, suddenly and without preamble said, "You must read Goethe's Faust *one of these days." We had a handsome edition of Goethe, and I picked out* Faust. *It poured into my soul like a miraculous balm.*
—C. G. Jung, Memories

Romantic philosophers visualized the universe as a living organism endowed with a soul pervading the whole and connecting its parts.
—Henri Ellenberger, The Discovery of the Unconscious

CHAPTER

Great Minds:
The Impact of Received Ideas

Romanticism as a protest against rationalism offers a parallel to Jung's emphasis upon achieving awareness and insight into the ways of the Western world. In fact, many of the same imaginative and visionary themes of the earlier romantic period were to engage Jung. Like the romantics of an earlier time, Jung saw his task as standing stoutly against the rationalism of his age. He wrote: "Today, our basic convictions have become increasingly rationalistic. . . . Nothing is more characteristic and symptomatic in this respect than the gulf that has opened between faith and knowledge" (*Undiscovered Self* 84–85). Repeatedly Jung stressed that the Western world has accorded priority to the extroverted thinking function. Romanticism fostered a recovery of the divine in the world of literature, and this mode of illumination and the flash of insight can be seen in several places in Jung's corpus.

Jung's own experience found its major motifs in the precursors of German, English, and French romanticism. The topics of the unconscious, individuation, inner "myth," anima/animus, archetype, androgyny, the shadow, alchemy, and enantiodromia (the correlation of opposites), to which Jung devotes so much attention, are all fore-shadowed by the earlier continental romantics. One wonders to what degree he connected with the experiences for which these notions stand and to what degree his own formulations are indebted to the romantic movement.

Jung openly acknowledged his debt to Schopenhauer, Kant, and Nietzsche, but much less directly to the members of the romantic movement apart from his beloved Goethe. Doubtless the best treatment of the connection between romanticism and depth psychology has been advanced by Henri Ellenberger in *The Discovery of the Unconscious*. Ellenberger points out that romanticism originated in Germany, achieving its highest development there between 1800 and 1830. It was a cultural reaction against the Enlightenment, which witnessed some radical shifts after the American and French Revolutions. It laid great stress upon the individual, unconscious motivation, and irrational factors. A basic datum of romantic philosophy was the notion of primordial phenomena. The German term for this is *Urphaenomene*, which refers to a series of metamorphoses. Among the *Urphaenomene* was the myth of the androgyne. Androgyny can be described as "a psychic personification which holds male and female in conscious balance" (Samuels, Shorter, and Plaut 22). Precisely this balancing of opposite psychic tendencies between consciousness and the unconscious is one of the hallmarks of Jungian thought.

In Plato's *Symposium*, Aristophanes describes the primordial human being composed of both sexes, which later became separated from each other and were searching for reunification. In later centuries numerous romantics revived the idea of the fundamental bisexuality of the human being. Ellenberger maintains: "The Romantic philosophic concept of the *Urphaenomene* not only reappears in Jung's work under the name of 'archetype,' but is to be found in Freud's as well. . . . There is hardly a single concept of Freud or Jung that had not been anticipated by the philosophy of nature and Romantic medicine" (205). What is striking is the existence of so many of the romantics' key ideas in Jung's formulations.

Ross Woodman, in an article titled "Literature and the Unconscious: Coleridge and Jung," compares the question put by the Hermit to the Ancient Mariner with Jung's own experience: "What flowed out of him was an account of loss of soul." Woodman contends that Jung's anima had reached his ego in such an inferior or primitive state that "he found himself in the condition of Keats' chameleon poet without an identity of his own. He simply withdrew entirely into the unconscious and was for a time swallowed up by it as Jonah was swallowed by the whale or the Mariner by that oceanic world 'below the kirk'" (366). As we have seen, Jung himself was nearly swallowed up by the raging power of the unconscious. In later years he was to stress the ways that the unconscious could become integrated into consciousness.

Jung was much more empathetic to the work of the romantics, as well as to the gnostics, hermeticists, and alchemists, than to certain forms of modern literature and art as exemplified by James Joyce and Pablo Picasso. It could be said that the romantics practiced a mode of active imagination before it was named. Jung was especially fond of E. T. A. Hoffmann's *The Golden Kettle* (*Der Goldne Topf*), about a "divided self" who develops in a one-sided manner. In the story a thirty-five-year-old music teacher falls in love with his fifteen-year-old pupil. As Jungians have interpreted this story, anima projection brings the teacher to the edge of suicide and insanity. Hoffmann's story is thought to reflect a similar experience in his own life. Typical of this tale and of so much of the romantic age, his life alternates between dream and reality. In Hoffmann's subsequent writing, his self-destructive projection becomes withdrawn, and through his creative endeavors, his pupil becomes his muse. This is but one illustration of transformation in literature that Jung incorporated to shape and forge his emergent psychology. He, of course, believed that it was necessary to attain self-consciousness, lest one succumb to the tidal wave of unconsciousness as various other creative persons, such as Nietzsche and Hölderlin, had done.

In 1950 Jung included Aniela Jaffé's Jungian analysis of Hoffmann's fairy tale in the German version of his *Psychology of the Unconscious* (*Gestaltungen des Unbewussten*). Jaffé writes: "[Anselmus] leaves his girlfriend, Veronica, in order to unite with a dream figure, the beloved little snake, Serpentina. In the end, he disappears into the fairy tale land of Atlantis. His yearning for the transcendent had completely alienated him from the world. For her part, Veronica marries a well-situated bureaucrat: thus, the split is complete" (*Was C. G. Jung a Mystic?* 29–30). In her commentary on *The Golden Kettle*, Jaffé points to the one-sidedness of the romantic movement. Extreme attitudes are frequently compensated by the emergence of the opposite extreme. This is the familiar Jungian theme of enantiodromia. Jaffé also shows that the romantics had lost the direct religious experience of the believing person and were searching for new, better ways to experience spirituality (38).

Jung was also attracted to the themes of romanticism because they reflected his own experience—intense inner images without faithful belief. The romantic frequently lives in the inner world of adventure. Earthly life is scorned as "self-destroying illusion" (ibid., 37). Also, the romantic is preoccupied with the theme of death. The split is between the magical or visionary world and the real world. Explaining the viewpoint of the romantic, Jaffé points out that "his concept of the process of individuation is also, in the final analysis, a preparation for death. . . . Everything which in life, reminds one of death: the night, dreams, the uncanny, sickness and solitude, the supernatural and the trance, attracts them with irresistible power. Beyond the limits of life they seek its origin and its worth, and this gives life its only meaning" (Jaffé, *Was C. G. Jung a Mystic?* 33, 38).

Clearly Jung was attracted to the romantics. Perhaps part of the reason is that they, like himself, had been attracted to the uncanny and the numinous. Looked at from another perspective, we once again see a reflection of the importance of Jung's mother's No. 2 Personality, which showcased her uncanny and numinous power.

Goethe, Schopenhauer, and Nietzsche

Jung was greatly attracted to Goethe. His interest in Goethe seems to have stemmed from the issues presented in the second part of *Faust*. There the split between Mephistopheles and Faust appears to mirror his own inner rift. Indeed, Jung explains how his mother, "or rather, her No. 2 personality" once said to him that he must read Goethe's *Faust*. He regarded Faust as being one-sided but taking the devil seriously. As Stanley Riukas states, "The reason why the devil should be taken 'seriously' is that Mephisto is just the 'better half' of Faust himself—the rebellious, the progressive aspect of one's diabolos, the tempter, the troublemaker, the creative element" (letter to author, Sept. 18, 1990). Jung puts it this way: "The real problem . . . lay with Mephistopheles, whose whole figure made the deepest impression on me, and who, I vaguely sensed, had a relationship to the mystery of the Mothers" (*Memories* 60).

Jung regards the second part of *Faust* as more than a literary exercise, being reminded of Goethe's words: "Now let me dare to open wide the gate / Past which men's steps have ever flinching trod" (ibid., 188–89). In this same connection there is a reference to the Golden Chain in alchemy, which consists of a series of great wise men beginning with Hermes of Trismegistus. This chain is thought to link earth with heaven. In view of its magical and transformative nature, this issue is purposefully left somewhat oblique.

John-Raphael Staude, in *Consciousness and Creativity*, has drawn several connections between Jung, Hesse, Goethe, and Nietzsche. Staude observes that there was more than an accidental similarity between Mephistopheles and Zarathustra. Staude is, of course, referring to the way Jung expressed the matter in *Memories*. In his autobiography Jung wrote: "Zarathustra was Nietzsche's Faust, his No. 2, and my No. 2 now corresponded to Zarathustra—though this was rather like comparing a molehill with Mount Blanc. And Zarathustra—there could be no doubt about that—was morbid. Was my No. 2 also morbid?" (*Memories* 102). He recognized that in an important respect he was like Goethe, Nietzsche, and a host of other creative persons. They all had "multiple" personalities. However, he could not quite bring himself to analyze the matter thoroughly.

Staude points out the crucial differences between Mephistopheles and Zarathustra. As he put it, "Goethe had managed to save his sanity by projecting both sides of himself (Faust and Mephisto) into his drama of the soul of modern man. Nietzsche, on the other hand, made the fatal mistake of identifying—over-identifying—with his mana personality Zarathustra/Dionysos" (Staude, *Consciousness* 117). Nowhere does Jung clarify his view of the difference between Goethe and Nietzsche on this important matter. Doubtless he thought a great deal about it with regard to his own situation. He wrote: "Just as Faust had opened a door for me, Zarathustra slammed one shut, and it remained shut for a long time to come" (*Memories* 103). He was aware that he, like his mother, possessed a mana personality—one exhibiting extraordinary and compelling power. Intuitively he may have sensed that he needed to avoid overidentifying with it. As time went on, he was to reflect intensely upon the causes of Nietzsche's psychological demise. Eventually, when faced with a similar crisis, he embarked upon an inner journey whose purpose was to activate the split-off images of the unconscious. Hence, his own inner healing was nurtured.

Even in his early days Jung had been highly interested in Schopenhauer's concept of the will. What interested him about Schopenhauer was not only his philosophy, which had a great affinity with Eastern thought, but also a concern in the philosopher's work that was closer to his own psychic experience. According to Staude, "From Schopenhauer, Jung got the idea of a universal will that might be purposive. This conception helped him understand his cousin [i.e., Hélène Preiswerk] 'because I thought I could trace clearly in her signs of something working in the unconscious toward a goal' " (Jung, cited in Staude, *Adult Development* 27).

Jung was interested in a variety of philosophers and religious mystics, and upon close examination, one can see that the experiences of these philosophers and mystics paralleled those of Jung. Swedenborg, the great Swedish mystic, clearly engrossed Jung for this reason. Leibniz, Kant, and Schelling were three men whose works Jung had read in his youth, but they were all quite unknown to Freud (Hostie, *Religion* 22). Jung was also fascinated by the writings of Novalis, another thinker who during childhood developed a second personality. For Jung, he anticipated the concept of creative illness (Ellenberger 672–73), with its gift of unusual clarity born through the agony of pain and suffering. "While still a child, Novalis developed a second personality of daydreaming and imagination. This personality grew, and while Novalis lived an apparently normal life as a mining engineer, he also proclaimed his poetic dream to be superior to any reality" (ibid., 168).

After his break with Freud, Jung returned to Schopenhauer and von Hartmann. Schopenhauer's great treatise was *The World as Will and Idea* (1883). Of it Jung was to comment, "I would ask the reader to replace the word 'idea' by 'primordial image,' and then he will be able to understand my meaning" (*CW* 6:446). *Primordial image* was virtually synonymous with and later largely replaced by the term *archetype*. Schopenhauer's view of life, reflecting to some degree the Eastern cycle of rebirth, was for Jung a needed corrective to the Western rationalism of his age. He wrote that Schopenhauer was "the first to speak of the suffering of the world, which visibly and glaringly surrounds us, and of the confusion, passion, evil—all those things which the others hardly seemed to notice and always tried to resolve into an all-embracing harmony and comprehensibility" (*Memories* 69).

At the same time, Schopenhauer stressed the inexorable aspects of ceaseless striving in which blind will is realized through us and in spite of us. For him man's life is permeated with illusion in much the same manner as Hindu *maya*. Schopenhauer wrote: "Every breath we draw wards off the death that is constantly intruding upon us. . . . In the end death must conquer, for we become subject to him through birth and he only plays for a little while with his prey before he swallows it up" (*World as Will and Idea*, bk. 4, sec. 57, cited in Thilly 499). Schopenhauer's vivid descriptions of the tenuous nature of life's experience stimulated Jung's own reflections on the schism between reality and illusion.

Doubtless, Schopenhauer was to stimulate Jung's later interest in Eastern religions, since he and they took suffering seriously. His somber picture of the universe confirmed Jung's own observations. "He spoke neither of the all-good and all-wise providence of a Creator . . . but [of the] blindness of the world-creating Will" (*Memories* 69). Jung's own observations as a youth of diseased and dying fish, mangy foxes, frozen or starved birds, and countless other tragedies had already confirmed for him firsthand Schopenhauer's theoretical formulations.

Eduard von Hartmann's *Philosophy of the Unconscious* (1869) anticipated to a considerable degree the writings of Jung. Von Hartmann sought to reconcile Hegel's intellectualism with the voluntarism of Schopenhauer. His philosophical speculations were based on the beginnings of an inductive scientific method. He found mechanism an inadequate explanation in need of supplementation. This was the operation of will in nature. "This will is, according to von Hartmann, governed by a purpose of which . . . it is unconscious" (Thilly 500). In his 1925–26 Seminar Jung acknowledged his indebtedness to von Hartmann, who as a young man he read assiduously.

Both Schopenhauer and von Hartmann had a concept of the unconscious elements in human personality, and Jung found them fascinating reading. Time and again he would seek guidance from persons whose life experience paralleled his own. The philosopher who stimulated him the most, however, was Nietzsche. Like Jung himself, Nietzsche was a pastor's son who had turned in the opposite direction. For Nietzsche, "He that humbleth himself shall be exalted" should be translated into "He that humbleth himself wishes to be exalted" (Ellenberger 273). Nietzsche's analysis of culture and his "transvaluation of values" provided a significant challenge for Jung. Not denying Nietzsche's valuable insights into the human situation, he was to pursue creating one's own "myth" as an alternative to the nihilism inherent in Nietzsche's position.

For Jung Nietzsche was a seer who possessed both prophetic and shamanic qualities. He did not analyze issues but spoke with the voice of an oracle. Ira Progoff has written: "Nietzsche was not merely a philosopher to him but a 'phenomenon' of the utmost significance. . . . Jung regards Nietzsche's falling into insanity as being intimately related to the other basic fact in Nietzsche's life, that Zarathustra had 'come' to him, had 'possessed' him, a few years before" (*Jung's Psychology* 31). Jung realized that Nietzsche was no irreligious man, but nevertheless, his God was dead. He accounted for this and the related phenomenon of Nietzsche's psychosis by his theory of libido. The energy that was formerly projected out upon God remained within the psyche, thus producing a disastrous dissociation of his personality. Jung concluded that for such a man it is dangerous to say that God is dead, because then he becomes God.

> The result was that Nietzsche himself split and he felt himself forced to call the other self "Zarathustra" or, at other times "Dionysos." In his fatal illness he signed his letters "Zagreus," the dismembered Dionysos of the Thracians. The tragedy of Zarathustra is that, because his God died, Nietzsche himself became a god; and this happened because he was no atheist. . . . Since it is a matter of tremendous energy, the result will be an equally important psychological disturbance in the form of a dissociation of personality. The disruption can produce a dual or multiple personality. (Jung, *Psychology and Religion* 103–5)

When Jung revised his Terry Lectures for publication in volume 11 of *The Collected Works*, he changed his original manuscript considerably. He linked the Nietzsche phenomenon to schizophrenia and included a reference to Nietzsche's inflation. He omitted any mention of how this eventuality had transpired, namely through dissociation that produced a dual or multiple personality. He had clearly stated this in his original version of the text. Intuitively Jung may have regarded this topic as being too close to home. As we have seen, Jung held that humankind has remained largely in a state of unconsciousness and that quite unconsciously is destroying old values. By contrast, he wrote, "Nietzsche thought himself quite conscious and responsible when he smashed the old tablets, yet he felt a peculiar need to back himself up by a revivified Zarathustra, a sort of alter ego, with whom he often identifies himself in his great tragedy *Thus Spake Zarathustra*" (*cw* 11:85). Jung's observation had been expressed in Nietzsche's own words: " 'Da, plotzlich, Freundin! wurde Eins zu Zwei Und Zarathustra gieng an mir vorbei. . . .' Then suddenly, friend, did one become two—and Zarathustra passed by me" (from the poem "Sils-Maria," probably dedicated to Lou Andreas-Salomé, cited in Ellenberger 169, 181).

With his keen perception, Jung saw precisely how men like Nietzsche, Schopenhauer, and Goethe, who had split-off multiple personalities, were in important respects like himself. He too was struggling with the issue of the crisis of meaning for modern man. He could see how Nietzsche became engulfed, having to take upon himself the burdens of divinity, which had hitherto been projected outward. In Jung's mind this was linked to the Dionysian "gods" of the unconscious emerging with relentless fury. He resolved to pursue his "experiment" of confronting the unconscious but to seek to effect a reconciliation between the conscious and the unconscious.

Several other factors arise. Jung perceived the danger for a man like Nietzsche to make a statement like "God is dead." "He becomes instantly a victim of 'inflation' " (*Psychology and Religion* 104). After his break with Freud, Jung, like Nietzsche, was the victim of inflation. Correspondent with his loss of footing, which he likened to the "loss of soul" experienced by the primitive, was a vibrant message of personality confirmation, somewhat as a compensation. He developed a sense of divine destiny, of the absolute rightness of what he was doing.

We recall that during his creative illness, Jung dreamed of the leaves on the fruitless tree being transformed into sweet grapes full of healing juices. "It was then that I ceased to belong to myself alone, ceased to have the right to do so. From then on, my life belonged to the generality" (*Memories* 192). Unlike Nietzsche, whose outlook isolated him from the mass of humanity, Jung sought to reconnect himself with nature and humankind through his encounter with the unconscious. This involved sand and oil painting, diary keeping, mandalas, and a host of other means that allowed his inner images to express themselves and attempt to heal the inner split of his psyche.

There are other points of comparison between Nietzsche and Jung. Not only did each man experience the effects of two personalities, along with incisive and creative insights linked to the phenomenon of splitting, but both experienced the phenomenon of inflation. In addition, Nietzsche identified with the wise old man of the mountains, and Jung, with the imaginal figure of Philemon. "In literature the personification par excellence of the wise old man is found in Nietzsche's Zarathustra. According to Jung, Nietzsche identified himself with the figure of Zarathustra, that is with the archetype of the wise old man. This would explain why Nietzsche developed such delusions of grandeur when he became psychotic" (Ellenberger 710). Nietzsche becomes "the prophet of a new era" (ibid., 276). Thus, Jung was enormously stimulated by the impact of Nietzsche's personality and his ideas, more than with those of any other single person. Ellenberger states it this way:

> Jung's theories are filled with concepts that can be traced, in more or less modified form, to Nietzsche. Such are Jung's reflections on the problem of evil, on the superior instinct in man, on the unconscious, the dream, the archetypes, the shadow, the persona, the wise old man, and many other concepts. Jung also gave an interpretation of Nietzsche's personality. Zarathustra, he said, was a secondary personality of Nietzsche, which had formed and slowly developed in his unconscious until it suddenly erupted, bringing with it an enormous amount of archetypal material. (278)

Obviously there were crucial differences between the two men as well. As Ellenberger notes (671), Jung was able to descend into Hades and emerge victoriously, while Nietzsche, not firmly anchored in reality and living alone, was overwhelmed by a formidable eruption of archetypal material. In his autobiography Jung indicated that his family assisted him with the process of maintaining his equilibrium at the time when he was threatened by a psychosis. He wrote: "My family and my profession remained the base to which I could always return, assuring me that I was an actually existing, ordinary person. . . . I was not a blank page whirling about in the winds of the spirit like Nietzsche" (*Memories* 189). As Jung saw it, Nietzsche had lost his footing because he possessed nothing other than his inner world of subjectivity.

Those less sympathetic to Jung's experience, like much of the psychoanalytic community, would go further. For instance, Nandor Fodor, in an unsympathetic commentary upon *Septem Sermones ad Mortuos*, refers to Jung's Christ "neurosis." He writes of "the next phase of Jung's psychotic imagery [when] Philemon appeared and associated to him as a mentor. . . . So Philemon had stepped out of Jung's dream and became a Daimon like that of Socrates or the spirit control of today's mediums" (77). Clearly, it is this quality of religious "inflation" that has most annoyed Jung's psychoanalytic critics. For instance, John Gedo writes:

> Jung had his "earliest dream," which preoccupied him for the rest of his life. This also involved descent into an underground cavern; here a magnificent golden throne occupied the center with a huge phallic shape of naked flesh upon it. His mother's voice warned him that this was the man-eater. The desperate need to idealize a male figure implied in this nightmare was what Jung had turned upon Sigmund Freud, only to find, instead of the Godhead, the archaeological science of psychoanalysis. He solved his dilemma by deciding that his own unconscious was divine. ("Magna" 79–80)

Gedo is not being quite fair. Jung did not decide that his unconscious was divine; his unconscious did! There is a big difference. One can observe Jung's tendency to identify himself repeatedly with an autonomous unconscious force that stems from his unconscious, but what are we to make of it? In a certain sense, given his situation, it was his salvation. As in the case of various other persons of creative genius, his inner struggle was obviously the source of his inspiration through agony and, at times, ecstasy. Jung himself refers to the matter in these terms: "These talks with the 'Other' were my profoundest experiences: on the one hand a bloody struggle, on the other supreme ecstasy" (*Memories* 48). Toward the end of *Psychology of Religion*, Jung explains:

> Religious experience is absolute. It is indisputable. You can only say that you have never had such an experience, and your opponent will say: "Sorry, I have." And there your discussion will come to an end. No matter what the world thinks about religious experience, the one who has it possesses the great treasure of a thing that has provided him with a source of life, meaning and beauty and that has given a new splendor to the world and to mankind. He has pistis and peace. Where is the criterion by which you could say that such a life is not legitimate, that such experience is not valid and that such pistis is mere illusion? (113).

Jung's appreciation for the primary datum of religious experience was evident. For him it was a different way of perceiving reality that was not to be reduced to anything else. This is why he valued the direct knowledge of archetypal structures so much more than the blind faith of "true believers." He recognized that disputes about ultimate matters were futile. Like William James, whom he greatly admired, he was saying in effect that we judge attitudes and lives by pragmatic criteria. In many other places throughout his writings, Jung took great pains to insist on the subjective character of human judgments. Intuitively, he realized that in value judgments one person's meat may be another's poison.

With the publication by James Jarrett of the notes of Jung's seminars presented from 1934 to 1939 on Nietzsche's *Thus Spake Zarathustra*, we have an extended analysis of the way in which a creative genius like Nietzsche was also under the aegis of unconscious forces. In Jung's view, the dark side of the shadow needed to be compensated by a recovery of harmony and balance. Jung attributed Nietzsche's psychological demise, in part at least, to his being the son of a Christian pastor and his consequent need to move psychically to the opposite polarity (enantiodromia). As Jung put it in his 1934 Seminar: "Well now, Nietzsche often speaks of contempt. . . . He means by 'contempt' a negative attitude dramatically expressed" (Jung, *Nietzsche's Zarathustra* 1:68). Jung continued: "The negative attitude of Christianity was against the flesh—that flesh should be overcome was the highest ideal even. But he says it reached even the soul; the soul

Jung as Modern Man in Search of a Soul

itself became meager, hideous, and famished because it lost the body. That statement does not coincide with the Christian teaching at all, where the more you overcome the body, the more you are supposed to become beautiful and fat in heaven. But psychologically you find that the soul really becomes thin because it loses its *raison d'être*" (68–69).

Jung's notion of the collective unconscious has literary implications, as does his concept of the archetype. "It is an all-embracing general symbol, and the self, the Superman, is also the ocean, according to *Zarathustra*. So the self is the whole collective unconscious, the origin and the end of life, the origin of rain and of all rivers, of the whole universe, the end of all distinctness" (ibid., 71).

Jung's View of Knowledge and Experience

In his Terry Lectures at Yale University in 1937, Jung stated: "Notwithstanding the fact that I have often been called a philosopher, I am an empiricist and adhere to the phenomenological standpoint." In theory he did not deny the validity of other considerations, but he stated that he was not "competent to apply them correctly" (*Psychology and Religion* 2). Unlike Freud, Jung readily acknowledged the function of philosophy in calling attention to unacknowledged assumptions. As he wrote: "It was a great mistake on Freud's part to turn his back on philosophy. Not once does he criticize his premises or even the assumptions that underlie his personal outlook. . . . I have never refused the bittersweet drink of philosophical criticism, but have taken it with caution, a little at a time. . . . At any rate, philosophical criticism helped me to see that every psychology—my own included—has the character of a subjective confession" (*Modern Man* 118). As Jung was a psychiatrist and not a philosopher, he did not formulate a theory of knowledge. Although some writers have referred to him as a philosopher, time and again he stated that he was no philosopher but an empirical scientist.

The key to his understanding of religious experience is that its basis is to be found in the images of the unconscious mind. Such experience he regarded as subjective and open to all sorts of mistaken value judgments. "No transcendental truth is thereby demonstrated, and we must confess in all humility that religious experience is extra ecclesiam, subjective, and liable to boundless error" (*CW* 11:105). It is true that religious and philosophical statements are subject to error.

Jung's statement, however, supposes that "scientific" statements deal with the truth of facts. What is overlooked is that truth does not consist of mere facts but value judgments as well.

Throughout his writings Jung proceeded from the assumption that experience is all of a psychic nature. This is explicitly stated many times in his writings. It is nowhere stated more clearly than in *Modern Man in Search of a Soul:* "The fact that all immediate experience is psychic and that immediate reality can only be psychic, explains why it is that primitive man puts the appearance of ghosts and the effects of magic on a plane with physical events. . . . All our knowledge is conditioned by the psyche which, because it alone is immediate, is superlatively real" (221). It is evident that Jung had read Kant and been influenced by his ideas. Kant was one of the first to explore the possibility of religion within the bounds of reason, rather than revelation, the traditional construct. Jung had great respect for Kant as a thinker of the first rank but used Kant's conceptions with considerable freedom. For instance, he likened Kant's "thing-in-itself" to his own rendering of the self. Furthermore, he disregarded Kant's basic postulate that while knowledge begins with experience it does not follow that it arises from experience. For Jung, knowledge arises from experience.

Knowledge for Jung is based on reality that has a basis in the psyche and is first known as a psychic image. "Psychic existence is the only category of existence of which we have immediate knowledge, since nothing can be known unless it first appears as a psychic image. Only psychic existence is immediately verifiable" (*CW* 11:480). Jung stated that to the extent that the world does not assume the form of a psychic image, it is virtually nonexistent. "This is a fact which, with few exceptions—as for instance in Schopenhauer's philosophy—the West has not yet fully realized. But Schopenhauer was influenced by Buddhism and by the Upanishads" (481). Especially in his mature years, Jung had a high regard for the religions of the East, in which there is direct knowing through life and no conflict between science and religion. "No science is there based upon the passion for facts," he wrote, "and no religion upon mere faith; there is religious cognition and cognitive religion" (480).

At one point in his career Jung sought to account for philosophical truth on the basis of his theory of psychological types. For instance, on his reasoning, a thinking type would espouse a very different life philosophy than an intuitive type. As a result, he was of the opinion that philosophers are merely sharing the results of their own subjectivity. In speaking of the way that philosophical statements are conditioned, he said, "A philosophical statement is the product of a certain time in a certain place, and not the outcome of a purely logical and impersonal procedure. To that extent it is chiefly subjective; whether it has an objective validity or not depends on whether there are few or many persons who argue in the same way" (ibid., 478). Or as Paul Stern has put it, "Jung's typology owed much to the work of the American philosopher William James. . . . Jung eagerly adopted the American's notion that every philosophy is built on subjective premises and that the history of philosophy is largely the history of the clash of human temperaments" (157, 158).

In theory, Jung did not hold the view that all truth is psychological and hence subjective. He was so impressed with unconscious determination, however, that he almost overlooked the fact that even though statements are conditioned, this still says nothing about their essential truth or falsity. From the time of the early Greek philosophers onward, ascertaining truth has not been a matter of majority opinion. That is to say, a neurotic person may espouse a theory that is true, while a well-adjusted person may come up with one that is false. In short, psychological conditioning factors need not, as he implied, limit philosophical truth to subjective appearances.

Empirical Science and Value Assumptions

For an empirical investigator, Jung had a great deal to say about metaphysics. These statements were remarkable for their ambiguity. At times he maintained that psychology and metaphysics were separate and distinct disciplines. His concern at those times was with what could be psychically experienced, while not denying the validity of other considerations, that is, alternative methods. At other times, he tried to show how metaphysical statements arise from the soul and are in the last instance psychological (*Two Essays* 267). In a period when the scientific study of religion has been greatly expanded, nearly all investigators would agree with Jung that both philosophy and religion have a psychological side that is subject to empirical investigation. Few if any would want to disagree with his belief that science is an instrument that can be used to get at the locked doors of the human psyche.

Jung described the empirical scientific method: "Scientific method must serve. It errs when it usurps a throne. It must be ready to serve all branches of science because each, by reason of its insufficiency, has need of support from the others. Science is the best tool of the Western mind and with it more doors can be opened than with bare hands. Thus it is part and parcel of our understanding, and only clouds our insight when it lays claim to being the one and only way of comprehending" (in Wilhelm 78). These words express a valuable insight that unfortunately Jung lost sight of at those other times when he tended to regard science as the only way of knowing. He does so in a later part of *The Secret of the Golden Flower*, where he writes: "To understand metaphysically is impossible; it can only be done psychologically. I therefore strip things of their metaphysical wrappings in order to make them objects of psychology" (ibid., 129).

Thus, on the one hand, Jung's empiricism ostensibly sought to remain within the confines of strictly scientific knowledge, which, as he maintained, is but one way of knowing. On the other hand, at times this same empiricism succeeded in becoming the only means of knowing (i.e., scientific reductionism). In his early writings he tried to regard psychology as an autonomous science unconcerned with any metaphysical position. In practice he was not always consistent with his theoretical position.

It should also be noted that Jung generally took a dim view of all philosophical and theological criticisms of his work. In a letter to Gebhard Frei, he wrote: "In my view it is quite perverse to criticize my scientific work, whose aim is to be nothing but scientific, from any standpoint other than that which is appropriate to it, namely the standpoint of scientific method" (Sept. 22, 1944, cited in White, *God and the Unconscious* 236). Jung thought that criticism of his work was inappropriate unless it was concerned with empirical facts. In this way he sought to defend himself from philosophical criticism, which he regarded as inappropriate. In his own defense, he assumed that because his aim was avowedly scientific, he had succeeded in staying within the limits of empirical science. Thus he believed that the only valid criticism of his work that could be offered must proceed on strictly scientific grounds.

In support of Jung's position, Jolande Jacobi has written: "Jung is as far from being a 'metaphysician' as any natural scientist ever was, for his statements always refer to empirically verified facts and are strictly limited to what is conceivable on the basis of experience. But here too, as in the natural sciences, experience leads to a boundary where our empirical knowledge ceases and metaphysics begins" (*Psychology of Jung* 61). In spite of its surface plausibility, Jacobi's statement does not adequately reflect the way Jung's writings abound with mystical and metaphysical conjectures. A central difficulty of a thoroughgoing empirical investigation on the magnitude that Jung has undertaken is that it necessitates value judgments about the nature of the person being investigated. Hence, the problem is not with Jung's empiricism insofar as it remains empirical, but with his quasimetaphysical assumptions.

Jung was very much aware that psychology was once a branch of metaphysics. He wrote: "True to its history where psychology was first of all metaphysics, then the study of the senses and their functions, then of the conscious mind and its functions, psychology identified its proper subject with the conscious psyche and its contents and thus completely overlooked the existence of the unconscious psyche" (Jung and Kerényi 98). As a rule Jung tended to regard metaphysics as conscious psychology that had not become aware of the existence of its unconscious determinants. For this reason, Jung contended that philosophic intellect is not a perfect and "unconditioned instrument," as philosophers like to think. On the contrary, he held that for the most part philosophers are merely sharing the results of their subjective fantasies.

Raymond Hostie has shown how Jung sought to justify his early agnosticism by an oblique reference to Kant. According to Hostie, Jung extended Kant's theoretical skepticism to include the practical realm so that he ended up with an absolute agnosticism in no way justified by the scientific data (Hostie, *Religion* 139). Possibly unknown to Jung, in his *Prolegomena to Any Future Metaphysics* Kant had made a distinction between metaphysical and empirical cognition. He wrote: "First, as concerns the sources of metaphysical cognition, its very concept implies that they cannot be empirical" (13).

We are now in a position to consider the implications of what has preceded. If Jung had consistently thought through the meaning of the distinction he made between empirical and metaphysical knowledge, he might well have arrived at Kant's conclusion. In that case, he would not have tried to derive metaphysical knowledge from experience. On the other hand, if he believed that metaphysics could be derived from experience, in order to be consistent he would have rejected the independent nature of metaphysics. Probably out of respect for Kant, he did not reject the metaphysical quest entirely.

From one standpoint, Jung's frequent appeal to the authority of Kant was somewhat strange, in view of his own appreciation of archetypes stemming from the unconscious and his frequent use of ambiguous and paradoxical language. Kant is a prime example of a strictly logical mind at work. He could brook no contradictions. On the other hand, Kant demonstrated little or no interest in the kind of imaginal thinking that was Jung's forte. As Stephanie De Voogd has put it: "Kant had no conception of what we, since Jung, call imagination; Goethe for his part was speaking from personal experience of his own creative imagination which was of a kind wholly lacking in Kant" (179).

According to Jung's theory, absolute and psychic reality are to be distinguished and kept apart, but in practice they come together. In one place Jung wrote, "The psychological explanation and metaphysical statement do not contradict one another any more than, shall we say, the physicist's explanation of matter contradicts the as yet unknown or unknowable nature of matter" (CW 11:238). In still another place in the same work Jung has metaphysical reality explainable as unconscious phenomena. He asserted: "Submission to any metaphysical authority is, from the psychological standpoint, submission to the unconscious. There are no scientific criteria for distinguishing so-called metaphysical factors from psychic ones. But this does not mean that psychology denies the existence of metaphysical factors" (ibid.). One may wonder whether Jung did not, in the last instance, regard such "so-called metaphysical factors" as being reducible to the psychic realm. He seemingly could not decide in his own mind whether all reality is psychic or whether there is reality that goes beyond this. He safeguarded himself by including the latter possibility. In earlier chapters we have seen how from childhood on he was of "two minds." We can now see how this double-mindedness found its way into many, if not most, of his theoretical formulations.

Jung was very much impressed by the fact that metaphysical statements have the reality of psychic fact. He believed that to the Western mind, which "compensates its well-known feelings of resentment by a slavish regard for 'rational' explanations, the obvious truth seems all too obvious, or else it is seen as an inadmissable negation of meta-

Jung as Modern Man in Search of a Soul

physical 'truth'" (*CW* 11:511). It is clear that Jung did not consider statements about the mind and its structure capable of establishing metaphysical truth. He wrote: "Psychology . . . holds that the mind cannot establish or assert anything beyond itself" (ibid., 476). His blanket statement is revealing. Here he betrays his distrust not only of metaphysical statements but of metaphysical truth as well.

Among metaphysicians there are just as many mistaken judgments as in other fields, but this is not to say that psychology needs to exercise active distrust of the methods employed by other disciplines. Such distrust is neither necessary nor warranted, as Jung himself seemed to sense. In seeking to counter the sometimes pretentious nature of conscious reason as shown in metaphysics, Jung went to the opposite extreme—that of favoring unconscious processes. It would appear that there is a need for a position between these two extremes, one that would incorporate both conscious and unconscious perspectives.

In all of the controversies in which he was involved, Jung always found it difficult to grasp the exact significance of any method other than his own. In his answers to the criticism of others, he sought to extricate himself from his difficulties in a number of ways. He stoutly maintained that to treat a metaphysical statement as a psychic process was not to say that it was merely psychic. He also pointed out that when we say *psyche* we are dealing with "the densest darkness that it is possible to imagine" (*CW* 11:296). In Jung's later writings, he was more careful to limit himself to the psychic sphere. In *Aion* he wrote: "Psychology, as I have said, is not in a position to make metaphysical statements. It can only establish . . . the symbolism of psychic wholeness" (198). Psychic wholeness is what Jung struggled to attain throughout his life. This was largely done through the very considerable attention he devoted to the study of symbolism.

For the most part, Jung was not sufficiently impressed with the limitations of psychology as a science. This has now been seen more clearly by psychologists and philosophers alike. In an article entitled "Metaphysics, Religion, and Psychotherapy," Orville Walters has cogently shown that it is the business of science to stand silent and claim no special competence on such matters as ethical discrimination and ultimate destiny. Walters has written: "Not everyone is willing to concede this inherent limitation in the nature of science. There is confidence that science will ultimately be able to provide a full explanation of the phenomena of the universe, including human behavior. This faith is responsible for most of the opposition toward permitting metaphysics to complement the incomplete world view that science now offers" (244). In a 1961 letter to me, Jung distinguished between hypothesis and hypostasis (Jung, *Letters* 2:583–84). He held that his psychology entertained a number of hypotheses in the tentative fashion appropriate to a scientific psychology and quite in contrast to the finality employed by philosophical absolutists and theological dogmatists.

Several studies in recent years, such as Homans's *Jung in Context* and Stolorow and Atwood's *Faces in a Cloud*, have shown that Jung was not an impartial scientist testing out new hypotheses. Both studies amply demonstrate that frequently a metapsychological system is an expression of its creator's most problematic subjective experiences. Throughout his life Jung was obsessed with the ghosts or demons of his unconscious. Now it can be said: He was a man who theorized to a large extent on the basis of his inner needs.

Jung as Modern Man in Search of a Soul

"Every pioneer is a monologist" until other people have tried out his method and confirmed his results.
—*C. G. Jung to Robert C. Smith*

CHAPTER 7

The Urgency of Spirituality: Jung's Relation to the Divine

In my research for this book, one of my main tasks was to investigate the connection between Jung's inner conflicts begun in childhood and the psychological, religious, and creative themes of his mature years. For Jung, religion was the intuitive psychotherapy of the ages. As we might expect, however, he was of two minds toward religion, just as he was of two minds toward his mother. Thus his investigations into the archaic dimensions of religion reflect, in my view, a fruitful revisiting and "reliving" of childhood trauma. Each of these exhibit the intuitive or numinous side of religion rather than its conceptual, ethical, or ritual dimension.

Focusing on religious experience somewhat in the manner of William James, Jung was one of the first "scientific investigators" to posit a universal or archetypal stratum for religious experience. His cross-cultural analyses drew a link between religious figures as diverse as the Buddha, Muhammad, Confucius, Zarathustra, Mithras, Attis, Kybele, and Mani, and also explored various esoteric cults. Unlike Freud, who theorized that dreams revealed repressed past experience, Jung viewed dreams as prospective and compensatory. Consequently, he provided theoretical undergirding for the exploration of dreams, astrology, parapsychology, and various other therapies of self-discovery. Jung's approach mirrors elements of the traditional modes of the ecstatic healer, which in times past and in more archaic societies have provided practical guidance to large numbers of people.

Growing up in a pastor's home, Jung knew the ways that Protestantism, following the main motifs of the age, had stressed the historical criticism of the Bible. Protestantism had, at the same time, become moralistic and pietistic. An important part of Jung's critique of Protestant Christianity was that it had neglected the symbolic dimension of religious life. During the Reformation, in the Protestant churches in Switzerland the altar was removed, along with all forms of sacramentalism. At the same time the preaching of the "Word of God" from the pulpit was emphasized. The result was that Protestantism became rationalistic and moralistic but failed to perform its therapeutic task. Catholicism, for its part, preserved the sacramental and numinous dimensions of religion but adopted an obscurantist view with regard to many of the other issues of the modern world. By preoccupying believers with participation in ritual, it continued to project attention outside the individual and neglected the task of dealing with the troublesome effects of the unconscious—a situation that Jung termed "modern man in search of a soul."

His own inner struggles and the problems of so many of his patients presented Jung with a formidable task. He sought to make connections between depth psychology and the issues of psychic healing hitherto neglected by Protestants and Catholics alike. Increasingly, he became a savant seeking to recover the symbolic aspects of life discarded in an age of rationalism and materialism.

Ever since Jung's Terry Lectures on Psychology and Religion at Yale University in 1937, many have seen him as a great defender of religion and its viability in the modern age. A simplistic contrast is made between Freud and Jung. One is regarded as religion's great enemy, the other its great friend. This assessment is mistaken if taken at face value, however. Like all oversimplifications, it distorts the true nature of a complex state of affairs. Possibly many people in the modern world have needed to project on Jung the role of religion's great revitalizer. This need may have arisen because of the devastating attacks visited upon traditional religion from so many quarters. Recent centuries have shaken the foundations of traditional religious belief. Apparently including himself, Jung adamantly stated that "modern man abhors dogmatic postulates taken on faith and the religions based upon them. He holds them valid only in so far as their knowledge-content seems to accord with his own experience of the deeps of psychic life" (*Modern Man* 239). On the same point, when an interviewer asked if he believed in God, Jung replied that he did not believe in God, he "knew" God. Such statements were given much attention and helped to build his reputation. The clear implication was that in modern society it was necessary to recover both the catharsis and the healing dimension that religion had traditionally afforded. Jung insisted that of his patients in the second half of life "there has not been one whose problem in the last resort was not that of finding a religious outlook" (ibid., 264).

There were those who challenged this popular view of Jung. One such person was Martin Buber. In his book *Eclipse of God*, Buber viewed Jung's work as containing a direct threat to religion and actually considered him more dangerous to religious thought than either Heidegger or Sartre. Buber claimed that Jung was identified with modern consciousness that "abhors" faith and promotes a perspective of "psychic immanence" (84).

Certainly Jung was greatly absorbed with religious issues throughout his life. It can be maintained that his interest in religion stemmed at least as much from his own inner conflicts as from his desire to be a therapist to Christianity, as Murray Stein contends in *Jung's Treatment of Christianity*. Jung is popularly known for his emphasis on achieving inner wholeness and psychic integration. His writings have illustrated the connection between unconscious processes and the healing through myth that comes from the spiritual traditions of world religions. No one has altogether satisfactorily linked Jung's own personal struggles with his insights into world spirituality, as

Stein points out (*Jung's Treatment* 2). Indeed, given the complexities of Jung's life, such is by no means an easy task.

After offering an illuminating discussion of how Jung has been understood by his interpreters and carefully tracing several of his personal crises through much of his life experience, Stein fails to apply his insights into Jung's personality conflicts to Jung's later writings on religion. With unusual clarity, Stein has usefully shown that Jung's interpreters tend to view him as an empirical scientist, a hermeneutical revitalist, a doctor of souls, or a post-Christian modern man. Stein finds all of these assessments deficient and offers a new interpretation based upon the assumption that Jung viewed his relationship to Christianity as a therapeutic one.

In my own view, Jung's contribution to the therapy of the Christian tradition was a matter of secondary importance for him. Peter Homans, following Heinz Kohut, John Gedo, and Philip Rieff, has emphasized Jung's narcissism and viewed him as a post-Christian modern man. Stein holds that this perspective "arises from their slanting the angle of focus too sharply in the direction of his personal existential dilemmas and psychological pathology" (*Jung's Treatment* 16). Jung's inner conflicts need to be viewed correctly even though they disclose personal pathology and its lifelong resolution. Although Jung pointed to some post-Christian problems and the way they could be addressed (e.g., the crisis of meaning and the question of death), he also made important contributions to the revitalization of spirituality in the modern age. Throughout his life and especially in works like *Answer to Job*, he thoroughly reinterpreted Christianity with such ambivalence that it is evident that he was *both* its friend and its enemy. This topic has been taken up by several of his interpreters, such as John Dourley, Jeffrey Satinover, and Homans. Looking at all the evidence, it is hard to gainsay the view that he pointed the way both for Christianity's renewal and for its "repudiation" (Homans, *Jung in Context* 184).

Dourley in *The Illness That We Are* presents a Jungian criticism of Christianity. In his first chapter Dourley addresses the issue of "Jung's ambivalence toward Christianity." Applying his insight to Jung's concept of myth, Dourley writes: "Jung understands the Christian myth to be a great gift to humanity. . . . [His understanding of myth] also reveals the elements of a continued and consistent criticism of Christianity" (*Illness* 9). Dourley is correct about Jung's ambivalence but fails to account for the underlying reason for it.

Jung had an unusual need to correspond with theologians, whose approval he feverishly sought and whose frequent criticisms were a source of consternation to him. One can note a similar thread in the quality of his relationships with his father, Freud, Victor White, Gebhard Frei, Raymond Hostie, and Martin Buber, as well as several others. Recriminations and accusations of misunderstanding came from both sides. In my correspondence with Jung when I was a doctoral student, I was struck by his passionate involvement with his own ideas. In Zurich some years later, a Swiss explained to me how even in his early professional years and throughout his career Jung had to fight an uphill battle for the acceptance of his ideas. This was especially true of an academic audience, where Jung's ideas met resistance and skepticism. In one of his letters to me, Jung likened himself to a heroic figure who has been constantly misunderstood. He wrote: " 'Every pioneer is a monologist,' until other people have tried out his method and confirmed his results. Would you call all the great minds which were not popular among their contemporaries, monologists, even that 'voice of one crying in the wilderness'?" (Jung, *Letters* 2:571).

By casting doubt on the paradigms of traditional monotheism and patriarchy, Jung showed how religious experience could be separated from traditional dogma and ritual. The ways he did this are complex in the extreme. One of his last works, *Answer to Job*, with its theme of the dark side of God and psychic suffering, in large measure reflects his own experience.

Modern Man in Search of a Soul

Gradually Jung became determined to make a scrupulous study of the psychic basis of religion. While others made a distinction between psychic experience and religious experience, he assumed that they are the same thing. As Hans Schär, in an early work on Jung, has written: "There has probably never been any doubt for Jung that religion is either a psychic occurrence and thus intimately connected with the total structure of the soul or it is nothing at all. He does not hesitate to regard religious experience as accessible to psychology, and he makes no distinction between religious processes and other psychic happenings" (56). While this bold assumption opened a whole new realm for psychic investigation, to assume, as Jung does, that religion can be explained by means of its psychic origin is to make a large assumption that goes almost unrecognized by him. This assumption is that all truth is of the same kind, facts to be discovered. It is interesting that the psychoanalyst Erich Fromm has recognized this deficiency in Jung's reasoning. In *Psychoanalysis and Religion* Fromm writes: "Jung's use of the concept of truth is not tenable. He states that 'truth is a fact and not a judgment,' that 'an elephant is true because it exists.' But he forgets that truth always and necessarily refers to a judgment and not to a description of a phenomenon" (15).

Increasingly, Jung became convinced that religion is primarily the result of unconscious forces. He wrote: "But religion is a vital link with psychic processes independent of and beyond consciousness, in the dark hinterland of the psyche" (Jung and Kerényi 101). Jung's views have a distinctive quality to them. In contrast to the views of others, he assumes that the unconscious is the locus of the religious function. He defines religion as "a relationship to the highest or strongest value, be it positive or negative. The relationship is voluntary, that is, you can accept, consciously, the value by which you are possessed unconsciously. That psychological fact which is the greatest power in your system is the god, since it is always the overwhelming factor which is called god. . . . As soon as a god ceases to be an overwhelming factor, he becomes a mere name" (*Psychology and Religion* 98). Jung assumes that deity is a psychic factor in the personality. Often, as we have just seen, following traditional usage, Jung refers to a god-image by the pronoun *he*, which would suggest that his idea of a god is masculine. By the same token, his colleague Erich Neumann dedicated his influential work *The Great Mother* to Jung, who is credited with being friend and master. The archetype of the feminine as a psychic factor of divinity and countless female expressions of divinity interested both men.

For the most part, Jung used the term *god* or *god-image* to describe a compelling psychic function, but he was by no means always careful in this respect and brought on stringent criticisms from theologians and philosophers. He believed that religion has an important psychological aspect, which he proposed to deal with from an empirical point of view. Frequently he maintained that he was restricting himself to the empirical observation of phenomena while refraining from any metaphysical or philosophical considerations.

With the appearance of *Psychological Types* in 1921, Jung's psychology took definite form and shape. He set forth his theory of types, including the two basic attitudes of extraversion and introversion and the four basic functions of thinking, feeling, sensation, and intuition. These functions were further subdivided into rational and irrational functions. *Psychological Types* is especially important because in it Jung endeavored to set forth some definitions that are crucial to an understanding of his psychology.

Joseph Campbell tells a delightful story in which the hearer is supposed to assume that he or she has been chatting with an unknown gentleman sitting in the next airplane seat:

> A stewardess stops by and respectfully addresses him as "Senator." When she leaves, you find that you are speaking to him with different feelings from those you had before, and not quite the same sense of ease. He has become for you what Jung has termed a "mana personality," one charged with the magic of an imposing social mask, and you are talking now not simply to a person, but to a personage or presence: a respectful American citizen conversing with a senator. The personae of the little scene will have changed—at least for your side of the dialogue. As far, however, as the Senator is concerned, he will still be the man he was before; and if he was putting on no airs then, he will be putting on no airs now. (*Myths to Live By* 67)

For Jung the archetype is an element of our psychic structure that represents certain instinctive premises in the dark primitive psyche and therefore is a necessary component in our psychic economy (Jung and Kerényi 110). He is of the opinion that archetypes do not consist of inherited ideas but of inherited dispositions to reaction (Jung, *Two Essays* 139).

Projection is defined as "displacing a subjective process out into an object," in contrast to introjection, which "consists in taking an object into the subject" (Jung, *Psychological Types* 582). Jung makes much of the compensatory law of enantiodromia, according to which every attitude in the unconscious calls up a compensatory attitude. Literally *enantiodromia* means "a running counter to." Jung explains that in the philosophy of Heraclitus this concept is used to designate the play of opposites, namely the view that maintains that everything that exists goes over to its opposite. He accounts for his interpretation by saying, "I use the term enantiodromia to describe the emergence of the unconscious opposite, with particular relation to its chronological sequence." Continuing the same topic, he writes: "This characteristic phenomenon occurs almost universally wherever an extreme, one-sided tendency dominates the conscious life; for this involves the gradual development of an equally strong, unconscious counterposition, which first becomes manifest in an inhibition of conscious activities, and subsequently leads to an interruption of conscious direction" (ibid., 542). He saw that no psychic equilibrium takes place without the compensation brought about by the regulatory function of the opposites. Jung is speaking to the question of how the divided self effects a process of creative resolution of opposites.

Given what we now know about the circumstances of Jung's childhood, the phenomenon Jung describes as enantiodromia would seem to be not merely the passing of one psychological mode over to its opposite. Rather, it is more accurately described as an attempted psychic resolution of the phenomenon of early childhood splitting. This has been explored by D. W. Winnicott, Jeffrey Satinover, W. R. D. Fairbairn, Melanie Klein, and others to explain the difference between the True Self and the False Self.

Jung saw fit to make a conceptual distinction between the soul and the psyche. He wrote: "By psyche I understand the totality of all the psychic processes, both conscious as well as unconscious; whereas by soul, I understand a definitely demarcated function-complex that is best characterized as a 'personality'" (*Psychological Types* 588). In his definition, the psyche is broader than, and includes, the soul, which for him constitutes only a certain "limited functional complex" (Jacobi, *Psychology of Jung* 5). Those familiar with thinking of soul in traditional religious categories should note Jung's unique and specialized use of the term. For Jung souls are separate personalities or, in Satinover's characterization, "split-off 'personified complexes' that exhibited a startling degree of autonomy" (Satinover, "Jung's Lost Contribution" 417).

Expanded Consciousness and the Transcendent Function

For Jung consciousness is "the relationship between the ego and the various mental contents." The conscious mind is based on and results from "an unconscious psyche which is prior to consciousness and continues to function together with, or despite consciousness" (*Integration of the Personality* 3, 13).

The three levels of the mind he distinguishes are the conscious, the secondary or personal unconscious, and the primary, collective, or absolute unconscious. The unconscious is regarded as prior to the conscious mind, and since it is autonomous, it has or "is" a law unto itself (ibid., 13).

For Jung, the more we become conscious of ourselves through self-knowledge and act on the basis of this knowledge, the more the personal unconscious superimposed on the collective unconscious will be diminished. "In this way there arises a consciousness which is no longer imprisoned in the petty, oversensitive, personal world of the ego, but participates freely in the wider world of objective interests" (*Two Essays* 187). His point is that a widened consciousness no longer needs to be compensated by unconscious countertendencies but is a function of the relationship to the world of objects.

The term *unconscious* is for Jung a "boundary concept" or *Grenzbegriff* (*Psychological Types* 613) used to describe that into which our consciousness cannot penetrate. Its function is compensatory to that of consciousness. The region of the unconscious, because of its hidden nature, can be reached only indirectly by means of symbols. "The symbol is, on the one hand, the primitive expression of the unconscious, while on the other hand, it is an idea corresponding to the highest intuition produced by consciousness" (in Wilhelm 105).

Beneath the personal unconscious, which corresponds to the Freudian conception with all its repressed wishes, desires, and impulses, Jung viewed a deeper level of what he termed the collective unconscious. In one of his most definitive statements about its nature, he wrote, "The collective unconscious is a part of the psyche which can be negatively distinguished from the personal unconscious by the fact that it does not, like the latter, owe its existence to personal experience and consequently is not a personal acquisition" (*Archetypes* 42). For him the personal unconscious consisted of complexes, while the collective unconscious consisted of inherited archetypes.

Religious concepts such as the idea of God were viewed as archetypes coming from the autonomous realm of the collective unconscious.

Humankind still lives in a sea of unconsciousness to a large extent, according to Jung, and has evolved out of unconsciousness far too little. This follows anthropologist Lucien Lévy-Bruhl's conception of participation mystique. Jung and Lévy-Bruhl are agreed that primitive mentality does not draw a clear distinction between subject and object and between reality within and reality without. "In so far as the difference between subject and object is not conscious, unconscious identity prevails. Then the unconscious is projected into the object, and the object is introjected into the subject, that is to say, made part of the subject's psychology" (in Wilhelm 122).

In an early work Jung wrote, "mankind wishes to live in God only their ideas which they project into God" (*Symbols* 111). He also wrote: "The gods of Greece and Rome perished from the same disease as did our Christian symbols. . . . On the other hand the gods of the strangers still had unexhausted mana" (*Archetypes* 14). With the development of consciousness, these projections are withdrawn, though the psychic energy still remains.

"Consciousness can hardly exist in a state of complete projection. At most it would be nothing but a heap of emotions. Through the withdrawal of projections, conscious knowledge slowly developed" (*Psychology and Religion* 100). Jung regarded the gaps that remain in actual knowledge to be instances of projections that still exist. As a result, he correlated the withdrawal of projections with the origin of subject-object knowledge.

The tendency toward greater self-consciousness is not without its dangers, Jung warned. He was of the opinion that it was better to avow our spiritual poverty and to acknowledge that our spiritual dwelling has fallen into disrepair than to feign a legacy to which we are not heirs. "The more powerful and independent consciousness becomes, and with it the conscious will, the more is the unconscious forced into the background. When this happens, it becomes easily possible for the conscious structures to be detached from the unconscious images" (in Wilhelm 85). Jung's analysis of modern consciousness contended that this is precisely what happened to Protestantism, with its stress on iconoclasm, which has had the effect of dissociating man from his unconscious. For this reason Jung appreciated the Catholic emphasis on the mediating power of symbols as having a positive effect upon psychic wholeness.

On this point Paul Tillich and Jung agree. Tillich has written:

> C. G. Jung has called the history of Protestantism a history of continuous "iconoclasm" ("the destruction of pictures," that is, of religious symbols) and, consequently, the separation of our consciousness from the subconscious of everybody. He is right. Protestants often confuse essential symbols with accidental signs. They often are unaware of the numinous power inherent in genuine symbols, words, acts, persons, things. They have replaced the great wealth of symbols appearing in the Christian tradition by rational concepts, moral laws, and subjective emotions. (xxiii)

The assumption here is that religious symbols proceed from archetypes in the unconscious. Jung and Tillich seem to agree that Protestant thought has all too often become moralistic and rationalistic and separated from its unconscious images.

Self was used by Jung to designate the sum total of conscious and unconscious existence (*Psychological Types* 585). He held that the self is "a magnitude superordinate to the conscious ego. It includes not only the conscious, but also the unconscious portion of the psyche and is therefore a personality, so to speak, which we too are" (*Two Essays* 186). As early as 1902 Jung dealt with the phenomenon of personified complexes in his doctoral dissertation, where he stressed both the splitting off of functions from the ego complex and the strong tendency of the psychic elements toward autonomy, which he terms autonomous complex. In another place he wrote that the self is not only the midpoint but also the circumference, taking in consciousness and the unconscious. Self is the center of the psychic totality, as the ego is the center of consciousness (*Integration of the Personality* 96). The goal of analytical psychology, which has been called psychic integration or individuation, calls for a shifting of the center of the personality from the ego to the self. *Self* is used by Jung in an exclusively psychological sense, which is quite different from the meaning the term has had in the history of philosophy. In another place Jung indicated: "Intellectually the self is no more than a psychological concept, a construct that serves to express an unknowable essence which we cannot grasp as such, since by definition it transcends our powers of comprehension. It might equally well, he tells us, be called the 'God within us' " (*Two Essays* 250).

The goal of Jung's psychology has been expressed succinctly by the term *individuation*. By it Jung refers to achieving true uniqueness and individuality as well as becoming one's own self. Such individuation then means coming to selfhood or self-realization and wholeness. This process of self-realization or coming to be a self is distinguished from the process whereby the ego becomes conscious. Jung has said his self is indistinguishable from a god-image. For him there is an analogy between self-realization or individuation and the realization of a god-image, which he says, expressed in religious or metaphysical terms, amounts to God's incarnation (*cw* 11:157).

For Jung "the transcendent function" is simply another name for the psyche's capacity for transformation and symbol formation. He writes: "This function of mediation between the opposites I have termed the transcendent function, by which I mean nothing mysterious, but merely a combined function of conscious and unconscious elements, or, as in mathematics, a common function of real and imaginary factors" (*Psychological Types* 145–46). Occasionally, almost in spite of himself, Jung used the term *transcendent* in its more usual meaning. For instance, late in his career he wrote: "These specific attainments are now gravely threatened . . . by the rationalistic hubris which is tearing our consciousness from its transcendent roots and holding before it immanent goals" (*Aion; cw* 9, pt. 2, p. 221).

The Dark Side of God and Psychic Suffering

Much attention has been focused on Jung's late work *Answer to Job*, published in 1951. In this work Jung turns the biblical account upside down and offers a highly subjective interpretation of it for modern man. Like *Septem Sermones ad Mortuos* which was written in 1916, the volume virtually wrote itself. It raises the issue of Job's helplessness and dependence, his possession by Yahweh-like states, and his defiance of a state of passive victimization. Apparently its production was of great therapeutic value for its author.

Unlike the account of Job that questions the earlier theodicy that the just are rewarded and the wicked punished, Jung's account pictures God as one who is easily provoked to acts of retaliation, both malicious and evil-intentioned. He writes: "It is not easy for [Job] to accept the knowledge that divine arbitrariness breaks the law. . . . He is up against a God who does not care a rap for any moral opinion and does not recognize any form of ethics as binding" (*cw* 11:369). Jung views Yahweh's conspiracy with Satan as both intolerable and despicable. The God of Jung's reconstructed hermeneutic includes and incorporates evil as part of his nature.

Answer to Job was a project that greatly interested Jung. Like many of his earlier writings, it poured out of him as though it came from an underground spring. Commentators have noted that this work, as indeed much of his creative writing, resulted from an activation of his own unconscious processes. It was begun in the Spring of 1951, when he was experiencing a debilitating illness. When the book was completed, his illness was over. To Aniela Jaffé in July 1951 he wrote: "If there is anything like the spirit seizing one by the scruff of the neck, it was the way this book came into being" (*Letters* 2:20).

To his great dismay, *Answer to Job* stirred up a hornet's nest of controversy. Several of his own associates, therapists like Neumann, found it stimulating yet controversial. Even for his closest colleagues, however, the line of argumentation Jung presented was unacceptable in a variety of ways. Others — mostly theologians, philosophers and Biblical scholars — fervently disputed its assumptions and presumptions.

In *Answer to Job* Jung deals with scriptural materials in a rather idiosyncratic manner. He makes no bones about the fact that the work grew directly out of his own subjective experience. Jung focuses on Yahweh as the First Cause of all that is. By the same token, *Answer to Job* extends rather than withdraws projections upon the "cosmic father." Much more than the scriptural text, Jung's late work reflects both conscious and unconscious anger toward divine tyranny. Nonetheless, Jung engages in an extended revitalization of the symbolic process. His main focus is the image of God rather than Job.

In particular, Jung concentrates on Yahweh's tyrannical stance toward Job. Identifying psychologically with Job, he both explains the situation from the victim's viewpoint and projects his feelings upon Yahweh. Throughout his life, as he discloses in his autobiography, Jung had much rage toward both of his parents. As I see it, he takes the scriptural narrative and runs with it in his own direction. This is a useful task insofar as his discourse is a redaction that refutes the implied assumptions of the biblical text. Job itself, however, is a book that disputes the then-accepted theodicy of divine reward and punishment. Although heretical in its day, it gained a measure of acceptance for being true to life. Hence, a further heresy, based on personal experience, that reacts to an original one seems worthy of examination.

In this late work of Jung, Yahweh receives the main attention of his servant Job. Jung's interpretation does not focus primarily on Job and the meaning of his experience for human existence, as in the biblical account. Jung's version is primarily about Yahweh viewed from the vantage point of Job as Jung understands him. Jung amplifies particularly those aspects of Job's experience that grow out of and resonate with his own experience. I am struck by Jung's assumption of dualistic anthropomorphism in regard to Yahweh's character. He asserts that the gods of antiquity "teemed with virtues and vices" (*CW* 11:371). As Jung puts it, Yahweh is "everything in totality. He is total justice and also its total opposite" (372). More important, he asserts that Yahweh is unconscious and needs conscious man, who, it would seem, can think his thoughts after him, and his own thoughts as well. Jung continues: "That is why the Creator needs conscious man even though from sheer unconsciousness he would like to prevent him from becoming conscious" (373).

There is an intrepid quality to Jung's interpretation. In certain important respects, for him man is infinitely superior to God, for man possesses the element of self-consciousness that God lacks. Looking ahead, it is this quality that leads Jung to posit the psychic necessity of the incarnation of the divine logos (the psychic equivalent of Sophia, or Wisdom) in the second part of his book. Divine reason must find its expression in a mythic incarnation in human form, as he sees it. For Jung this implies that God is relative to humans and desperately needs human beings to fulfill the divine intention.

For Jung the "Book of Job places this pious and faithful man, so heavily afflicted by the Lord, on a brightly lit stage where he presents his case to the eyes and ears of the world" (*CW* 11:375). Thus Job comes to doubt the dominant theodicy that obedience will be rewarded and disobedience will be punished. However, Jung does not put it quite that way. For him "Yahweh was influenced by one of his sons, by a doubting thought and made unsure of Job's faithfulness" (375). He reminds his reader that in Persian tradition Ahriman proceeded from one of Ormuzd's doubting thoughts (375n5).

Jung presents a picture of a dualistic deity of infinite power and anthropomorphic qualities but limited compassion and self-consciousness. Yahweh's anthropomorphism is in conflict with his omniscience. Whatever the divine attributes, and they are many, Jung is deeply impressed by the inconsistencies in Yahweh's behavior. He puts the matter even more pointedly when he asserts: "From the human point of view Yahweh's behavior is so revolting that one has to ask oneself whether there is not a deeper motive hidden behind it" (*CW* 11:375).

In an almost uncanny way Jung spoke of the feminine expression of the divine. In *Answer to Job* he presents, among other things, a theory of the repression of and reemergence of the feminine principle in the history of religious thought. The second half of *Answer to Job* is taken up with the way that Sophia serves as a compensatory principle for the divine indwelling of the human. There Sophia is viewed as the feminine Anthropos, the counterpart of the masculine principle (*CW* 11:439). Jung notes that the original man who was created in the divine image had, according to Jewish tradition, two wives, just like his heavenly prototype. That is, Adam had Lilith (who is a satanic correspondence to Sophia) and Eve, just as Yahweh had Sophia and Israel. Jung views the emergence of Christianity as a form of compensation. As he puts it, "It was the men of the last few centuries before Christ who, at the gentle touch of the pre-existent Sophia, compensate Yahweh and his attitude, and at the same time complete the anamnesis of Wisdom" (396). Jung observes that Yahweh was preparing to become man, through his good son Christ, while Satan, the bad son, is excluded, expelled, and seen "as lightning" to "fall from Heaven" (Luke 10:18).

Jung also speaks of the relationship of Mary to Sophia. He calls attention to the feminine nature of the Holy Ghost, whose nature is personified by Sophia. Sophia is symbolized by the dove, the bird belonging to the love goddess. In antiquity the love goddess was in most cases the mother of the young dying god. In the Catholic tradition Mary eventually becomes the Queen of Heaven, representing another version of the sacred marriage (*hieros gamos*) motif. This tradition of Mary may be viewed as a compensation for the emerging male patriarchalism as it arose in early Christianity. As Jung puts it: "Mary, as the bride, is united with the son in the heavenly bridal-chamber and as Sophia with the Godhead" (*CW* 11:182). Protestant-ism, of course, did not develop the compensatory aspects of Mary veneration. On the present religious scene, we are witnessing the re-emergence of the goddess theme among those feminists who are in-vestigating the feminine aspects of the divine.

An ongoing body of interpretative literature on *Answer to Job* has been produced by a diverse group of writers. Shortly after the book was written, Victor White vigorously objected to Jung's attempt to "transfer our personal splits and ills to our gods and archetypes, and put the blame on them" (White, Plaut, and Spiegelberg 77–78). Jung shrugged off the force of White's observation, but in the light of recent studies of Jung's personal history it is now clear that Father White saw profoundly into the way that Jung was personally using psychological projection (see Jung, *Letters* 2:238n1). In a way that Jung does not, White interprets Job as a man who must grow up, one who has ignored the dictates of his psychological and spiritual nature. White also calls attention to the way in which Jung fails to reflect the transformation that occurs in Job's consciousness (White, *Soul and Psyche* 235).

In White's analysis of *Answer to Job*, several points emerge: Job according to Jung is superior to Yahweh. He possesses the self-consciousness that Yahweh lacks. God becomes man not for the sal-vation of mankind but rather "for his own self-improvement" (ibid.). Unfortunately he only incarnates the "light side," to the neglect of the "dark," so that the incarnation is equally one-sided. In summary White states: "There are . . . signs that God is learning better the dark, feminine side of his all too masculine nature" (236).

A very different interpretation of *Answer to Job* is found in Harry Slochower's article "Freud as Yahweh in Jung's *Answer to Job*," which appeared in *American Imago*. Slochower, a psychoanalytic writer, has tried to show how Jung unconsciously linked Yahweh with Freud and his own father. He cites Jung's revealing letter to Freud of Octo-ber 28, 1907, in which Jung expresses his desire for Freud as well as his fear that a sexual attack of his youth may be repeated symbolically with Freud. Slochower admits that Jung's study involves "theologic-religious and mythic motifs" that he does not propose to examine.

He does maintain, however, that the conflicts within Job and within Yahweh pertain to Jung's own conflicting attitudes.

With considerable perception Slochower writes: "In the last decade of his life, Jung makes a final attempt to meet this problem, this time in a passionate tract *Answer to Job*. In it, his veneration and desire for Freud, mixed with envy and fear, are transferred on to the relation between Job and the Hebraic God, Yahweh" (8). Slochower also tries to link "a complicated web of motives" with Jung's attempt to reach out for "help" against being "overwhelmed" by Freud's personality. "Jung maintained his desire for, interlaced with envy and fear of attachment to Freud, to the end" (ibid.).

Slochower makes several points. First, Jung anthropomorphizes Yahweh. Especially Slochower calls attention to the ways in which "*Answer to Job* incorporates an ardent wooing of Yahweh, a near-despairing plea that Yahweh respond, that he 'answer' Job, above all, that he answer with love. And the author's bitter complaint is that it is precisely love which this Hebraic deity lacks" (18). Second, Slochower goes on to point out Yahweh's and Job's displacement by Christ. Jung makes the point in *Memories* that Job "is a kind of prefiguration of Christ. The link between them is the idea of suffering. Christ is the suffering servant of God, and so was Job" (216). Third, both Yahweh and Job, whom Slochower postulates to be Freud and Jung, are combined into a single personality. As Jung puts it, "Yahweh's intention to become man, which resulted from his collision with Job, is fulfilled in Christ's life and suffering" (*Answer to Job*, cited in Slochower 20).

In my opinion, Slochower is on the right track but does not quite succeed in presenting a totally compelling interpretation. To me, it seems that Freud is viewed as Yahweh and that Jung views himself as Job. There would clearly seem to be large amounts of projection of Jung's own experience upon Yahweh. But is Slochower correct that Jung displaces this upon Christ? The psychic mechanism is projection in still another form. In this way Job (for Jung an innocent victim) becomes Christ, that is, the innocent victim who redeems the world.

In presenting a Jungian answer to Slochower's article, C. Jess Groesbeck acknowledges the new considerations that Slochower has opened up for further study and calls attention to a matter that

Slochower's innovative article ignored, namely the importance of the lost or split feminine for Jung. In part II of *Answer to Job*, Jung suddenly turns his attention away from Yahweh and Satan to apocalyptic issues of merger with Christ, who is seen as the successor of Job. We can, I believe, read this shift of attention on Jung's part first as reenactment of the identity issue with his father and later Freud (Slochower's contention) and secondly as reenactment of his problems with the split feminine (to some extent Groesbeck's and also my own contention). Very possibly this is all unconscious on Jung's part. Jung himself in *Answer to Job* does not speak directly of the split feminine. On the contrary, he launches into a complex set of late biblical issues involving John's view of the divine child, the second Adam, and various topics in the Epistles of the New Testament as well as the Book of Revelation.

The real issues that underlie these disguised concerns are a preoccupation with Sophia (a feminine source of divinity), the *complexio oppositorum* as a definition of the self, and the sacred marriage at one place of the Lamb with his bride (*cw* 11:447) and at another place of Yahweh with Sophia (448). Jung includes innumerable quotations from the nineteenth and twenty-first chapters of the Book of Revelation. These represent a vision of a city "built foursquare" and "of pure gold, clear as glass, and so were its streets." The final vision of the relation of Christ to the church Jung describes as a "uniting symbol" (447). It would seem that underneath it all, Jung projected his basic childhood conflicts upon numinous mystical symbols in ways that may not have resolved Job's dilemma but therapeutically assisted in Jung's own quest for individuation. As we have seen, Jung developed a lifelong preoccupation with reconstructing religious identity and incorporating the feminine dimension into his life and writings.

Unwittingly Jung discovered a phenomenon that cuts across the ages. Even if he read his own psychic experience into the account, he was apparently one of the pioneers in investigating the psychological aspects of cosmic and psychic balance. When the image of the divine becomes overly one-sided, somehow it has to be balanced by its opposite in the unconscious. Contrary to his own words, Jung developed a highly idiosyncratic concept of God because of his anger toward his father, Freud, and the traditional Christian idea of God as all good. But equally important, if not more so, what captivated

Jung as Modern Man in Search of a Soul

him was the god-image derived from his mother, which was ruthless, primitive, magical, and filled with numinous power. Both directly by intention and indirectly in his life and writings, Jung has greatly illuminated our understanding of the function of persona, mana personality, and what he termed personality inflation. As we have seen, he knew about these matters firsthand. A close reading of the features of Jung's life shows that he became aware of inflation as a phenomenon in his mother's, his own, and countless of his patients' lives. It grows out of inner fantasies that produce one-sidedness of personality development. It is, of course, closely linked to Jung's conception of anima and animus. There is obviously a great difference between viewing oneself in an exaggerated manner and inflating the importance of others. For Jung "inflation is a regression of consciousness into unconsciousness. This always happens when consciousness takes too many conscious contents upon itself and loses the faculty of discrimination" (cw 12, cited in Samuels, Shorter, and Plaut 82).

To my knowledge, no one has thus far thoroughly explicated the ways that the image of the split feminine impinged upon Jung's writings on religious themes, although we may safely assume that its impact was considerable. In this connection Groesbeck reminds us that Jung's "split feminine images" were contained in the connection he made between Sophia and Israel. By the same token, according to Groesbeck, Jung viewed Christ as the integration of Yahweh and Job. Groesbeck concludes: "The split feminine images seem to be a part of a split that is healed in the tranformation into Christ" ("Jungian Answer" 252). Here we have another of the many reasons religion was so important for Jung. Even into Jung's adulthood and old age, Christ represented the uniting symbol of his life, signifying wholeness and integration.

In his perceptive review of *Memories* Winnicott wrote: "What must be remembered, I think, is that Jung himself spent his life looking for his own self, which he never really found since he remained to some extent split (except insofar as this split was healed in his work on his autobiography)" (review 454). Winnicott stated that his own expertise as a child psychoanalyst was particularly pertinent to those chapters of *Memories* concerning Jung's childhood. Had he been more familiar with Jung's later writings, Winnicott doubtless would have seen how the motif of self-healing through symbolic transformation is to be found in much of what Jung has written, including *Answer to Job*.

In the process of growing up, achieving wisdom came to assume great importance for Jung. After his break with Freud in a very troubled period of his life, he identified with Philemon, whom he viewed as the personification of wisdom. In later years too, the pursuit of inner wisdom affording a gnosticlike certainty became a lifelong quest. The very writing of *Answer to Job* was beneficial to Jung and had a salutary effect at a time of infirmity and ill health in old age. It had the effect of making contact with the numinous dimension, and this was for Jung a metaphor of healing. It perplexed him greatly that so many of his colleagues, and many of the philosophers and theologians whom he knew, were so greatly angered by what he wrote.

Answer to Job was an idiosyncratic interpretation. More than forty years later, with the challenge of postmodernism upon us, we may be somewhat more charitable toward such interpretations of Scripture. Or are we? In any case, we may have to wait for another creative genius of Jung's stature to take up the issue again with similar—but, I hope, even greater—magnitude of vision.

As we have seen, the strands composing Jung's contribution to religious studies are complex. In this chapter we have explored some of the connections between Jung's profound interest in divergent forms of spirituality and the needs of his own life experience. We have noted that his prodigious output and keen insight into the links between psychology and religion would have been much less had he not had the unique life experiences he did. We have further seen that there is considerable evidence that Jung was of many minds toward religion. As few others have, he perceived the spiritual problems of modern man with unusual acuity. At the same time, he was aware of the ongoing need of people living in any age for a sense of transformed and ecstatic consciousness. As a physician of the soul, Jung focused his genius on the intuitive or numinous side of religion, which for centuries had been eroded by the winds of modernity. On the positive side, Jung viewed certain aspects of religion as a means to overcome personal fragmentation, split-off autonomous contents, and inner dissociation. In this respect he can be viewed as a pioneering bridge-thinker. His eclectic approach to his patients mirrors those elements of the ecstatic healer of times past through the re-

Jung as Modern Man in Search of a Soul

newal of the symbolic dimensions of religion. To an unusual degree, then, Jung was a synthesizer in an age of analysis.

There seems to be little doubt that Jung's highly creative use of religious images was for him a largely unconscious mode of intuitive psychotherapy. That is to say, on one level, his investigations into the archaic dimensions of religious experience and the impersonal aspects of archetypal symbolism seem to represent an ongoing response to childhood traumas, some of which he was never able to face directly. In a way they represent a lifelong revisiting and imaginative extension and exploration of earlier experiences. On still another level, his queries into hitherto neglected aspects of world spirituality have opened up a host of new lines of inquiry, discussion, and interpretation for investigators.

But if . . . horses . . . had hands, or were able to draw with
their hands and to do the works that man can do, horses would
draw the forms of gods like horses.
—Xenophanes, Fragment 15

CHAPTER 8

Self & Myth: A Modern Integration

More than any other single figure of our time, Jung
has linked personal and cosmic myth in the discipline of the history
of religions. Myth for him was not an outmoded or inauthentic form
of expression. He linked people to the wisdom of the ages, helping
them through the various crises of the life cycle from birth to death
and allowing them to participate in a cosmic drama beyond themselves. In Jung's view the major mythical visions of the world are
essentially similar. They embody archetypal images that differ only in
the details of their expression. The underlying pattern they express
remains constant. In this regard Joseph Campbell has acknowledged
his direct debt to Jung and has followed Jung's lead in his own explo-

rations. Jung's writings for Campbell have focused attention upon the largely unconscious myth that informs a cultural vision. For instance, Campbell in his classic work *The Hero with a Thousand Faces* has shown that the central features of the world's great myths, from Marduk to Indra to Superman, bear remarkable similarities. Further, Campbell has written: "The inward journeys of the mythological hero, the shaman, the mystic, and the schizophrenic are in principle the same: and when the return or remission occurs, it is experienced as a rebirth: the birth, that is to say, of a 'twice-born' ego, no longer bound in by its daylight-world horizon" (*Myths to Live By* 230).

Jung's first work in this field, *Symbols of Transformation*, revealed that his own concept of libido differed markedly from Freud's. As we saw in chapter 4, his results were diffuse in the extreme. *Symbols of Transformation* was written at top speed, as was *Answer to Job*. After writing *Symbols of Transformation*, Jung came to examine his own view of the myth of the hero. At the very time that he experienced his psychic breakdown or creative illness, he posed the question of his own myth. He sought, as it were, the key that would open the gates of the world's mythology. Freud had wanted him to focus upon a specific topic in the history of mythology. Jung, however, wanted to deal with myth in a broad and wide-ranging manner, to consider types and patterns of myths. His efforts, which contributed to his break with Freud, sought to explain the myths of the past but, most important, became crucial to both his understanding of world cultures and his view of personality theory.

Reflecting upon his efforts, Jung wrote some memorable words about the nature of myth. The question for him began as a personal query. He asked: "In what myth does man live nowadays? In the Christian myth, the answer might be. 'Do you live in it?' I asked myself. 'To be honest, the answer was no. For me, it is not what I live by.' 'Then do we no longer have any myth?' 'No, evidently we no longer have any myth.' 'But then what is your myth—the myth in which you do live?' At this point the dialogue with myself became uncomfortable, and I stopped thinking. I had reached a dead end" (*Memories* 171). Christian myth and its psychoanalytic countermyth no longer worked for Jung, so he embarked upon his "descent into the unconscious" to uncover his own myth, which was to embody elements of unconscious contents analogous to the religious traditions of mankind. Of one thing Jung seemed assured: man cannot live without a myth or overarching vision of the world. For a considerable period of time Jung's myth embodied a preponderance of unconscious contents (descent, rebirth, myth of the hero, the wise old man, etc.), but eventually the mythical themes of inner transformation were to be partially replaced by those of inner integration and the reconciliation of opposites.

There is a question whether Jung referred to a monotheistic deity in any sense equivalent to the usage of religious thinkers and theologians. For instance, the issue is raised in John Gedo's article "Magna Est Vis Veritatis Tuae et Praevalebit" (Great Is the Power of Your Truth, and It Shall Prevail)," whose title comes from a letter from Jung to Freud, written on November 11, 1908. In a footnote Gedo refers to a discussion of his paper at a meeting of the San Francisco Psychoanalytic Society in 1975. There Erik Erikson pointed out that Philip Rieff in *The Triumph of the Therapeutic* had been inexact in characterizing Jung's private religion as "God-centered." According to Erikson, Jung's understanding was, in fact, closer to certain Eastern faiths that do not conceptualize a definite deity. Repeatedly Jung stated that in his view *imago dei* (image of the divine) is neither a theological nor a metaphysical concept but an empirical one. For him God was "an autonomous complex" (letter to R. C. Smith, June 29, 1960, in Jung, *Letters* 2:570–73).

Jung does not say that his notion of the imago dei is, as Erikson holds, closer to the impersonal construct of Eastern religions. His concept would seem to cut across the East-West dichotomy. In answer to some questions I posed to him in 1960 with regard to his dispute with Martin Buber, he wrote: "How does the God complex behave in different individuals and societies? How does the Self-complex compare with the *Lapis Philosophorum* in Hermetic Philosophy and with the Christ-figure in patristic allegories, with Al Chadir in Islamic tradition, with Tifereth in the Kabbala, with Mithras, Attis, Odin, Krishna, and so on?" (Jung, *Letters* 2:571).

The Spiritual Problem of Modernity

One of the more perceptive contributions of Jung lies in the way he identified and analyzed the peculiar spiritual problems that beset those who live in the modern world. This may be described in part as the decline of man's image-making power.

Earlier ages had been able to project with great certainty upon deities outside themselves. For many in the modern world, including Jung himself, this was no longer a living option. The "acids of modernity" had eroded the source of cosmic certainty and wholeness. In his discussion of the rise of consciousness, he had considerable success in tracing the changes of worldview that had taken place over the centuries. His knowledge of cross-cultural parallels, the ancient world, the medieval period, the Enlightenment, the romantic period, and down to the present, especially with regard to applicable myths and symbols, was impressive. Most important, he brought a knowledge of the changes in the psyche occasioned by the changes in understanding the outer world. Jung's view of consciousness was thoughtful and evolved out of conversations with colleagues like Erich Neumann, Heinrich Zimmer, and Richard Wilhelm.

Jung's essay "The Spiritual Problem of Modern Man" is an ambitious venture into lucid explication of the peculiar problems besetting those persons interested in understanding issues such as the quest for meaning in our time. Jung contends that modern man, unlike his predecessors, is conscious to a superlative degree. "He alone is modern who is fully conscious of the present" (*CW* 10:75). Jung contends that earlier ages lived in a state of unconsciousness that engulfed them and in which they unconsciously projected their need for divinity outside themselves. Gradually, as projections were withdrawn, they came to live entirely in the present and entirely in consciousness, ignorant of unconscious influences. From his perspective, modern consciousness has been bought at a high price, so far as the psyche is concerned. As he puts it, "Modern man has lost all the metaphysical certainties of his medieval brother" (81).

As we saw in chapter 6, the single philosopher who shaped Jung's thought more than any other was Friedrich Nietzsche. For the dramatic statement of the crisis of selfhood, all later writers, including Freud, Jung, Buber, Heidegger, Jaspers, Sartre, and the other existentialists, are indebted to Nietzsche for his penetrating statements about the death of God. A prophet in the sense that he perceived things that other mortals only dimly glimpsed, Nietzsche was to perceive with clarity the consequences of a civilization without transcendent moorings. Jung was to perceive its therapeutic consequences. Though Nietzsche saw that God was dead for modern Western man, he was haunted by the issue throughout his writings. It was the cause of both his despair and his cosmic loneliness. In fact, Jung attributed Nietzsche's psychosis to his loss of spiritual moorings and withdrawal of projections (*Psychology and Religion* 103f.). For Nietzsche, God is dead, and man has slain him. His phrase "Gott ist tot" represents the climax of a development that has its roots at the very beginning of modern consciousness. Although explanations for this phenomenon vary, there is general agreement that mankind's image-making power has long been on the decline.

Jung's account of the declining effect of the image of God is based on the belief that images of the divine no longer hold their former meaning. He has said: "That the gods die from time to time is due to man's sudden discovery that they do not mean anything, that they are made by human hands, useless idols of wood and stone. In reality, however, he has merely discovered that up till then he has never thought about his images at all" (*CW* 9, pt. 1, p. 13). Jung notes the growth of psychological interest over the past decades as an indication that modern man is turning from outward material things to inner processes. "The psychological interest of the present time is an indication that modern man expects something from the psyche which the outer world has not given him: doubtless something which our religion ought to contain, but no longer does contain, at least for modern man" (*CW* 10:83).

Jung contrasts the perspective of objective knowledge with that of subjective experience, that is, the pursuit of science with that of faith, which has constituted the central perspective of Western forms of religion. In an early passage he insists: "Modern man abhors faith and the religions based upon it" (*CW* 10:84). Martin Buber, in his attack upon Jung's writings as panpsychism, was especially offended by this phrase. Buber contended that Jung extended the dominant trend of modernity by his gnosticism and by relegating the divine to an archetype of the unconscious. Jung, for his part, was convinced it could not be otherwise.

Jung's analysis of the decline of man's image-making capacity, if not his solution to the problem, has contributed to our understanding of this issue. His point is that if something is devalued in consciousness, it causes a compensation in the unconscious. Hence his stress upon the principle operative within the psyche is known as enantiodromia. Western consciousness in his view is one-sided, relative, and questionable. "The gods whom we are called upon to dethrone are the idolized values of our conscious world" (*CW* 10:88). One of these, which he regards as at the crux of the spiritual problem, is "to be found in the fascination which the psyche holds for modern man." Jung maintains that the ways in which psychic forces "transform the life of peoples and civilizations . . . are unforeseen and unforeseeable" (92).

Jung points out that in antiquity the man of the Greco-Roman world boldly cast off his defunct Olympian gods and turned instead to the mystery cults of Asia. Parallels are to be observed in our own age, even though the God of the West is still a living person for vast numbers of people (ibid.). As Jung sees it, in a scientific age with its accompanying depersonalization, there is increasingly an urgent need for a transformation of spiritual consciousness. Religious exclusivism and the intolerance it engenders receive harsh words from his pen. As he puts it, this is the view that sees "Christianity as the only truth and the white Christ the only redeemer" (89). Yet the implication is clear that with the drift from a theological perspective to a psychological one, a rash of new spiritualities has eventuated. Developments since Jung's death would seem to bear this out.

Empirical Science or New Religion?

In the 1950s Martin Buber maintained that Jung had deified the soul of man. He wrote: "One would grasp Jung's idea better if one said that from now on the Godhead no longer takes the place of the human self as it did in mankind up till now. Man now draws back the projection of his self on a God outside of him without thereby wishing to deify himself (as Jung here emphasizes, in contrast to another passage, in which . . . deification is clearly stated as a goal)" (*Eclipse of God* 86). In response to such criticisms of self-deification, Jung wrote, "I have been accused of 'deifying the soul.' Not I but God himself has deified it! I did not attribute a religious function to the soul. I merely produced the facts which prove that the soul is a *naturaliter religiosa*, i.e., possesses a religious function" (*Psychology and Alchemy* 13).

In Jung's reply to Buber, he cited an article in the *British Medical Journal* for February 9, 1952, which said, "Facts first and theories later is the keynote of Jung's work. He is an empiricist first and last" (cited in Jung, *Symbolic Life* 664).[1] Jung declared that this point of view had his approval. Throughout his writings he placed great stress upon the fact that he was primarily an empirical scientist. For example, in *Psychology and Religion* he set forth the limitations of his perspective: "Inasmuch as religion has a very important psychological aspect, I am dealing with it from a purely empirical point of view, that is, I restrict myself to the observation of phenomena and I refrain from any application of metaphysical or philosophical considerations. I do not deny the validity of other considerations, but I cannot claim to be competent to apply them correctly" (2).

Few would disagree with Jung's belief that science is not the only way of knowing. Unfortunately, at other times he does tend to regard science as the only way of comprehending. He does so in a later chapter of *The Secret of the Golden Flower*, when he writes, "*To understand metaphysically is impossible; it can only be done psychologically. I therefore strip things of their metaphysical wrappings in order to make them objects of psychology*" (ibid., 129; emphasis added). Thus, on the one hand, Jung's empiricism seeks to remain within the confines of strictly scientific knowledge, which is but one way of knowing. On the other hand, there are times when this same empiricism succeeds in becoming, as Buber indicated, the only possible metaphysic. It should be added in fairness that the statements cited above were written at an early period, when Jung maintained an agnostic attitude with regard to religion. In his later years, as a result of much criticism from philosophers, he became more cautious about making such statements.

A related question involves whether Jung remained within the charmed circle of empirical science, as he maintained, or whether he was setting forth either a new religion or a psychological replacement for the role religion had occupied in the past. He was frequently queried on this point. In his correspondence he disavowed either being a prophet or possessing a new revelation. Buber accused him of setting forth a new religion of psychic immanence. Buber's point was that by taking the image of the divine entirely into the human sphere, Jung had confined the divine to a psychic archetypal image. The dispute was fraught with accusations and misunderstanding as well as some legitimate differences in perspective.

Philip Rieff in *The Triumph of the Therapeutic* claims that Jung dismissed a theological perspective as outmoded and substituted a therapeutic one. Rieff puts it this way: "As Jung well knew, all modes of faith appear slightly fraudulent in the age of science, a coming to gods who are not there" (109). It is not clear that Jung's ideas embody the sort of reductionistic paradigm shift that Rieff has laid out. Many theologians have found Jung's ideas profoundly illuminating. By the same token, so have many who are seeking expanded modes of consciousness and new forms of religious expression, freed from the patriarchal consciousness of traditional Christianity. As Murray Stein has expressed it, "This new religion for modern man, which was centered on the self and the psyche, has been hailed by some with enthusiasm . . . and denounced by others with quasi-prophetic zeal" (*Jung's Treatment* 14).

A central difficulty of Jung's approach, whether it is regarded as empirical or as an alternative mode of spirituality, is that it provides a comprehensive worldview of man, his nature, and his place in the world. As such, it necessitates certain value judgments about the nature of the man who is being investigated. Such a devoted follower as Jolande Jacobi could see this no more than Jung himself. She wrote: "The difficulty for psychology lies in the fact that proceeding from and never leaving an empirical basis, it penetrates into a realm in which the expressions of language, derived from experience, are perforce inadequate and must remain a mere approximation. Considered from this standpoint Jung is as far from being a 'metaphysician' as any natural scientist ever was" (*Psychology of Jung* 61).

One can question whether the difficulty is that psychology penetrates into a realm in which the expressions of language are inadequate or whether what constitutes the good life is in the end a matter of personal assessment and judgment. Another important question is why expressions of language are inadequate. Jacobi (systematizing Jung) assumes that they are inadequate because a human being is a psychological complexity, but another possibility is that a human being, in the deepest meaning of selfhood, defies all attempts at objectification.

Christian or Post-Christian?

Even today there is considerable disagreement among scholars as to whether Jung was a Christian of sorts or a post-Christian. He characterized his view as follows: "My own position is on the extreme left wing in the parliament of Protestant opinion." Also, he stated his conviction that "there must be protestants against the Catholic

Church, and protestants against Protestantism" (*cw* 11:347). There is a sense in which he was a protestant against the extreme iconoclasm that had demolished an appreciation of the symbolic aspects of religion and reduced it to simplistic homilies and pious moralism.

As a therapist, Jung employed a methodological strategy that was profoundly and intentionally eclectic. He tried to relate patients back to their faith traditions if possible, but if this was not an option, as often it was not, he endeavored to get them to pursue a solitary spiritual path. This led Jung into a kind of spiritual solipsism, believing that the self is the only reality that can be known. Hans Schär, in an early appreciative book on Jung's religious significance, makes this very point.

> Contradictions . . . derive from Jung himself. It is Jung who is full of praise for a rigidly dogmatic and hierarchical Church and who in the same book counsels those who want personal experience of religion to quit the Church. It is Jung who praises the wisdom and beauty of ecclesiastical dogma and immediately after, to prove his thesis, cites heretics and heresiarchs whom the Fathers of the Church—the very men who created the dogma—condemned as the Devil's brood. It is Jung who sends people back into the Catholic Church so that the confessional shall protect them from the dangers of introspection and then extols Meister Eckhart, who rescued God, heaven, and hell from projection into the world at large and lodged them in his own soul, thereby stimulating the intensive study of the self and the world within. (198)

There is a certain double-mindedness in Jung's resistance to "laying so much as a finger on dogma" and in one "whose psychology consistently attacks all submission to orthodoxy in the sense of a *sacrificium intellectus*" (ibid.). I strongly suspect that Jung's being of two minds about such a straightforward matter stems from the childhood origins of his Personalities No. 1 and No. 2. As a therapeutic strategy it can perhaps be justified, but the matter seems to go deeper than that and to embody an inner contradiction in his primary perceptions of the world.

Peter Homans, heavily influenced by Rieff's assertion that Jung made a paradigm shift from theological to psychological man, maintains that Jung was post-Christian. However, Homans maintains that after Jung abandoned the Christianity of his father's church, he never reaffirmed a Christian commitment. Jung himself considered himself a Christian (of sorts), although he felt obliged to clarify the issue. Like many modern Swiss, he accepted the role of the church for baptisms, marriages, and funerals, but not much else. After his inner transformation concerning the role of myth, Jung seems to have considered himself in some remote sense a Christian. Always curious about what theologians thought, nonetheless in his mature years he stayed as far away from institutional religion as possible.

Inner religious images were of course a matter of supreme interest to him, one might even say virtually an addiction, throughout his life. He was especially sensitive to the ways in which Protestant thought had forsaken the healing dimension of religion. One is struck by the ways in which Jung was both a modern man and a religious man. For the traditional Christian, these two ways of relating to the world had been thought to be antithetical, but not for Jung. In a sense Jung was both Christian and post-Christian. For him metaphysics grounded in traditional religion was part of a long-gone age of certainty that could no longer be revived. Modern depth psychology, for all its tentativeness, was in his view suited to take its place. Its dynamic view of the psyche was suited to individuation and the healing of the psyche. In an age in which absolutes had vanished and yet persons showed unmistakable evidence of one-sidedness, he came to appreciate spiritual perspectives embodying psychic harmony and balance. Jung came to value the self as a substitute for the integration and wholeness that religions had supplied in an earlier age.

As he wrote in *Psychology and Religion*, "The place of deity appears to be taken by the wholeness of the human" (*CW* 11:82). Satinover exposits this point: "In Jung's view the self becomes a kind of sophisticated psychological euphemism for God (and is generally treated as such in the Jungian movement)" ("Mirror" 31). Homans also claims that Jung pursued a pattern of assimilation and repudiation of the conflicts in his mind between two modes of experiencing religion (*Jung in Context* 129). Homans takes these modes to be the personal-mystical-narcissistic mode, which Jung assimilated, and the traditional mode, which he repudiated. There is a dual movement in Jung's visionary experiences of myth, but Homans's schema, while suggestive, misses the mark.

Rather than being related to Jung's narcissism, as Homans holds, the assimilation/rejection motif that Jung so frequently displayed should, I believe, be related primarily to his split between Personalities No. 1 and No. 2 and to his mother's Personalities No. 1 and No. 2. His lifelong fascination with numinosity is maternal and not paternal. Thus, it would seem to follow that his repudiation of traditional Christianity is connected at least as much with his mother and her inner split (as well as his own) as with his failure to identify with his father. To put it another way, the quest for alternative spiritualities, so widespread today, can be viewed as a symbolic return to the mother rather than the father. As we have seen, Jung's rejection of patriarchal paternalism has many parallels in the modern world. In spite of many inconsistencies on his part, his life and vision have strongly appealed to those interested in pursuing the implications of an alternative mode of spiritual self-realization. His repudiation of traditional Christianity (or better still, his efforts to supersede it when it produces pathology and not health) has several sources. One of the most important is connected with his failure to identify with his father, for which he blames the moribund and sterile nature of Christian institutionalism.

Jung's intense religious images would seem to stem from the experience of his own inner dissonance. It is part and parcel of an elaborate process of visionary or active imagination whereby mythical connections were set in motion. In another way, his rejection of traditional Christianity stemmed from his analysis of modern society and its unique spiritual problems.

The new literature on Jung has called attention to the phenomenon of his "polytheism." Interpreters like David Miller and James Hillman have insisted that Jung was no monotheist but the author of a polytheistic perception of the world. This polytheistic and multifaceted outlook has informed the popular Jungian vision of reality. Miller has discussed polytheism in the same context as polymorphousness, polysemousness, and polyarchy. According to him, "Psychologically, polytheism is a matter of the radical experience of equally real, but mutually exclusive aspects of the self" (5). Miller, who is deeply indebted to Hillman, has pointed out that "by polytheizing his psychology, Hillman provides theology the opportunity to save itself from psychologizing its monotheism" (61). Throughout his writings, Hillman also has taken particular delight in playing with words in imaginative and innovative ways. For example, one of Hillman's influential books is entitled *Re-Visioning Psychology*. Following

Jung's lead in coining new meanings and in imaginative amplification, these writers have taken Jung's thought in several new directions. Historians and psychologists of religion are well aware, as was Jung, that religious polytheism is on the rise in modern society. I shall not here attempt to explicate the implications of a polytheistic vision of reality, however. One form of thought that is fashionable in academic circles not only announces the death and the rebirth of God and the gods but proclaims a crisis in truth and meaning as well. The signification of this will continue to be a subject for serious study. It seems to me that the observations of Miller and Hillman on Jung's "polytheism" need to be understood in the larger context of his "psychic polytheism." What I have in mind is along these lines: As with his primary relationships, which were earlier and more central, so also the "gods" of his inner life would seem to be rooted in his unique life experience.

Although Freud and Jung were once known to joke about polymorphous perversity, in his essay "The Spiritual Problem of Modern Man" Jung was less than enthusiastic about the growth of such movements as spiritualism, astrology, and theosophy. Ironically, since his death, his name has been invoked on behalf of a host of New Age phenomena. He once wrote that: "the gods whom we are called upon to dethrone are the idolized values of our conscious world. Nothing, as we know, discredited the ancient gods so much as their love scandals, and now history is repeating itself" (CW 10:88).

Jung himself reflected the crisis of meaning in the present age. As he saw it, Nietzsche was overwhelmed by the loss of an absolute. He himself recoiled from a position of outright nihilism, believing as he did that a religious attitude was necessary to confront the modern crisis of meaning.

The Symbolic Power of Gnosticism and Alchemy

In Jung's studies he was especially interested in considering esoteric topics. Unlike Freud, who in his writings on religion limited himself to issues of religious authority, superego, and religious ritual in the Judaeo-Christian world, Jung focused upon archetypal motifs in both East and West. Folk traditions, with their extensive use of magic and shamanic practices, greatly interested him. Almost as a lifelong hobby he was to study the representatives of mystical traditions—especially persons such as Meister Eckhart, Angelus Silesius, Nicholas of Cusa, Nicholas of Flue, Leo Frobenius, and John of the Cross. In these he found substantiation for many of his beliefs about the presence of the imago dei in the soul of man.

Jung was deeply conscious of the psyche's need for psychic balance and integration. He believed that most cultures had accomplished just that through traditional modes of spirituality and healing. Religious mysticism of both East and West and the phenomena of gnosticism and alchemy held particular fascination for him. He once said: "If anyone ignorant of the psychology of the unconscious wants to get a picture of the true state of affairs, I recommend the study of Christian mysticism and Hindu philosophy. He will find the clearest effects of the antinomy of the unconscious" (*On the Psychology of the Spirit* 23). This advice Jung himself followed.

Some interpreters have dismissed Jung's interest in the perspective of Eastern ideas as peripheral to his life and thought. For instance, Homans writes: "He did write a number of short articles on Eastern religions, but his purpose was to emphasize what the West lacked. He did not share the interests of the historian of religion. Rather, he was predominantly concerned with the Christian faith" (*Jung in Context* 187). I do not agree. Jung sought to understand archetypal patterns in diverse cultures, and he traveled to Africa, India, and the western United States to visit diverse tribal communities. His interest in non-Western thought was far from tangential to his overall enterprise. His collaboration with classicists, anthropologists, and historians of religion is impressive by any account. He wrote original pieces in collaboration with Heinrich Zimmer, Richard Wilhelm, D. T. Suzuki, and W. Y. Evans-Wentz. In the last decades of his life Jung returned to the study of Christian symbols. Even then, as Harold Coward has pointed out, "the idea of karma and rebirth continued to play a central role in the development of Jung's thinking" (96; see also Jung, *Memories* 317–26).

One of the topics we have explored in this study is the degree to which Jung throughout his life sought to overcome personal fragmentation, splitting of autonomous contents, and inner dissonance. In this regard Coward's observation in his study *Jung and Eastern Thought* is of particular interest. Coward writes: "Jung's encounter with Eastern thought is complex, and in some respects can be described as a love/hate relationship" (96). We note that these very emotions characterized his relations earlier with his father and then with Freud.

Archetypal symbols produced by patients during treatment greatly impressed Jung. He found counterparts to these in the religions of the East. The opposition of forces made a deep and lasting impression on him. Tao gives rise to the opposite reality principles, darkness and light, yin and yang. Many of Jung's European patients produced mandalas during therapy, and he was impressed to find mandala symbolism in Chinese and Tibetan culture as well as several other places. He viewed it as confirmation of his psychological theories regarding the natural healing processes within the self.

Jung's friend of many years, Richard Wilhelm, returned from China in the late 1920s. When Wilhelm shared with Jung his version of *I Ching* and *The Secret of the Golden Flower,* Jung marveled, for the European world did not know such texts existed. *The Secret of the Golden Flower* presented Chinese yoga as a fusion of Taoist and Mahayana Buddhist sources, which became the basis of an instinctive preparation for death and also a transition to detached consciousness. Although reluctant to write a commentary on a Chinese text, when urged to do so by Wilhelm, Jung held that the Chinese classic when stripped of its archaic setting reveals the powers of growth latent in the psyche. Further, he firmly believed that the East taught a higher understanding than the West, namely understanding through life.

Jung became convinced that there was nothing to be gained through a crass imitation of the psychological wisdom of the East through the practices of Indian, Chinese, or Tibetan yoga. He wrote: "Western imitation of the East is doubly tragic in that it comes from a psychological misunderstanding as sterile as are the modern escapades in New Mexico, the blissful South Sea islands, and Central Africa, where 'primitivity' is being staged in all seriousness, in order that western civilized man may covertly slip out of his menacing duties, Hic Rhodus hic salta" (in Wilhelm 80). Rather than send missionaries to foreign peoples, our task, he insisted, is to recover the foundations of our own Western culture.

Jung's study of religion included a detailed examination of the early church fathers, including the gnostics. He regarded their religious experience as even more significant than the experience of those who chose the way of credal orthodoxy. In his view the loss of gnosis is the cause of much modern psychic difficulty. "The loss of *gnosis*, i.e., knowledge of the ultimate things, weighs much more heavily than is generally admitted. Faith alone would suffice too, did it not happen to be a charisma whose true possession is something of a rarity, except in spasmodic form. Were it otherwise, we doctors could spare ourselves much thankless work" (*Psychology and Religion: West and East; cw* 11:192). Jung may be right that the loss of certainty may weigh heavily upon the assessment of modern consciousness. He used this kind of analysis to account for pseudo-gnostic movements like theosophy, spiritualism, anthroposophy, astrology, parapsychology, and Christian Science. If he were living today, he would probably relate it to several similar movements.

Carl Raschke has linked the Dionysian gnosis of our culture, which is spawning several new cult movements, with the name of C. G. Jung. He writes: "Jung . . . perhaps more than any other seminal mind since Plotinus in antiquity, served to give legitimacy to esoteric and Gnostic concepts with a well-wrought theory that the famous renegade student of Freud wanted accepted as being somehow 'scientific.' . . . Jung made the murky symbols of spiritual discernment seem plausible with a flair that religious cultists lacked and philosophers would never have bothered to cultivate" (143–44). Raschke continues: "Why was Jung preoccupied with recondite, bizarre, and antiquated cults? In one respect his obsession had to do with his studied distaste for the basic motifs of Western thought. . . . He preferred Oriental wisdom . . . to Occidental logic and scientism. . . . But the nub of Jung's attitude toward the Western mind was his passion to find the *unifying factor* for both conscious and unconscious experience" (146; emphasis added). The concepts Jung pioneered have, in a narcissistic society, taken so many directions that he would doubtless say his intuitions were right in ways he never intended. In *The Undiscovered Self* Jung wrote that "religion means dependence on and submission to the irrational facts of experience" (cited in Raschke Kirk, and Taylor 23). Elsewhere in the same volume Jung states: "You can take away a man's gods, but only to give him others in return" (*Undiscovered Self* 77).

We are now in a position to appreciate more fully the role of Jung's childhood rituals as a means of solace in his early introverted isolation and sporadic attempts to overcome his dissociation. His own experience of gnosticlike visions, as illustrated in *Septem Sermones ad*

Mortuos, served to fuel his interest for several years thereafter in the quest for inner certainty.

Throughout the course of his work with patients, Jung discovered their spontaneous production of "archetypal" motifs during the work of active imagination. Through painting, dream recall, sand play, and various other innovative therapeutic techniques, the unconscious was encouraged to emerge more forcefully, whereupon patients produced repressed and compensatory sides of their personalities. The parallels with the productions from religious history were quite remarkable. For instance, the materials uncovered disclosed an unmistakable psychic origin of mythic materials such as mandalas. Jung found confirmation of many of his findings through researchers in mythology and the history of religions such as Karl Kerényi, Heinrich Zimmer, and Richard Wilhelm.

In *Psyche and Symbol* Jung cited the instance of a "hard-boiled" scientific rationalist who produced mandalas in his dreams and wakeful fantasies. He said that the man had to consult a court psychiatrist as he was about to lose his reason because suddenly he was assailed by the most amazing dreams and visions. Jung believed that the man's confusion resulted from the fact that he was in a clash between two equally real worlds, one external and the other internal, a fact that could no longer be denied. In Jung's own words:

> When one hears such a confession, and the patient wants to understand himself better, some comparative knowledge will be most helpful. When the hard-boiled rationalist mentioned above came to consult me for the first time, he was in such a state of panic that not only he himself but I also felt the wind coming over from the side of the lunatic asylum! As he told me of his experiences in detail he mentioned a particularly impressive dream. I got up and fetched an ancient volume from my bookself and showed it to him, asking: "You see the date? Just about four hundred years old. Now watch!" I opened the book at the place where there was a curious wood-cut, representing his dream almost literally. "You see," I said, "your dream is no secret. You are not shocked by a pathological insult and separated from mankind by an inexplicable psychosis. You are merely ignorant of certain experiences within human knowledge and understanding." It was worth seeing the re-

lief which came over him. He had seen with his own eyes the documentary evidence for his own sanity. (*Psyche and Symbol* xii, xv)

My own correspondence with Jung on this point is worth citing. In a letter of July 8, 1960, I had suggested that he was not as immune to the charge of being "a modern gnostic" as he would like to make out. Surely, I wrote, he was not a gnostic in the classical sense, for he posited no ultimate duality between good and evil; but he must admit that there were gnostic elements in his writings. Malcolm Diamond had called my attention to this, I noted, when he mentioned in a letter to me how Jung described the healing of a scientist by his own knowledge of the mandalas. In an unpublished letter of August 2, 1960, Jung replied that Diamond's letter indicated a misunderstanding of the facts he was describing. Jung contended that his own knowledge of mandalas was good for nothing in this instance but that the therapeutic factor was that the patient could discover it in himself. Jung added the caution that his scientific statements should not be treated by philosophical criticism. He went on to explain that he regarded philosophy as an inadequate method that leads to the wrong conclusions.

The vindictive tone of Jung's letter took me by surprise. Indeed, at the time when Jung's correspondence was being edited, Gerhard Adler did not want to publish this letter that Jung had written to me, probably because it shows Jung in an unfavorable light. When Jung felt that he was being misunderstood, his blunt, rather ruthless side came out. He wrote that he did not wish to continue such a fruitless conversation and indicated that I would do him a favor if I did not even mention the fact that he had written to me!

My reply reminded Jung that he had once said that the trouble with Freud was that he was unwilling to drink the bittersweet of philosophical criticism. "My impression is that you are also unwilling to do this if the point of view is at variance with your own" (unpublished letter from R. C. Smith to C. G. Jung, Aug. 9, 1960). The letter continued:

You have made it perfectly obvious in all that you have written that you are not a philosopher but an empirical scientist. . . . I have no desire to misrepresent you on that account. With regard to what Diamond said, I should add that I understand full well that healing only takes place when persons discover things for themselves and do not rely merely on the therapist's knowledge, however, I was merely citing the way Diamond gave me the reference. Certainly you will have to admit, there are many times when a therapist's theory affects the conceptions of his patients. Regardless of all that, the question I was really pointing to was whether gnosis or faith brings about the deeper healing. Obviously, you have your opinion and I have mine. But the very fact that we do represents value judgments on both our parts. So you see you can not avoid such philosophical assumptions.

Ernest Wallwork, a psychoanalyst and colleague in the American Academy of Religion, has reminded me of the intense rivalry and competition that existed between Freud and Jung. Perhaps the fact that I mentioned Freud in connection with the "bittersweet of philosophical criticism" led him to reply to my challenge. In any case, in a final letter to me on August 16, 1960, Jung stressed the difference between scientific hypothesis and metaphysical hypostasis: "Hypothesis is that all psychical products referring to religious views are comparable on the basis of a fundamental similarity of the human mind. This is a scientific hypothesis. The Gnostic, Buber accuses me to be, makes no hypothesis, but a hypostasis in making metaphysical statements. When I try to establish a fundamental similarity of individual psychical products and alchemistic or Gnostic noumena, I carefully avoid making a hypostasis, remaining well within the boundaries of the scientific hypothesis" (Jung, *Letters* 2:583–84). Jung was well advised to make a distinction between hypothesis and hypostasis. In actual practice he blurred this important distinction time and again. For this reason he was criticized by various philosophers and theologians.[2]

What is important for us to see in this connection is not the use that Jung has made of mandalas and other psychic symbols but the value he placed upon gnosis in the process of healing. While all therapeutic healing depends on the person's becoming aware of that which is hidden, the aim and goal of treatment are matters of judgment, where the therapist's own presuppositions enter in.

Many psychologists have maintained that in matters touching upon the issue of ultimacy, the psychologist as psychologist is well advised to maintain a respectful silence. The reasoning goes something like this: Religion concerns issues on which persons of sound mind and genuine sincerity have legitimate differences. These same psychologists would maintain that Jung's therapeutic approach has too closely identified inner knowledge (gnosis) with inner healing as a mode of deliverance. It is just such an identification that several of his critics reject.

The wounded surgeon plies the steel
That questions the distempered part;
Beneath the bleeding hands we feel
The sharp compassion of the healer's art.
—*T. S. Eliot,* "*East Coker*"

Wherever we find the creative principle in the Great
Individual and in the child . . . we venerate it as the hidden
treasure that in humble form conceals a fragment of the
godhead.
—*Erich Neumann,* Art and the Creative Unconscious

CHAPTER 9

Creativity & Healing:
Jung's Relation to His Inner Daimon

In this chapter we will consider some of the ways that Jung nourished the process of creative healing in his own life. We will examine some of the major motifs that interested him, such as the effect of the daimon, the inner dream voyage of the shaman as a traditional healer, and the use of symbolism as a means of evoking feelings of both ecstasy and unity. Distinct as many of these themes are, we will seek to reconstruct several of the elements of Jung's exploration of visionary creativity.

Earlier we saw that various psychiatrists have begun to debate how to interpret Jung's discussion of Personalities No. 1 and No. 2 and to ask to what degree they constitute both pathology and the potential for creative resolution. Now we are in a position to appreciate more fully Jung's great interest in the figure of the shaman as one who was in touch with his own and his people's brokenness and the powers of the spirit world. To a remarkable degree Jung was able to empathize intuitively with the life situation of the shaman as a "wounded healer." During childhood he had experienced inner helplessness and numinosity, which were to serve as a lifelong impetus for his creativity. The dissociation of Personalities No. 1 and No. 2 was to be the precursor of many of his most important discoveries.

The Unconscious Impulse toward Wholeness

In *Memories* Jung explains that his "inner voice" was an unconscious impulse that propelled him forward to new destinies, the very source of his creativity. The question of whether Jung's "psychic discoveries" were the result of his vision, as he contends, or an intuitive response to his unconscious determinants is at issue. Time and again, the urge to create takes charge in his life. It propels him forward to ever new explorations. He regrets that he has offended many people throughout his long life but protests that he is misunderstood: "Since my contemporaries, understandably, could not perceive my vision, they saw only a fool rushing ahead" (*Memories* 356). Jung acknowledges his impatience in *Memories*: "I had no patience with people — aside from my patients. I had to obey an inner law which was imposed on me and left me no freedom of choice. Of course, I did not always obey it. How can anyone live without inconsistency?" (357). Nonetheless, an inconsistency occasioned by a change in perspective is one thing; one reflecting inner dissociation is quite another. We are concerned here, I believe, with the latter.

Anthony Storr, in an article entitled "Individuation and the Creative Process," states that although Jung seems to have denied it, the individuation process and the creative process are closely analogous (329). Storr holds that both artists and scientists are concerned with bringing about new syntheses, and with the integration of opposites. By calling to mind all kinds of imaginal processes, Jung was effecting a process of natural healing of inner rifts or split-off aspects of consciousness. One can amplify Storr's observation with regard to Jung's own creativity. Not only is creativity linked to the integration of opposites and the production of new syntheses, but it is linked as well in Jung's life to the activation of "the inner daimon," "the split feminine," and the process of symbol making and mythmaking. These factors represent creative attempts to effect psychic healing.

According to James Hillman, the creative instinct is "that immense energy coming from beyond a man's psyche which pushes him to self-dedication via one or another specific medium, to devotion to his own person in its becoming through that medium, and which brings with it a sense of helplessness and increasing awareness of its numinous power" ("On Psychological Creativity" 362). Much creativity is based on the recall of unconscious images, which in turn reveal unconscious conflicts. To some considerable extent, then, creativity is an attempted resolution of inner processes. It is the healing of inner rift, the dissonance that arose in childhood. As Edwin Wallace reminds us: "Every theoretical system in psychology, as Jung . . . pointed out, has an element of its creator's psyche; furthermore, each system is partly its originator's attempt at self-cure" ("Freud's Mysticism" 203). Or, as Jung frequently put it, every psychology has the character of a subjective confession.

We will recall that in the analytic situation Jung's approach was most unorthodox. For the most part he was not occupied with questions of psychological method. He believed the therapist should study dream theory and psychological theory with care but then put theory aside and listen to the individual sufferer. It was axiomatic for Jung that the therapist could take the client no further than that person had already journeyed. If one was to assist the client in descending into the "depths of hades," empathy and insight on the therapist's part became essential. In effect, the therapist, for Jung, was necessarily concerned with relating the person to the numinous dimensions of the self.

Part of his vision of therapeutic healing was that he viewed the therapist's participation (countertransference) of great value in the healing process. Unlike the Freudians, who saw the therapist's countertransference as a problem, Jung believed that the therapist's own unconscious not only assisted but was crucial to healing. Doubtless, his great gift as a therapist was his intuitive ability to perceive a problem, as it were, before the patient began to speak, yet he was readily bored with the tedium of analytic work (Storr, *C. G. Jung* 10).

When Jung speaks of *daimon*, he is employing a Greek term with a particular history of meaning in Greek thought to apply to irrational impulses. *Daimon* is not at all the same as conscience. *Daimon* does not refer to happiness, although obedience to the daimon may be necessary for self-fulfillment. In its psychological meaning, *daimon* implies a dependence upon irrational forces. Thus, to ignore one's daimon or unconscious impulses would signal psychic disharmony. The philosopher David Norton in a somewhat similar vein has written: "Eudaimonia is both a feeling and a condition. . . . It signals that the present activity of the individual is in harmony with the daimon that is his true self" (5). The term *daimon* was first made famous by Socrates and Plato. In Greek and Roman culture (especially in Stoicism) over time it took on several connotations, referring especially to psychic intervention by a host of anonymous supernatural beings. In the view of the classicist E. R. Dodds, in some ages the daimons grow closer. Thus, periods of profound social change and upheaval are thought to unleash a host of troublesome psychic forces that have been previously projected outward onto the cosmos (Dodds, *Pagan and Christian* 37-68; see also Dodds, *Greeks and the Irrational* 39-45).

Some interpreters of Jung have viewed human experiences as essentially lonely but heroic struggles against life's antinomies. Life, then, becomes "the encounter of the single individual with his own god or daimon, his struggle with the overpowering emotions, affects, fantasies and creative inspirations and emotions that come from within" (von Franz 13-14). This would appear to be another way of saying that one is gripped by one's numinous inner experiences.

Recent studies have called attention to unconscious motivations in the lives of both Freud and Jung. In spite of their discoveries, these pioneers of the psyche were to a large degree unconscious of their inner motivations. In their respective personality structures, several unconscious factors seem to form a constellation conveniently termed the daimon.

In an article entitled "Psychotherapy and the Daimonic," Rollo May has defined *daimonic* as "any natural function in the individual that has the power of taking over the whole person." He gives sex, eros, anger, rage, and craving for power as examples. May points out that the daimonic can be either destructive or creative. Writing as an existential psychotherapist, he says, "The principle is, identify with that which haunts you, not in order to fight it off, but to take it into yourself; for it must represent some rejected element in you" (196).

May follows Jung's analysis of anima and animus as denied aspects of the self. In this connection he calls attention to the ambivalent meaning of the very term *anima* (or *animus*), which means "both a feeling of hostility, a violent, malevolent intention (animosity) and also animate, to give spirit, to enliven." He argues that "the denied part of you is the source of hostility and aggression, but when you can through consciousness integrate it into your self-system, it becomes the source of energy and spirit which enlivens you" (200). May's exposition of the destructive or creative aspects of the daimonic is useful to our inquiry. In his own life, Jung was integrating unacceptable impulses into the wider frame of consciousness. As Jung understood it, the daimon was not a spirit external to himself but the effect of the collective unconscious. What early peoples thought of as spirit possession he viewed as the archetypal or collective unconscious.

In his book *Healing and Wholeness*, John Sanford has a chapter on the "ecstatic healer." Sanford seeks to show how chapter 6 of *Memories*, on Jung's creative illness, was a "shamanic type of experience." Sanford states: "There is no indication that he became ill at this time, evidently because he was able to understand enough of what his experience meant. Had this understanding and development not taken place, he would certainly have become ill" (70). One can disagree with Sanford on this point and insist that illness can, and sometimes must, be a necessary prelude to the healing process. Healing frequently begins when one is initiated into the process of accepting and probing the depths of the psychic process.

John-Raphael Staude, in *Consciousness and Creativity*, has observed that the growth of consciousness and creativity frequently emerges out of the experience of a symbolic death and rebirth. He writes: "This process may take the form of an encounter with a second personality (or daimon) within the self, or as Jung has described this experience—which he calls the 'individuation process'—as part of the development of the personality as a whole" (113). Typically there is a descent into the depths of unconscious material and a rebirth into a larger frame of consciousness.

Joe McCown writes: "The shaman is a broken-hearted individual who has learned to mend hearts—his own and others. . . . The shaman is someone who has been through a schizophrenic episode and knows how to guide others through such episodes (voyages)" (444).[1] In archaic societies the shaman is an initiate who has been on an inner voyage and knows how to conduct others on similar journeys. Typically he is regarded as a reliable guide to the underworld. He is to be relied upon for the very reason that he has recovered his soul force. McCown raises the question of whether persons like Carl Jung, Fritz Perls, and R. D. Laing were not "contemporary shamans." Further, he writes: "It may be that when Laing asks for 'guides' to conduct persons through 'transcendental experiences' (schizophrenic voyages) he is asking for physicians and priests who are also modern shamans, men who from their own experience know something of the labyrinthine ways of madness" (445).

Jung frequently expounded on the phenomenon of the power associated with the shaman or medicine man that allowed him to practice his magic with such force. Time and again Jung stated that it was an axiom that every relatively independent portion of the psyche has the character of a personality and that it personifies itself as soon as it is given a chance. Additionally, Jung drew a parallel between moderns and primitives. He wrote: "If an important component is projected on a human being he becomes mana, extraordinarily effective—a sorcerer, witch, werewolf, or the like. The primitive idea that the medicine-man catches the souls that have wandered away by night and puts them in cages like birds is a striking illustration of this" (*cw* 10:68). He was correct to emphasize how the mechanism of projection performed a similar function in both primitive and modern cultures. With regard to mana, Jung was to write that it "adheres to the desired mid-point of the personality . . . that ineffable something betwixt the opposites, or else which unites them, or the result of conflict, or the product of energic tension: the coming to birth of personality, a profound individual step forward, the next stage" (*cw* 7:228).

Transformative Symbols

Susan K. Deri, a leading psychoanalyst who died in 1983, has made a major contribution to the close connection between symbolization and creativity. She explained that the creative principle underlies human life but is nowhere systematically treated in the Freudian psychoanalytic literature. Traditionally it has been treated under the heading of sublimation, as a method of instinctual aim displacement. In a closely reasoned book, *Symbolization and Creativity*, Deri referred to the "early good fit" between child and mother. In describing the role of the mother, she employs Imre Hermann's concept of "dual-union" to refer to the primary relationship between the mother and the infant. Quite deliberately she prefers this term to Mahler's now fashionable term *symbiosis* (Deri 6). From a psychoanalytic perspective, she then proceeds to discuss the capacity of symbols to point beyond themselves and reach into another realm, that realm that cannot be spoken about directly.

Deri makes the point that in Freud's view symbols both connect and separate: "A symbol is formed when the real, concrete object is unavailable, or has to be given up, but connection with it is still desired. Symbolization facilitates separation from primary 'objects' by keeping connected with them via symbol-bridges. The symbol is *la presence d'une absence*" (106). After discussing Freud's view of symbols, she proceeds to elucidate the view of Erich Neumann, one of Jung's closest associates. Deri discusses Neumann's *Art and the Creative Unconscious*, in which Neumann calls attention to the analogy between the creative principle of the unconscious and the elemental creative principle found in nature. Like Jung and Neumann, Deri also views archetypes as prototypal dimensions of the collective, transpersonal unconscious. The thread connecting dreams, fantasies, hallucinations, and various forms of art is also sympathetically explored.

As her own view of symbolization is somewhat similar to that of Jung, Deri writes appreciatively of Jung's references to the "numinous" or "fascinating quality of the nonpersonal eternal" archetypes (121). Especially highlighted is Neumann's sentence "The creative power of the unconscious seizes upon the individual with the autonomous force of an instinctive drive" (Neumann, *Art* 98). The point is made that such activation of the unconscious can lead to "ecstatic frenzy or psychosis" (Deri 122). It is this autonomous force that Jung refers to as the transcendent function.

Both Jung and Neumann speak of being seized by the power of the unconscious. Elsewhere Jung speaks of this as the power of the daimon. Throughout his writings he indicates that earlier ages spoke of "spirits" but that our age can speak of the power of the unconscious. Freud viewed the unconscious as a receptacle of repressed wishes, but Jung saw this motivating source as prospective, in that it determines the individual's future destiny. Deri reminds us, however, that "Freud's own views were not that totally different from Jung's with regard to inherited psychic tendencies" (122). According to Deri, a person's capacity for symbolization defines his or her creativity or lack thereof. Symbol-making is by no means a random activity but is "the specifically human way of creating order and connectedness within the person's psychic organization, as well as the means of bridging from the inside to the outside" (5).

The word *symbol* is derived from the Greek verb *symballein*. Literally, it means "to bring together" or connect in a meaningful way. It is striking and understandable that Jung, who was inwardly split from early childhood, should play such a key role in formulating symbolic meaning in our time. For those aspects of reality that cannot be known directly, the symbol serves to unite several meanings. For that reason symbols express multivalence, in that they have different and multiple meanings at different levels. For instance, according to the church historian Cyril Richardson, the fish symbolized baptism, the Eucharist, the conversion of the gentiles, the coming kingdom, the Resurrection, and the Savior simultaneously. Among the many symbols to which Jung calls attention are the cross in Christianity, the phallus or lingam in Hinduism, and the lotus in Buddhism.

Mircea Eliade, who followed Jung closely in this connection, has pointed out, first, that symbols are multivalent. Second, in early society symbols are always religious because they point to something real or to a structure of the world. In archaic cultures the real is equivalent to the sacred. Third, religious symbols are capable of revealing those aspects of the real that are not evident on the level of immediate experience (Eliade and Kitagawa 97f.).

Irene Champernowne, a Jungian therapist for many years, tells of a short but vivid dream she once had. She dreamed of a sailing boat cruising down a broad river. In her dream she knew that Dr. Jung was in the boat as it rounded a bend in the river and that he had died at the moment a clock struck midnight. She was saddened and awakened. After a period of active imagination on the dream, she recalled a conversation with Dr. Jung years before in Zurich. He had related the story of a difficult woman patient who had once come to him for a consultation because of insomnia. Jung found the woman tense, rigid, and unreceptive. Feeling discouraged at the end of the consultation by his inability to reach the woman, he remembered a little tune, a song of maidens sailing on the Rhine that his mother used to sing to him as a child. Jung asked the woman if she liked sailing as together they watched one of the sailing boats on Lake Zurich through the window. The woman replied simply that she did not sail. Jung, of course, loved sailing and began to explain to her the way the wind filled out the sails and the way the sails could be adjusted to catch the wind. As he spoke about the receptivity of the sails and how life could be compared to a sailboat, the woman relaxed. He explained that the wind would take us along if we put ourselves in its way. Then the therapeutic consultation was over.

At the time Jung was appalled by the futility of the interview and was rather ashamed that he had spoken at length of sailing. As a result he did not send a report to the woman's psychiatrist in Paris. Some years later he met the other psychiatrist, who told him he had a bone to pick with him: he had sent a patient suffering from insomnia to him but had not received a progress report. From the woman the other psychiatrist had been unable to discover what treatment Dr. Jung had given her. "I only could discover that you talked about sailing boats," he added. But the woman's insomnia had given way, and she had slept, so whatever the treatment, it had worked. In relating the story to Champernowne, Jung offered no explanation of what had happened to the woman. But he did say to her in a confiding tone, "If a little tune comes into your head, follow it" (Champernowne, *Creative Expression* 20–21). In a refreshing manner Champernowne summarizes: "The symbol can carry the contradictory and ambivalent nature of reality when a concept cannot. For instance, water as a symbol is something that can quench thirst or drown us by flood. Light can illuminate or blind us. Wind is both the breath of life or a destroying hurricane. The opposites can be contained in symbol. This is why we need the symbolic life" (7–8).

In a work published posthumously, Jung's lead article, "Approaching the Unconscious," has a section entitled "Healing the Split." There he viewed symbols as natural attempts to reconcile and reunite opposites within the psyche (Jung et al., *Man and His Symbols* 90). His point was that by themselves symbols do not effect the needed synthesis, but they point in that direction.

In chapter 1 we noted the importance for Jung of his "phallic" or "intrusive mother" (Satinover's insightful and descriptive clinical terms). On this same topic Deri has stated unequivocally that "the intrusive mother who is demanding rather than giving crowds out the child's spontaneous creativity from the 'potential space' between herself and the child" (267). This type of mother both overstimulates her offspring and singles them out for special attention, thus reinforcing their sense of uniqueness and self-importance. Such a mother wants to realize her magical illusions about herself through her children. Satinover also elaborates the details of such a relationship.

Winnicott, too, has been much appreciated by contemporary theorists for his contribution to the understanding of imaginal objects, and the role of play and fantasy in the developmental process. Intuitively in childhood, and then again after the break with Freud, Jung had the good sense to participate in direct confrontation with his unconscious images. From one perspective inflation has its perils, but insofar as it facilitates the process of activation of the unconscious, it has its merits as well.

Visionary Creativity as Inner Healing

In modern times frequently a distinction is made between creativity and productivity, but just as often the two are conjoined. In prior ages creation was regarded as a divine act, as in many of the stories of the creation of the world. Man and woman are frequently regarded as co-creators together with divine agency. In the modern world, being creative has become a matter of great importance in the scale of values. James Hillman points out that "the term 'creativity' is very modern. Before the enlightenment, when we were all God's creatures living in His creation, the word creative in the sense of 'creativity' was hardly used in English. 'Creative' as 'productive' entered usage only in 1803 with the Romantic affirmation of individuality. Now that God is dead . . . creativity is carried more and more by man, and the word has become a conceptual symbol holding projections of hope and individuality" ("On Psychological Creativity" 359). From a Freudian perspective, creativity originates in conflicts, which spring from more fundamental biological drives. According to Freud, childhood experiences are very important in accounting for the creative product. Creative work disguises the nature of the conflict and is, to some extent, its resolution.

In Jung's case it seems reasonable to assert that his creativity stemmed at least partially from childhood conflict, which until the publication of *Memories* was disguised and is, even now, a subject of debate and considerable confusion among commentators. Additionally, creative work itself is an attempted resolution of internalized inner conflict. In the psychoanalytic literature, Freud's theory has been subject to a variety of modifications and additions. Ernst Kris has added to the Freudian perspective the importance of the primary process in the formal mechanisms of creativity (*Psychoanalytic Explorations* 13). One may object that true creativity is not as straightforward a matter as either Freud or Kris took it to be. That is to say, they considered the use of the primary process in creativity to be "a regression in the service of the ego" (Kris, cited in Arieti, *Intrapsychic Self* 334). Such explanations simply fail to account for the kind of creativity that Jung exemplified.

Silvano Arieti, a leading authority on schizophrenia, points out that Jung made a significant contribution to the problem of creativity by distinguishing between psychological and visionary creativity. Arieti writes: "In the psychological mode the content of the creative product is drawn from the realm of human consciousness" and "submits the material to a direct, conscious, purposeful aim" (*Intrapsychic Self* 335). Jung distinguishes several features in each mode. The psychological mode nowhere transcends the bounds of psychological intelligibility. It is directed and purposeful. The artist's work is an interpretation and illumination of the contents of consciousness. By contrast, in the visionary mode "the experience that furnishes the material for artistic expression is no longer familiar." The material determines its own form. Visionary works "impose themselves upon the author; his hand is, as it were, seized and his pen writes things that his mind perceives with amazement.... The work brings its own form" (*Contributions to Analytical Psychology* 235–36).[2]

The visionary mode clearly interested Jung the most. In this mode the content originates not from the lessons of life but from the timeless depths, the archaic level of personality that he terms the collective unconscious. This is the way he put it: "We mean by collective unconscious, a certain psychic disposition shaped by the forces of heredity; from it consciousness has developed" (*Modern Man* 190). In the visionary mode the creative person is at the mercy of a reemergent content.

The creative person is frequently conscious of an alien will or intention beyond his or her comprehension. This is what has been termed by Jung an autonomous complex and is a detached portion of the psyche that leads an independent life. Its psychic energy has been withdrawn from conscious control. Jung's own life provides an excellent case study of this principle, for as we have seen, his dissociation began early in the conflict with his parents and produced a lasting split in his personality structure. His separation from Freud triggered a prolonged psychic disruption, from which he gradually emerged to produce some of his best and most creative writing.

All of Jung's later work embodies this visionary aspect of his personality. This is the reason Jung's life is fascinating but his personality theory is frequently misleading. Let us take one example. In an essay called "Psychology and Literature" in *Modern Man in Search of a Soul* he writes, "Any reaction to stimulus may be causally explained, but the creative act, which is the absolute antithesis of mere reaction will forever elude human understanding" (177). As we noted earlier, Jung held that there is a creative instinct that is possessed by all, operating in much the same way that Abraham Maslow's self-actualization principle does. This autonomous creative complex is for Jung entirely separate from the complexes rooted in psychopathology. The source of this creative complex resides in the archetypal motifs found in the collective unconscious.

It would seem that the source of creative productions of all kinds is quite complex and not readily subject to facile explanations. Indeed, in these pages I am by no means arguing for a simple reductionism of Jung. All that is being argued is that the *motivation* for creativity often comes from the need to heal psychic wounds. By the same token, this does not account for the *source* of the power and gifts to accomplish the healing; this remains a mystery, as Jung and Freud both say. Thus, one can argue, instead, that in a person of genuine talent it is to be explained neither as "a regression in the service of the ego" (traditional Freudianism) nor in the facile descriptions of traditional Jungianism.

In a 1945 letter to P. W. Martin, Jung wrote: "The main interest of my work is not concerned with the treatment of neuroses but rather with the approach to the numinous. But the fact is that the approach to the numinous is the real therapy and inasmuch as you attain to the numinous experiences you are released from the curse of pathology" (Jung, *Letters* 1:376). Jung thought that suffering was by no means a curse if it involved confronting the truth about life.

This brings us face to face with the conceptual confusions that exist in Jung's writings. To a considerable degree Jung himself realized the search for the soul as a mode of realizing inner creativity. When it came to putting down his thoughts on paper, he frequently floundered or misled the reader. The matter becomes clearer if we recognize the large extent to which his theoretical writings are an explication of his autobiographical experience. Jung's profound inner ambivalence led him to separate the psychological from the ontological on one level but to conjoin them on another level (see Smith, "Empirical Science"). Throughout his writings he holds that metaphysics can be understood psychologically, but then, when pressed, he backs off such claims. The philosopher will readily dismiss such ambivalence as muddled, but it is a further demonstration of the autobiographical character of much of Jung's work.

I strongly suspect that Jung's unconventional ideas, expressed by a passionate interest in gnosticism, alchemy, Indian and Chinese yoga, and the Tibetan and Egyptian Books of the Dead and similar treatises, had a similar psychic origin, in that they mirror his inner conflicts and pose a resolution. Jung's later concepts, such as the mandala, *coincidentia oppositorum*, the androgynous self, and synchronicity, embody a quality of diffuseness or dissociation that at the same time points in the direction of an inner unity yet to be fully realized.

Contrary to his own words, Jung succeeded in projecting a myth about himself composed of many diverse and conflicting images. In addition, many people have projected myths of their own upon him. Thus, he has been viewed variously as empirical scientist, philosopher, healer of the soul, and mystic, and in most studies of his life, Jung has been either idealized or villainized.

The theme of the reconciliation of opposites, so often recited in Jung's work, would also seem to embody the element of coming to terms with unconscious contents that need to be reunited into the larger frame of consciousness. Dissociation does have its value as a spur to creativity in a way not dissimilar to Lacan's notion of the "presence of an absence." As Storr has pointed out in *The Dynamics of Creation*, "Creative people show a wider than usual division in the mind, an accentuation of opposites. It seems probable that when creative people produce new work they are in fact attempting to reconcile opposites in exactly the way that Jung describes" (233).

As Erich Fromm has said, "Psychology can show us what man is not. It cannot tell us what man, each one of us, is. The soul of man, the unique core of each individual, can never be grasped and described adequately. It can be 'known' only inasmuch as it is not misconceived. The legitimate aim of psychology thus is the negative, the removal of distortions and illusions, not the positive, the full and complete knowledge of a human being" (in Leibrecht 33). We will recall that Jung used the term *self* to designate the totality of being, that sum total of conscious and unconscious existence. For him the self is "a term that is meant to include the totality of the psyche in so far as this manifests itself in an individual. The self is not only the centre, but also the circumference that encloses consciousness; it is the centre of this totality, as the ego is the centre of consciousness" (*Integration of the Personality* 96). In another place Jung said, "The term 'self' seemed to me a suitable one for this unconscious substrate, whose actual exponent in consciousness is the ego" (*CW* 11:259). For Jung the goal of psychological development is self-realization or individuation. As we saw in the previous chapter, according to Jung's theory the self is indistinguishable from a god-image. This image is generally seen in the mandala, which has the status of a "uniting symbol."

What is new in the modern situation, in Jung's view, is that this symbol of deity has been taken by the wholeness of the individual. "A modern mandala is an involuntary confession of a peculiar mental condition. There is no deity in the mandala, nor is there any submission or reconciliation to a deity. The place of the deity seems to be taken by the wholeness of man" (*CW* 11:82). According to Jung, this is an answer of the unconscious psyche that can no longer project the idea of deity as an autonomous entity. When the self is withdrawn from projection, "the self then functions as a union of opposites and thus constitutes the most immediate experience of the Divine which it is psychologically possible to imagine" (261).

Vocation is the calling to genuine selfhood. In contrast to the traditional Christian idea that the believer must imitate the life of Christ, Jung insists that it is the issue of single-minded integrity that counts. Each person must seek to live life as truly as Christ lived his: "We protestants must sooner or later face this question: Are we to understand the 'imitation of Christ' in the sense that we should copy his life and, if I may use the expression ape his stigmata; or in the proper sense that we are to live our own proper lives as truly as he lived his in all its implications? It is no easy matter to live a life that is modelled on Christ's, but it is unspeakably harder to live one's own life as truly as Christ lived his" (*cw* 11:340). There is the risk of coming into contact with unconscious forces as well as the risk of making mistakes.

Jung believed that the reason so few are willing to take the lonely difficult path that leads to integration, inner realization, and selfhood is that mankind is still in a stage of childhood, a stage that cannot be skipped. "The great majority of people," he wrote, "need authority, guidance, and laws. This fact cannot be overlooked. The Pauline overcoming of the law is possible only for the man who knows how to set his soul in the place of conscience. Only a very few are capable of doing this. . . . And these few tread this way only from inner necessity, not to say compulsion, for the way is narrow as a knife-edge" (*Two Essays* 251).

Unlike Freud, who stressed the role of the superego (a father derivative), Jung frequently described himself as ruthless (in much the same way that his mother's No. 2 Personality was ruthless). Here one detects echoes of Nietzsche's Overman as well as elements of antinomianism. For Paul the law was overcome but not totally dispensed with. It is doubtful that Paul would agree with setting one's soul in the place of conscience. In any case, the function of conscience is to be transformed and made a matter of inner decision. Jung's integrated self sets aside conscience as a court within the soul that concerns itself with the distinction between right and wrong.

On the other hand, Jung's explication of the meaning of vocation is admirable. He writes: "True personality is always a vocation and puts its trust in it as in God. . . . The fact that many a man who goes his own way ends in ruin means nothing to one who has vocation. He must obey his own law, as if it were a demon whispering to him of new and wonderful paths. Anyone with a vocation hears the voice of the inner man; he is called" (*cw* 11:175–76). Jung is, of course, referring to the inner law of compulsion that pursues the creative individual bent upon fulfilling his or her destiny. The self that is considered by Jung to be the bridal unification of good and evil is nothing less than the call of individuation or personal vocation.

Jung saw that individuation or the coming-to-be of the self must be distinguished from egocenteredness and autoeroticism. He has written that individuation is "a process by which a man can create of himself that definite, unique being that he feels himself at bottom to be." Explaining the same point further, he has said: "But the self comprises infinitely more than a mere ego, as the symbolism has shown from of old. It is as much one's self, the other selves, as the ego. Individuation does not shut one out from the world but gathers the world to oneself" (*Spirit and Nature* 435).

Many of Jung's patients were in the second phase of life and had lost a sense of life's meaning. In his article "Stages of Life" in *Modern Man in Search of a Soul* he speaks of the dual stages of waxing and waning. The psychological requirements of the first stage and the second stage are diametrically opposed. In the first stage of life the horizon is rising, as one begins a career, marries, and raises a family. In the second half of life one's energies and one's possibilities are declining. The sun is setting, as it were, in the west. Traditionally persons in this phase of life need more time for solitude to face the issue of their finitude and impending death.

To persons in the sunset of life, Goethe's words apply: "Turn inward, it is within that you will find the center in which no man of noble mind can doubt. You will want for no rule, your independent conscience is the sun of your ethical day" (cited in Schmid 247).[3] Karl Schmid has written: "Thomas Mann's Doctor Faustus is a brilliant attempt to describe these two aspects of Faust's pact with the Devil: creative for the German artist Leverkuhn, but destructive for his nation. We share the feelings of Zeitblom, the humanist: admiration for the creative aspect, horror for the destructive aspect" (247). Like so many aspects of life's rich experience creativity itself can be seen as a two-edged Sword of Damocles. In ancient Greece, Damocles was forced to sit at a banquet under a sword suspended by a single hair to demonstrate the precariousness of the king's fortunes. In the modern world we tend to think of creativity as an unmitigated good, but it has its negative side as well.

In one of his more insightful moments, Jung wrote:

Every one of us gladly turns away from his problems; if possible, they must not be mentioned, or, better still, their existence is denied. We wish to make our lives simple, certain, and smooth, and for that reason problems are taboo. We want to have certainties

Jung as Modern Man in Search of a Soul

and have no doubts—results and no experiments—without even seeing that certainties can arise only through doubt and results only through experiment. The artful denial of a problem will not produce conviction; on the contrary, a wider and higher consciousness is required to give us the certainty and clarity we need. (*CW* 8:389).

Postscript

In *The Wounded Jung* we have considered several of the ways in which Jung pioneered therapeutic approaches to achieve inner integration. Thus the expression of creativity in its many forms became for him an important part of his vision of wholeness.

We have seen how Jung's life embodied a search for the self, a striving for closure, a healing of an inner rift, a reconciliation of opposites. One can question whether such closure was ever achieved or whether it could be. In my view it was not. Had it been, I believe we would not have witnessed the dynamism of Jung's output of ideas that are both original and creative. His visionary and literary creativity continued right into his later years, with the writing of *Answer to Job* and his autobiography.

In childhood Jung had profound feelings of abandonment, damaged self-esteem, and long periods of loneliness, which eventuated in his lifelong explorations of what he was the first to term introversion. During his descent into the unconscious, he daily confronted his unconscious images through a variety of creative means, such as journal keeping and the painting of inner images, many of which represented mandalas. These he took to be the first signs of a coming period of psychic integration.

Jung's inner conflicts spurred him on to master whole libraries of arcane knowledge and the traditions of symbolic sacred lore to answer the questions posed by his work with patients. He wrote in an oblique style that has more than frustrated even many of his sympathetic readers. He himself was bothered endlessly by the difficulty that he had in getting many of his basic ideas across to readers. In contrast to Freud, whose style was straightforward and lucid, Jung for the most part wrote in a diffuse manner, and the connections he makes are at times extremely convoluted.

Carl Meier, one of Jung's associates, relates a story from antiquity of Chiron's wound. The wound was caused by an arrow Herakles intended for Elatos, one of the other centaurs. The arrow wounded Chiron in the knee, producing lameness in the healer. On the arrow was venom from the Hydra, and though Herakles attempted to cure the wound, his attempt failed. Chiron was unable to heal himself and so suffered the pain of an incurable wound (Meier, *Ancient Incubation*, 9). The story can be applied to Jung's own experience. Not only does the wound signify his lifelong need for healing and wholeness, but over time the wound is transformed so that it becomes the very thing that heals, and on this account it is divine. Jung encouraged such an account by responding in creative ways to the numinous forces emerging from the unconscious.

Throughout these pages I have tried to demonstrate that dissociation and inner splits are directly and genuinely related to the creative process. The phenomenon described is gaining increasing recognition among therapists.

Jung frequently said that his life embodied the elements of agony, pain, and suffering as well as moments of ecstasy. Late in life he wrote: "The daimon of creativity has ruthlessly had its way with me" (*Memories* 358). In responding to the creative drive within, he was to endeavor to realize the reconciliation of opposites that so frequently engaged him in his writings and with his patients.

Introduction

1. It is generally thought that Jung's autobiography originally included a chapter on Toni Wolff that was later deleted. The lengthy correspondence between Jung and Wolff was destroyed after her death. Their forty-year relationship has been candidly discussed in several of the biographies but interpreted quite differently. For the time being, part of the story remains hidden in unpublished materials.

2. Unpublished C. G. Jung Oral History Archive, at the Francis A. Countway Library of Medicine in Boston, Massachusetts. The statement is also recounted in Lewis Mumford's review of *Memories* in the *New Yorker*, written a short time after Jung's autobiography appeared.

1: Mother No. 1 & Mother No. 2

1. Transcript of an interview of Ruth Bailey, Jung's housekeeper, in the Jung Oral History Archive, Countway Library.

2. The original English-language transcript of *Memories* was a gift of Dr. James S. Cheatam to the Countway Library.

3. Many times throughout his life Jung reported that he heard voices and conducted conversations with imaginary or inanimate objects. I remember a conversation that I had some years ago with a Jungian analyst, riding back to Zurich from an Eranos conference in Ascona. The topic turned to the subject of Jung's habit of talking to the pots and pans at his beloved Bollingen. That is, I mentioned, precisely the sort of thing done by persons living in societies that take animism seriously. The analyst, in whose car I was riding, thought that it was strange that I was amazed at Jung's practice of animism in the modern world!

4. Transcript of Bailey interview, Jung Oral History Archive, Countway Library.

3: Jung and Freud

1. The German title was *Wandlungen und Symbole der Libido* (1911). The work's first English title was *Psychology of the Unconscious* (1916). Later it was retitled *Symbols of Transformation.*

2. Although Jung had never met Miller, he took her fifteen-page report of dreams and visions, published in Geneva in 1906, and expanded it into a book of more than four hundred pages.

4: Creative Illness

1. According to Sabina Spielrein, she and Jung had spoken of having a child named Siegfried (Fisher 479).

2. Jung was familiar with several of the various numerological meanings of the number twelve in antiquity, such as the twelve apostles, the twelve tribes of Israel, the twelve months of the year, the twelve signs of the Zodiac, the twelve gates of the heavenly Jerusalem, and the twelve times twelve of the blessed who will adore the Lamb of God. At the time none of these meanings satisfied him, but one fantasy kept returning, namely that something that was dead was also alive (*Memories* 172).

3. Jung uses the term *logos* for the thinking function and *eros* for the feeling function. This is an example of gender stereotyping that feminists have complained about in Jung's writings.

4. Daniel Noel has called my attention to the fact that Jung refused to call any of this "art."

5: The Lost Feminine

1. Marilyn M. Metzl, associate clinical professor at the University of Kansas, used this phrase as the title of a 1991 presentation at a conference on Creativity and Madness for the American Institute of Medical Education. In a telephone conversation with me, Dr. Metzl emphasized the fact that Jung had analyzed both his wife, Emma, and Toni Wolff.

2. Transcript of an interview of Fowler McCormick in the Jung Oral History Archive, Countway Library.

3. Transcript of an interview of Susanne Trüb in the Jung Oral Histroy Archive, Countway Library.

4. In *The Great Mother* alone, Neumann includes twenty-four citations calling attention to Bachofen.

8: Self & Myth

1. In this connection Daniel Noel called my attention to Hillman's use of the phrase "empirical disguise" (in "Pandaemonium of Images" in *Healing Fiction*) as a way of interpreting this phenomenon on Jung's part.

2. The Buber-Jung controversy and its implications are discussed in Robert C. Smith, "A Critical Analysis of Religious and Philosophic Issues between Buber and Jung," doctoral diss., Temple University, 1961.

9: Creativity & Healing

1. McCown recalls how R. D. Laing in *The Politics of Experience* points out that the root etymological meaning of *schizophrenia* is *schiz*, "broken," and *phrenos*, "soul" or "heart."

2. For an extended discussion of the psychological and visionary modes, the reader should consult Philipson, esp. pt. 2, pp. 103–35.

3. Goethe's original reads: "Sofort nun wende dich nach innen, das Zentrum findest du da drinnen, woran kein Edler zweifeln mag. Wirst keine Regel da vermissen, denn das selbstständige Gewissen ist Sonne deinem Sittentag."

Alchemy. A traditional means of magical transmutation and transformation. Many societies have had the idea of the transformation of base elements into gold and also of psychic dross into a different reality. These concepts fascinated Jung, especially in the latter part of his career.

Ambivalance. The existence of mutually contradictory feelings or thoughts about the same person. This study contends that Jung himself had such feelings about both of his parents.

Amplification. Imaginal expansion upon unconscious contents as a vital part of the therapeutic healing process.

Androgyny. Possessing both male and female characteristics and holding them in balance.

Anima. A Jungian term referring to unconscious feminine characteristics in the male personality.

Animus. The masculine component of the female personality. According to Jungian theory, animus is represented in an archetype that symbolizes the collective experiences of women with men.

Archetype. An inherited structural component of the mind that stems from the accumulated experience of humankind.

Collective unconscious. The deep layer of the unconscious that Jung posited was part of the collective inheritance of the race.

Compensation. The self-regulatory manner in which conscious and unconscious operate both to include and to exclude aspects of the personality.

Complex. A term coined by Jung to refer to a collection of images and ideas that comprises the multilayered aspects of the personality.

Coniunctio. An alchemical symbol in which dissimilar elements are united.

Dissociation. The process by which aspects of the personality are split off from the personality and assume lives of their own.

Elan vital. A term first used by the philosopher Henri Bergson to indicate the creative vital force of the personality.

Empiricism. The theory that knowledge is based on verifiable sense observation. Jung was regarded by many other investigators as a mystic, but he stoutly maintained his stance as an empiricist.

Enantiodromia. The necessary opposition that is a governing principle of psychic life. Heraclitus first used this term to indicate that all life eventually went over to its opposite. Jung also frequently spoke of the *coincidentia oppositorum.*

Extrovert. A person whose primary locus for action is the outer or external world of other persons.

Gnostic. The tendency in early Christianity to find salvation through intuitive "knowledge" or insight. The history of religions offers many examples of initiation into the sacred mysteries. Gnostic themes abound in Jung's writings, but he vigorously denied that he was a gnostic.

Hieros gamos. Sacred marriage. Jung frequently used the concept to refer to the internal marriage of masculine and feminine aspects of a person's psyche.

Hypostasis. A dogmatic assertion not based on empirical evidence.

Hypothesis. A testable proposition about behavior that states an expected outcome based on assumptions about personality factors or conditions.

Imago. The idealized image of a key person in one's developmental process, such as the mother.

Immanence. A theological term that refers to the divine within.

Individuation. The lifelong process of becoming a distinct and unique individual.

Inflation. The tendency of the personality to overcompensate for inner deficiencies by exaggerating some aspects of the personality.

Integration. The means by which hitherto unconscious contents are incorporated into a larger frame of consciousness, thereby enabling the personality to achieve a greater sense of balance.

Introjection. The process of incorporating either another individual's or a group's standards into one's own value structure.

Introvert. A term coined by Jung to denote an individual who sees the primary source of meaning in the inner world of dreams and images.

Libido. A term originally used by Freud to refer to sexual energy but expanded by Jung to refer to psychic energy and to denote a much wider range of social and creative activities.

Logos. A term used in antiquity to refer to the source of divine reason. Frequently *logos* (divine word) was contrasted with *eros*, or the sensual aspect of life.

Mana personality. A person endowed with exceptional, compelling, and persuasive power, and in some cases "numinous" elements. In traditional societies these features of "divine power" were typically possessed by visionaries, prophets, seers, and shamans.

Mandala. A term from the Sanskrit that means "magic circle." Jung believed the mandala appeared at precisely that point when inner psychic healing was taking place. In his own experience and those of his patients, mandalas were connected to the integration process.

Mythological themes. For Jung, myth was not a fiction to be explained away but rather an inner lived reality. He stoutly believed that we all create our own inner myths. For him they represent archetypes stored in the collective unconscious.

Narcissism. Excessive self-love and overvaluation of the self. To date, Peter Homans, following Heinz Kohut, has presented the most extensive study of narcissistic elements in Jung's personality.

Nekyia. The term used by Henri Ellenberger to refer to Jung's descent into the depths of the unconscious after his break with Freud. The history of religions also affords numerous examples in which the soul undertakes a journey into the world of the spirits.

Numinosum. A term coined by Rudolf Otto that refers to the dual feeling of sacred power and uncanniness. In spite of Jung's troubled childhood, his encounter with the numinous dimension of his existence proceeded through a variety of creative means.

Persona. In classical drama the mask worn by an actor to indicate the role to be played. In Jungian terminology it is the official face or side that we show to the world.

Personal unconscious. The strata of the unconscious that represents largely repressed elements previously a part of consciousness.

Primordial image. An archetypal idea, such as the original, unconscious mother image in the child. Jung thought that such motifs were ultimately derived from the collective unconscious.

Projection. A defense mechanism in which unacceptable impulses and desires are attributed to others.

Psychosis. A severe mental disorder characterized by a partial or complete withdrawal from reality.

Quaternity. A fourfold structural interpretation of reality that characterized Jung's cosmological speculations and also his typology.

Regression. A defense mechanism in which there is a personality reversion to an earlier stage of development.

Sacrifice. The tendency to deprive oneself of that which is realistically needed to function in the world. For Jung, thoroughgoing consciousness requires sacrifices of various kinds.

Schizophrenia. Literally "split mind"; the condition formerly known as dementia praecox. *Schizophrenia* is a rather general term referring to psychotic reactions characterized by withdrawal from reality and accompanied by behavioral disturbances.

Shadow. A term coined by Jung to refer to the unpleasant "dark" side of the personality that one would like to have hidden from others.

Split feminine. A term used in recent Jungian literature to refer to the process of dissociation and splitting of some feminine personality qualities.

Synchronicity. A term used by Jung to refer to events that occur at the same time but, in his view, without causal connection.

Transcendence. A theological term that refers to divinity as being beyond or apart from rather than a part of the self.

Transcendent function. The ability of the psyche to mediate opposites by means of the process of symbolization. For Jung this was a natural process that was assisted by dreams and fantasy.

Transformation. One of the goals of the life process that is the outcome of initiation, descent into the unconscious, and other means of becoming immersed in unconscious processes.

Undoing. An unconscious defense mechanism in which guilt is counteracted by such means as acts of atonement, sacrifice, and expiation.

Unio mystica. Feelings of spiritual oneness. Typically such feelings involve oneness with God, nature, or the universe as a whole.

Books

Adler, Gerhard. *Studies in Analytical Psychology*. New York: Norton, 1948.

Arieti, Silvano. *The Interpretation of Schizophrenia*. 2d ed. New York: Basic Books, 1974.

———. *The Intrapsychic Self*. New York: Basic Books, 1967.

———, ed. *American Handbook of Psychiatry*. 2d ed. New York: Basic Books, 1974.

Barnaby, Karin, and Pellegrino D'Acierno, eds. *C. G. Jung and the Humanities: Toward a Hermeneutics of Culture*. Princeton, N.J.: Princeton University Press, 1990.

Bennet, E. A. *Meetings with Jung: Conversations Recorded during the Years 1946–1961*. Zurich: Daimon Verlag, 1985.

Brome, Vincent. *Freud and His Early Circle*. New York: William Morrow, 1968.

———. *Jung: Man and Myth*. New York: Atheneum, 1978.

Browning, Don S. *Religious Thought and the Modern Psychologies*. Philadelphia: Fortress Press, 1987.

Buber, Martin. *Eclipse of God: Studies in the Relation between Religion and Philosophy*. Translated by Maurice S. Friedman et al. New York: Harper and Bros., 1952.

———. *The Knowledge of Man: Selected Essays*. Edited with an introductory essay by Maurice S. Friedman. Translated by Maurice S. Friedman and Ronald G. Smith. New York: Harper and Row, 1965.

Cady, Susan, Marian Ronan, and Hal Taussig. *Sophia: The Future of Feminist Spirituality*. San Francisco: Harper and Row, 1986.

Campbell, Joseph. *The Hero with a Thousand Faces*. Cleveland: World, 1970.

———. *Myths to Live By*. New York: Viking Press, 1972.

———, ed. *Myths, Dreams, and Religion*. New York: E. P. Dutton, 1970.

———, ed. *The Portable Jung*. New York: Viking Press, 1971.

Carotenuto, Aldo, ed. *A Secret Symmetry: Sabina Spielrein between Jung and Freud*. Translated by Arno Pomerans, John Shepley, and Krishna Winston. New York: Pantheon Books, 1982.

Carson, Anne, ed. *Goddesses and Wise Women: The Literature of Feminist Spirituality, 1980–1991. An Annotated Bibliography*. Freedom, Calif.: Crossing Press, 1992.

Champernowne, Irene. *Creative Expression and Ultimate Values*. London: Guild of Pastoral Psychology, 1973.

————. *A Memoir of Toni Wolff*. Foreword by Joseph L. Henderson. San Francisco: C. G. Jung Institute of San Francisco, 1980.

Chapman, J. Harley. *Jung's Three Theories of Religious Experience*. Lewiston, N.Y.: Edwin Mellen Press, 1988.

Charet, F. X. *Spiritualism and the Foundations of C. G. Jung's Psychology*. Albany, N.Y.: State University of New York Press, 1993.

Clift, Wallace B. *Jung and Christianity: The Challenge of Reconciliation*. New York: Crossroad, 1982.

Coward, Harold. *Jung and Eastern Thought*. Albany, N.Y.: State University of New York Press, 1985.

Cox, David. *Jung and St. Paul*. New York: Association Press, 1959.

Daly, Mary. *Beyond God the Father: Toward a Philosophy of Women's Liberation*. Boston: Beacon Press, 1973.

————. *Gyn/Ecology: The Metaphysics of Radical Feminism*. Boston: Beacon Press, 1978.

————. *Pure Lust: Elemental Feminist Philosophy*. Boston: Beacon Press, 1984.

Deri, Susan K. *Symbolization and Creativity*. New York: International Universities Press, 1984.

Diamond, Malcolm. *Martin Buber: Jewish Existentialist*. New York: Oxford University Press, 1960.

Dodds, E. R. *The Greeks and the Irrational*. Berkeley: University of California Press, 1951.

————. *Pagan and Christian in an Age of Anxiety*. Cambridge: Cambridge University Press, 1965.

Donn, Linda. *Freud and Jung: Years of Friendship, Years of Loss*. New York: Charles Scribner's Sons, 1988.

Dourley, John P. *C. G. Jung and Paul Tillich: The Psyche as Sacrament*. Toronto: Inner City Books, 1981.

————. *The Illness That We Are: A Jungian Critique of Christianity*. Toronto: Inner City Books, 1984.

Dry, Avis M. *The Psychology of Jung: A Critical Interpretation*. New York: John Wiley and Sons, 1961.

Edinger, Edward F. *The Creation of Consciousness: Jung's Myth for Modern Man*. Toronto: Inner City Books, 1984.

————. *Ego and Archetype: Individuation and the Religious Function*. New York: G. P. Putnam's Sons, 1972.

Eliade, Mircea. *Myths and Mythical Thought*. Lucerne, Switz: EMB, 1976.

Eliade, Mircea, and Joseph M. Kitagawa, eds. *The History of Religions: Essays in Methodology*. Chicago: University of Chicago Press, 1959.

Ellenberger, Henri F. *The Discovery of the Unconscious: The History and Evolution of Dynamic Psychiatry*. New York: Basic Books, 1970.

Engelsman, Joan Chamberlain. *The Feminine Dimension of the Divine.* Philadelphia: Westminster Press, 1979.

Ferguson, Marilyn. *The Aquarian Conspiracy: Personal and Social Transformation in the 1980's.* Rev. ed. Los Angeles: J. P. Tarcher, 1987.

Fordham, Michael. *Jungian Psychotherapy: A Study in Analytical Psychology.* New York: John Wiley and Sons, 1978.

———. *New Developments in Analytical Psychology.* London: Routledge and Kegan Paul, 1957.

Freud, Sigmund. *Collected Papers.* 5 vols. Edited and translated by Joan Riviere. New York: Basic Books, 1959.

———. *The Complete Letters of Sigmund Freud to Wilhelm Fliess, 1887–1904.* Edited and translated by Jeffrey Moussaieff Masson. Cambridge, Mass.: Harvard University Press, 1985.

———. *The Interpretation of Dreams.* Edited and translated by James Strachey. New York: Avon Books, 1965.

———. *New Introductory Lectures on Psychoanalysis.* Trans. by W. J. H. Sprott. London: Hogarth Press, 1933.

———. *On the History of the Psycho-analytic Movement.* In *The Standard Edition of the Complete Psychological Works of Sigmund Freud,* edited by James Strachey, 14: 3-66. London: Hogarth Press, 1957.

Freud, Sigmund, and Karl Abraham. *A Psycho-analytic Dialogue: The Letters of Sigmund Freud and Karl Abraham, 1907-1926.* Edited by Hilda C. Abraham and Ernst L. Freud. Translated by Bernard Marsh and Hilda C. Abraham. New York: Basic Books, 1965.

Freud, Sigmund, and C. G. Jung. *The Freud-Jung Letters: The Correspondence between Sigmund Freud and C. G. Jung.* Edited by William McGuire. Translated by Ralph Manheim and R. F. C. Hull. Princeton, N.J.: Princeton University Press, 1974.

Frey-Rohn, Liliane. *From Freud to Jung: A Comparative Study of the Psychology of the Unconscious.* Translated by Fred E. Engreen and Evelyn K. Engreen. New York: C. G. Jung Foundation for Analytical Psychology, 1974.

Friedman, Maurice S. *Martin Buber: The Life of Dialogue.* Chicago: University of Chicago Press, 1955.

Fromm, Erich. *Psychoanalysis and Religion.* New Haven, Conn.: Yale University Press, 1950.

Frosch, John. *The Psychotic Process.* New York: International Universities Press, 1983.

Gay, Peter. *Freud: A Life for Our Time.* New York: Norton, 1988.

Gedo, John E. *Portraits of the Artist.* New York: Guilford Press, 1983.

Gedo, John E., and George H. Pollock, eds. *Freud: The Fusion of Science and Humanism.* New York: International Universities Press, 1976.

Girard, Réné. *Job: The Victim of His People.* Translated by Yvonne Freccero. Stanford, Calif.: Stanford University Press, 1987.

Goldenberg, Naomi. *Changing of the Gods: Feminism and the End of Patriarchal Religions*. Boston: Beacon Press, 1979.

———. *The End of God*. Ottawa: University of Ottawa Press, 1982.

———. *Returning Words to Flesh*. Boston: Beacon Press, 1990.

Greenberg, Jay R., and Stephen A. Mitchell. *Object Relations in Psychoanalytic Theory*. Cambridge, Mass.: Harvard University Press, 1983.

Grotnick, Simon A., and Leonard Barkin, eds. *Between Reality and Fantasy*. New York: Jason Aronson, 1978.

Grotstein, James S. *Splitting and Projective Identification*. New York: Jason Aronson, 1985.

Halifax, Joan. *Shaman, the Wounded Healer*. New York: Crossroad, 1982.

———. *Shamanic Voices: A Survey of Visionary Narratives*. New York: Dutton, 1979.

Hannah, Barbara. *Jung: His Life and Work*. New York: G. P. Putnam's Sons, 1976.

Heisig, James W. *Imago Dei: A Study of C. G. Jung's Psychology of Religion*. Lewisburg, Pa.: Bucknell University Press, 1979.

Henderson, Joseph L. *Thresholds of Initiation*. Middletown, Conn.: Wesleyan University Press, 1967.

Hillman, James. *Healing Fiction*. Barrytown, N.Y.: Station Hill Press, 1983.

———. *The Myth of Analysis: Three Essays in Archetypal Psychology*. Evanston, Ill.: Northwestern University Press, 1972.

———. *Re-Visioning Psychology*. New York: Harper and Row, 1975.

Hoeller, Stephan A. *The Gnostic Jung and the Seven Sermons to the Dead*. Wheaton, Ill.: Theosophical Publishing House, 1982.

Hogenson, George B. *Jung's Struggle with Freud*. Notre Dame, Ind.: University of Notre Dame Press, 1983.

Homans, Peter. *The Ability to Mourn: Disillusionment and the Social Origins of Psychoanalysis*. Chicago: University of Chicago Press, 1989.

———. *Jung in Context*. Chicago: University of Chicago Press, 1979.

Hostie, Raymond, S.J. *Religion and the Psychology of Jung*. Translated by G. R. Lamb. London: Sheed and Ward, 1957.

Humbert, Elie G. *C. G. Jung: The Fundamentals of Theory and Practice*. Translated by Ronald G. Jalbert. Wilmette, Ill.: Chiron, 1984.

Isbister, J. N. *Freud: An Introduction to His Life and Work*. Cambridge, Eng.: Polity Press, 1985.

Jacobi, Jolande. *Complex/Archetype/Symbol in the Psychology of C. G. Jung*. Translated by Ralph Manheim. New York: Pantheon Books, 1959.

———. *The Psychology of Jung*. Translated by K. W. Bash, with a foreword by C. G. Jung. New Haven, Conn.: Yale University Press, 1943.

Jacques, Elliot. *Work, Creativity, and Social Justice*. London: Heinemann, 1970.

Jaffé, Aniela. *The Myth of Meaning in the Work of C. G. Jung*. Translated by R. F. C. Hull. Zurich: Daimon Verlag, 1984.

———. *Was C. G. Jung a Mystic?* Edited by Robert Hinshaw, assisted by Gary Massey and Henriette Wagner. Translated by Diana Dachler and Fiona Cairns. Einsiedeln, Switz.: Daimon Verlag, 1989.

Jones, Ernest. *The Life and Work of Sigmund Freud*. 3 vols. New York: Basic Books, 1955.

Jung, C. G. *Aion: Researches into the Phenomenology of the Self. Collected Works*, vol. 9, pt. 2. Translated by R. F. C. Hull. London: Routledge and Kegan Paul, 1959.

———. *Analytical Psychology Notes of the Seminar Given in 1925 by C. G. Jung*. Edited by William McGuire. Princeton, N.J.: Princeton University Press, 1989. [The text edited is that of the original transcript prepared by Cary F. de Angulo.]

———. *Answer to Job*. In *Collected Works*, vol. 11, pp. 355–470. Translated by R. F. C. Hull. New York: Pantheon Books, 1958.

———. *The Archetypes and the Collective Unconscious. Collected Works*, vol. 9, part 1. Translated by R. F. C. Hull. Princeton, N.J.: Princeton University Press, 1959.

———. *Aspects of the Feminine*. Translated by R. F. C. Hull. Princeton, N.J.: Princeton University Press, 1982.

———. *Civilization in Transition. Collected Works*, vol. 10. Translated by R. F. C. Hull. New York: Pantheon Books, 1964.

———. *The Collected Works of C. G. Jung*. Vols. 1–13, 16, 18. Edited by William McGuire, Sir Herbert Read, Michael Fordham, and Gerhard Adler. Translated by R. F. C. Hull (except for vol. 2, which was translated by L. Stein in collaboration with Diana Riviere). Princeton, N.J.: Princeton University Press, 1953–79.

———. *Contributions to Analytical Psychology*. Translated by H. G. Baynes and C. F. Baynes. London: Kegan Paul, 1928.

———. *The Integration of the Personality*. Translated by Stanley Dell. London: Routledge and Kegan Paul, 1940.

———. *Letters*. Vol. 1, 1906–50; vol. 2, 1951–61. Edited by Gerhard Adler and Aniela Jaffé. Translated by R. F. C. Hull. Princeton, N.J.: Princeton University Press, 1973.

———. *Memories, Dreams, Reflections*. Recorded by Aniela Jaffé. Edited by Aniela Jaffé, R. F. C. Hull, and Richard Winston. Translated by Richard Winston and Clara Winston. New York: Vintage Books, 1961.

———. *Modern Man in Search of a Soul*. Translated by W. S. Dell and Cary F. Baynes. New York: Harcourt, Brace and Co., 1933.

―――. *Nietzsche's Zarathustra: Notes of the Seminar Given in 1934–1939.* 2 vols. Edited by James L. Jarrett. Princeton, N.J.: Princeton University Press, 1988.

―――. *On the Psychology of the Spirit.* Translated by Hildegard Nagel. New York: Analytical Psychology Club of New York, 1948. [Two lectures given at Ascona, Switzerland, in August 1945.]

―――. *Psyche and Symbol.* Edited by Violet S. de Laszlo. Translated by Cary Baynes and R. F. C. Hull. New York: Doubleday, 1957.

―――. *Psychological Aspects of the Mother Archetype.* In *The Basic Writings of C. G. Jung,* edited with an introduction by Violet S. de Laszlo, translated by R. F. C. Hull, 327–60. New York: Modern Library, 1959.

―――. *Psychological Types.* Translated by H. Godwin Baynes. London: Kegan Paul, 1923.

―――. *Psychology and Alchemy.* Translated by R. F. C. Hull. Princeton, N.J.: Princeton University Press, 1968.

―――. *Psychology and Religion.* Terry Lectures. New Haven, Conn.: Yale University Press, 1938.

―――. *Psychology and Religion: West and East. Collected Works,* vol. 11. Translated by R. F. C. Hull. New York: Pantheon Books, 1958.

―――. *Psychology of the Unconscious: A Study of the Transformations of the Libido.* Translated with an introduction by Beatrice M. Hinkle. New York: Dodd, Mead, 1916.

―――. *Spirit and Nature.* Papers from the Eranos Yearbooks. Translated by R. F. C. Hull. New York: Pantheon Books, 1954.

―――. *The Symbolic Life: Miscellaneous Writings. Collected Works,* vol. 18. Translated by R. F. C. Hull. Princeton, N.J.: Princeton University Press, 1976.

―――. *Symbols of Transformation: An Analysis of the Prelude to a Case of Schizophrenia. Collected Works,* vol. 5. Translated by R. F. C. Hull. New York: Pantheon Books, 1956. [Originally published as *Wandlungen und Symbole der Libido* in 1911. The fourth edition in German was extensively revised in 1952 and published by Rascher Verlag, Zurich.]

―――. *Two Essays on Analytical Psychology. Collected Works,* vol. 5. Translated by R. F. C. Hull. Princeton, N.J.: Princeton University Press, 1966.

―――. *The Undiscovered Self.* Translated by R. F. C. Hull. Boston: Little, Brown, 1957.

―――. *Word and Image.* Edited, with chronology, by Aniela Jaffé. Translated by Krishna Winston. Princeton, N. J.: Princeton University Press, 1979.

Jung, C. G., and Sigmund Freud. *The Freud-Jung Letters: The Correspondence between Sigmund Freud and C. G. Jung.* Edited by

William McGuire. Translated by Ralph Manheim and R. F. C. Hull. Princeton, N.J.: Princeton University Press, 1974.

Jung, C. G., and C. Kerényi. *Essays on a Science of Mythology*. Translated by R. F. C. Hull. London: Routledge and Kegan Paul, 1951.

Jung, C. G., et al. *Man and His Symbols*. Edited by C. G. Jung and, after his death, M.-L. von Franz. London: Aldus Books, 1964.

Kant, Immanuel. *Prolegomena to any Future Metaphysics*. Edited by Paul Carus. Chicago: Open Court, 1902.

Kaufmann, Walter A. *Freud versus Adler and Jung: Discovering the Mind*. Vol. 3. New York: McGraw-Hill, 1980.

———. *The Portable Nietzsche*. New York: Viking Press, 1961.

Kelsey, Morton T. *Christo-Psychology*. New York: Crossroad, 1984.

———. *Healing and Christianity in Ancient Thought and Modern Times*. New York: Harper and Row, 1973.

Kerr, John. *A Most Dangerous Method: The Story of Jung, Freud, and Sabina Spielrein*. New York Random House, 1993.

Klein, Dennis B. *Jewish Origins of the Psychoanalytic Movement*. New York: Praeger, 1981.

Klein, Melanie, and Joan Riviere, eds. *Love, Guilt, and Reparation*. New York: Norton, 1964.

Kohut, Heinz. *The Analysis of the Self*. New York: International Universities Press, 1971.

———. *The Search for the Self*. New York: International Universities Press, 1978.

Kris, Ernst. *Psychoanalytic Explorations in Art*. Madison, Conn.: International Universities Press, 1962.

———. *Selected Papers of Ernst Kris*. New Haven, Conn.: Yale University Press, 1975.

Laing, Ronald David. *The Politics of Experience*. New York: Pantheon Books, 1967.

Leibrecht, Walter, ed. *Religion and Culture: Essays in Honor of Paul Tillich*. New York: Harper and Bros., 1959.

Martin, Luther H., and James Goss, eds. *Essays on Jung and the Study of Religion*. Lanham, Md.: University Press of America, 1985.

McGuire, William, and R. F. C. Hull, eds. *C. G. Jung Speaking: Interviews and Encounters*. Bollingen Series 97. Princeton, N.J.: Princeton University Press, 1977.

Meier, Carl Alfred. *Ancient Incubation and Modern Psychotherapy*. Evanston, Ill.: Northwestern University Press, 1967.

———. *Jung's Analytical Psychology and Religion*. Carbondale, Ill.: Southern Illinois University Press, 1977.

———. *Soul and Body: Essays on the Theories of C. G. Jung*. Santa Monica, Calif.: Lapis Press, 1986.

Mendelson, Edward. *Early Auden*. New York: Viking Press, 1981.

Miller, David. *The New Polytheism.* New York: Harper and Row, 1974.

Modell, Arnold H. *Object Love and Reality: An Introduction to a Psychoanalytic Theory of Object Relations.* Madison, Conn.: International Universities Press, 1968.

Moore, Robert L., ed. *Carl Jung and Christian Spirituality.* New York: Paulist Press, 1988.

Moore, Robert L., and Murray Stein, eds. *Jung's Challenge to Contemporary Religion.* Wilmette, Ill.: Chiron, 1987.

Moreno, Antonio. *Jung, Gods and Modern Man.* Notre Dame, Ind.: University of Notre Dame Press, 1970.

Nagy, Marilyn. *Philosophical Issues in the Psychology of C. G. Jung.* Albany, N.Y.: State University of New York Press, 1991.

Neumann, Erich. *Art and the Creative Unconscious.* 4 vols. Translated by Ralph Manheim. Princeton, N.J.: Princeton University Press, 1959.

———. *The Great Mother: An Analysis of the Archetype.* Translated by Ralph Manheim. Bollingen Series 47. Princeton, N.J.: Princeton University Press, 1963.

———. *The Origins and History of Consciousness.* Translated by R. F. C. Hull. Bollingen Series 42. Princeton, N.J.: Princeton University Press, 1954.

Noll, Richard. *The Jung Cult: Origins of a Charismatic Movement.* Princeton, N.J.: Princeton University Press, 1994.

Norton, David L. *Personal Destinies: A Philosophy of Ethical Individualism.* Princeton, N.J.: Princeton University Press, 1976.

Nouwen, Henri J. M. *The Wounded Healer: Ministry in Contemporary Society.* New York: Doubleday, Image Books, 1990.

Papadopoulos, Renos K., and Graham S. Saayman, eds. *Jung in Modern Perspective.* London: Wildwood House, 1984.

Perry, John Weir. *Roots of Renewal in Myth and Madness.* San Francisco: Jossey-Bass, 1976.

Philipson, Morris. *Outline of a Jungian Aesthetic.* Evanston, Ill.: Northwestern University Press, 1963.

Progoff, Ira. *The Death and Rebirth of Psychology.* New York: Julian Press, 1956.

———. *Jung's Psychology and Its Social Meaning.* Introduction by Goodwin Watson. New York: Julian Press, 1953.

Rainey, Reuben M. *Freud as Student of Religion.* Missoula, Mont.: Scholars Press, 1975.

Raschke, Carl A. *The Interruption of Eternity: Modern Gnosticism and the Origins of the New Religious Consciousness.* Chicago: Nelson-Hall, 1980.

Raschke, Carl A., James A. Kirk, and Mark C. Taylor, eds. *Religion and the Human Image.* Englewood Cliffs, N.J.: Prentice-Hall, 1977.

Rieff, Philip. *The Triumph of the Therapeutic: Uses of Faith after Freud.* New York: Harper and Row, 1966.

Roazen, Paul. *Freud: Political and Social Thought*. New York: Alfred A. Knopf, 1968.

——. *Freud and His Followers*. New York: Alfred A. Knopf, 1975.

Ruether, Rosemary R. *New Woman/New Earth*. New York: Seabury Press, 1975.

Samuels, Andrew. *Jung and the Post-Jungians*. London: Routledge and Kegan Paul, 1985.

Samuels, Andrew, Bani Shorter, and Fred Plaut. *A Critical Dictionary of Jungian Analysis*. London: Routledge and Kegan Paul, 1986.

Sanford, John A. *Healing and Wholeness*. New York: Paulist Press, 1966.

Schär, Hans. *Religion and the Cure of Souls in Jung's Psychology*. Translated by R. F. C. Hull. Bollingen Series 21. New York: Pantheon Books, 1950.

Schmid, Karl. *Evil*. Edited by the Curatorium of the C. G. Jung Institute, Zurich. Evanston, Ill.: Northwestern University Press, 1967.

Schoeps, Hans-Joachim. *The Religions of Mankind*. Translated by Richard Winston and Clara Winston. Garden City, N.J.: Anchor Books, 1968.

Schur, Max. *Freud: Living and Dying*. New York: International Universities Press, 1972.

Sedgwick, David. *The Wounded Healer: Countertransference from a Jungian Perspective*. London and New York: Routledge, 1994.

Smelser, N. J., and E. H. Erikson, eds. *Themes of Work and Love in Adulthood*. Cambridge, Mass.: Harvard University Press, 1980.

Smith, Robert C., and John Lounibos, eds. *Pagan and Christian Anxiety: A Response to E. R. Dodds*. Lanham, Md.: University Press of America, 1984.

Staude, John-Raphael. *The Adult Development of C. G. Jung*. Boston: Routledge and Kegan Paul, 1981.

——, ed. *Consciousness and Creativity*. Berkeley, Calif.: Ross Books, 1977.

Steele, Robert S. *Freud and Jung: Conflicts of Interpretation*. London: Routledge and Kegan Paul, 1982.

Stein, Murray. *Jung's Treatment of Christianity: The Psychotherapy of a Religious Tradition*. Wilmette, Ill.: Chiron, 1985.

Stern, Paul J. *C. G. Jung: The Haunted Prophet*. New York: George Braziller, 1976.

Stevens, Anthony. *Archetypes: A Natural History of the Self*. New York: William Morrow, 1982.

Stolorow, Robert D., and George E. Atwood. *Faces in a Cloud: Subjectivity in Personality Theory*. Northvale, N.J.: Jason Aronson, 1979.

Storr, Anthony. *C. G. Jung*. New York: Viking Press, 1973.

——. *The Dynamics of Creation*. New York: Atheneum, 1972.

———. *The Essential Jung*. Princeton, N.J.: Princeton University Press, 1983.

Sugg, Richard P., ed. *Jungian Literary Criticism*. Evanston, Ill.: Northwestern University Press, 1992.

Sulloway, Frank J. *Freud: Biologist of the Mind*. New York: Basic Books, 1979.

Thilly, Frank. *A History of Philosophy*. Revised by Ledger Wood. New York: Henry Holt, 1951.

Tillich, Paul. *The Protestant Era*. Chicago: University of Chicago Press, 1951.

Trüb, Hans. *Heilung aus der Begegnung: Eine Auseinandersetzung mit der Psychologie C. G. Jungs*. Edited by Ernst Cichel and Arie Sborowitz. Stuttgart: Ernst Klett Verlag, 1952.

Ulanov, Ann Belford. *The Feminine in Jungian Psychology and in Christian Theology*. Evanston, Ill.: Northwestern University Press, 1971.

Vincie, Joseph F., and Margareta Rathbauer-Vincie. *C. G. Jung and Analytical Psychology: A Comprehensive Bibliography*. New York: Garland, 1977.

Vitz, Paul C. *Sigmund Freud's Christian Unconscious*. New York: Guilford Press, 1988.

von Franz, Marie-Louise. *C. G. Jung: His Myth in Our Time*. Translated by W. H. Kennedy. New York: G. P. Putnam's Sons, 1975.

Waley, Arthur. *The Way and Its Power: A Study of the Tao Te Ching and Its Place in Chinese Thought*. New York: Grove Press, 1958.

Wehr, Demaris S. *Jung and Feminism: Liberating Archetypes*. Boston: Beacon Press, 1987.

Wehr, Gerhard. *Jung: A Biography*. Translated by David M. Weeks. Boston: Shambhala, 1988.

White, Victor. *God and the Unconscious*. Foreword by C. G. Jung and appendix by Gebhard Frei. London: Harvill Press, 1952.

———. *Soul and Psyche: An Inquiry into the Relationship of Psychotherapy and Religion*. New York: Harper and Bros., 1960.

Whitmont, Edward C. *The Symbolic Quest: Basic Concepts of Analytical Psychology*. New York: G. P. Putnam's Sons, 1969.

Wilhelm, Richard, trans. *The Secret of the Golden Flower*. Translated and explained from Chinese to German by Richard Wilhelm. Foreword and commentary by C. G. Jung. Text translated from the German by Cary F. Baynes. New York: Harcourt, Brace and World, 1962.

Winnicott, D. W. *Collected Papers, through Paediatrics to Psychoanalysis*. New York: Basic Books, 1958.

———. *The Maturational Processes and the Facilitating Environment*. London: Hogarth Press, 1965.

Atwood, George E., and Robert D. Stolorow. "Metapsychology,
Reification, and the Representational World of C. G. Jung."
International Review of Psychoanalysis 4, no. 1 (1975): 197–214.
Atwood, George E., and Silvan S. Tomkins. "On the Subjectivity of
Personality Theory." *Journal of the History of the Behavioral Sciences* 12
(1976): 166–77.
Avens, Robert S. "The Image of the Devil in C. G. Jung's Psychology."
Journal of Religion and Health 16, no. 3 (1977): 198–222.
Billinsky, John M. "Jung and Freud (The End of a Romance)." *Andover
Newton Quarterly* 10, no. 2 (1969): 39–43.
Carotenuto, Aldo. "Jung's Shadow Problem with Sabina Spielrein." In
*The Archetype of Shadow in a Split World: Proceedings of the Tenth
International Congress for Analytical Psychology* [Berlin, 1986], edited
by Mary Ann Mattoon, 241–61. Zurich: Daimon Verlag, 1987.
Christ, Carol. "Some Comments on Jung, Jungians, and the Study of
Women." *Anima* 3, no. 3 (Spring Equinox 1977): 66–69.
Clark, Robert A., M.D. "Buber and Jung." *Inward Light* [Washington,
D.C.] 49 (Fall 1955): 29–32.
De Voogd, Stephanie. "C. G. Jung: Psychologist of the Future,
'Philosopher' of the Past." *Spring* (1977): 175–82.
Dinnage, Rosemary. Review of *A Secret Symmetry: Sabina Spielrein
between Jung and Freud*, edited by Aldo Carotenuto. *Times Literary
Supplement*, Dec. 10, 1982, 1351–52.
Ebon, Martin. Review of *Memories, Dreams, Reflections*, by C. G. Jung.
International Journal of Parapsychology 5, no. 4 (Autumn 1963):
427–58.
Farber, Leslie H., M.D. "Martin Buber and Psychiatry." *Psychiatry* 19,
no. 2 (May 1956), 109–20.
Fisher, David James. Review of *A Secret Symmetry: Sabina Spielrein
between Jung and Freud*, edited by Aldo Carotenuto. *Partisan Review*
51, no. 1 (1984): 473–80.
Fodor, Nandor. "Jung's Sermons to the Dead." *Psychoanalytic Review* 51
(1970): 74–78.
Fordham, Michael. "Memories and Thoughts about C. G. Jung."
Journal of Analytical Psychology 20, no. 2 (1975): 102–13.
Friedman, Maurice S. "Healing through Meeting: Martin Buber and
Psychotherapy." *Cross Currents* 5, no. 1 (Winter 1955): 297–310.
Gedo, John E. "The Air Trembles, for Demi-Gods Draw Near."
American Imago 38, no. 1 (Spring 1981): 61–80.
———. "Magna Est Vis Veritatis Tuae et Praevalebit." *Annual of
Psychoanalysis* 7 (1979): 53–82.
Goldberg, Jonathan J. "A Jungian Critique of Harry Slochower's
Paper." *American Imago* 38, no. 1 (Spring 1981): 41–55.

Goldenberg, Naomi. "Archetypal Theory after Jung." *Spring* (1975): 199–219.

———. "A Feminist Critique of Jung." *Signs: Journal of Women in Culture and Society* 2, no. 2 (Winter 1976): 443–49.

———. "Feminism and Jungian Theory." *Anima* 3, no. 3 (Spring Equinox 1977): 14–17.

Gordon, R. "Death and Creativity: A Jungian Approach." *Journal of Analytical Psychology* 22, no. 2 (1977): 106–24.

Groesbeck, C. Jess. "The Analyst's Myth: Freud and Jung as Each Other's Analyst." In *Money, Food, Drink, and Fashion and Analytic Training: Depth Dimensions of Physical Existence*, Proceedings of the Eighth International Congress for Analytical Psychology, edited by John Beebe, 199–225. Fellbach-Oeffingen, West Germany: Verlag Adolf Bonz GmbH, 1983.

———. "A Jungian Answer to 'Yahweh as Freud.'" *American Imago* 39, no. 3 (Fall 1982): 239–54.

Gulick, Walter B. "Archetypal Experiences." *Soundings* 64, no. 3 (Fall 1981): 237–66.

Harding, M. Esther. "Jung's Contribution to Religious Symbolism." Paper read before the Analytical Psychology Club of New York, 1959.

Heisig, James W. "Jung and Theology: A Bibliographical Essay." *Spring* (1973): 204–55.

———. "The VII Sermones: Play and Theory." *Spring* (1972): 206–18.

Hillman, James. "On Psychological Creativity." *Eranos Jahrbuch* 35 (1966): 349–410. Also in *Schopfung und Gestallung*. Zurich: Rhein-Verlag, 1967. 359–81.

Homans, Peter. "Narcissism in the Jung-Freud Confrontations." *American Imago* 38, no. 1 (April 1981): 81–95.

Hostie, Raymond, S.J. "Religion and the Psychology of Jung." *Journal of Analytical Psychology* 3, no. 1 (Jan. 1958): 59–71.

Hubback, Judith. "VII Sermones ad Mortuos." *Journal of Analytical Psychology* 11, no. 2 (July 1966): 95–111.

Jaffé, Aniela. "The Creative Phases in Jung's Life." *Spring* (1972): 162–90.

———. "Details about C. G. Jung's Family." *Spring* (1984): 35–43.

———. "God—Eclipse or Transformation?" *Inward Light* [Washington, D.C.], 19, no. 50 (Spring 1956): 18–21.

Jung, C. G. "Reply to Buber." Translated by Robert Clark. *Spring* (1957): 3–9, published by the Analytical Psychology Club of New York. Originally published as "Chronik: Religion und Psychologie." *Merkur* 51 (May 1952): 467–73.

Khan, M. Masud R. "Secret as Potential Space." In *Between Reality and Fantasy*. Edited by Simon A. Grotnick and Leonard Barkin, 259–70. New York: Jason Aronson, 1978.

Kirsch, James. "Jung's Transference on Freud: Its Jewish Element." *American Imago* 41, no. 1 (Spring 1984): 63–83.

Lambert, Kenneth. "Analytical Psychology and Historical Development in Western Consciousness." *Journal of Analytical Psychology* 22, no. 2 (April 1977): 158–74.

Leavy, Stanley A. "A Footnote to Jung's 'Memories.' " Review of *Memories, Dreams, Reflections*, by C. G. Jung. *Psychoanalytic Quarterly* 33, no. 4 (1964): 567–74.

Leowald, Hans W. "Transference and Countertransference: The Roots of Psychoanalysis." Review of *The Freud-Jung Letters: The Correspondence between Sigmund Freud and C. G. Jung*, edited by William McGuire. *Psychoanalytic Quarterly* 46, no. 3 (July-Oct. 1977): 514–27.

Marcovitz, Eli. "Jung's Three Secrets: Slochower on 'Freud as Yahweh in Jung's *Answer to Job.*' " *American Imago* 39, no. 1 (Spring 1982): 59–72.

Martin, Stephen A. "The Creative Process and Healing." *Psychological Perspectives* [published by the C. G. Jung Institute of Los Angeles] 11, no. 1 (Spring 1980): 30–37.

May, Rollo. "Psychotherapy and the Daimonic." In *Myths, Dreams, and Religion*, edited by Joseph Campbell, 196–210. New York: E. P. Dutton, 1970.

McCown, Joe. "Shamanism: The Art of Ecstasy." *Encounter 39* (Autumn 1978): 435–46.

Moore, Thomas W. "Psychology, Typology, and the Wise Old Man." Review of *Jung: A Biography*, by Gerhard Wehr. *New York Times Book Review*, Feb. 14, 1988, 22.

Mumford, Lewis. "The Revolt of the Demons." *New Yorker*, May 23, 1964, 155–85.

Noel, Daniel C. "Veiled Kabir: C. G. Jung's Phallic Self-Image." *Spring* (1974): 224–42.

Oeri, Albert. "Some Youthful Memories of C. G. Jung." Translated by Lisa Ress Kaufman. *Spring* (1970): 182–89.

Plaut, A. "Jung and Rebirth." *Journal of Analytical Psychology* 22 (1977): 142–57.

Rank, Berta, and Dorothy MacNaughton. "A Clinical Contribution to Early Ego Development." *Psychoanalytic Study of the Child* 5 (1950): 53–65.

Satinover, Jeffrey. "At the Mercy of Another: Abandonment and Restitution in Psychosis and Psychotic Character." *Chiron* (1985): 47–86.

———. "Jung's Lost Contribution to the Dilemma of Narcissism." *Journal of the American Psychoanalytic Association* 34, no. 2 (1986): 401–39.

———. "Jung's Relation to the Mother." *Quadrant* 18, no. 1 (1985): 9–22.

———. "The Mirror of Doctor Faustus: The Decline of Art in the Pursuit of Eternal Adolescence." *Quadrant* 17 (Spring 1984): 23–38.

———. "The Myth of the Death of the Hero: A Jungian View of Masculine Psychology." *Psychoanalytic Review* 73, no. 4 (1986): 149–61.

Shengold, Leonard. "The Freud/Jung Letters." In *Freud and His Self-Analysis*. Edited by Mark Kanzer and Jules Glen, 187–201. New York: Jason Aronson, 1979.

Singer, June. "Jung as a Spiritual Teacher." *ReVISION* 8, no. 2 (1986): 41–47.

Slochower, Harry. "Freud as Yahweh in Jung's *Answer to Job*." *American Imago* 38, no. 1 (Spring 1981): 3–39.

Smith, Robert C. "Empirical Science and Value Assumptions: Lessons from C. G. Jung." *Journal of Religion and Health* 16, no. 2 (1977): 102–9.

Stein, Murray. "The Significance of Jung's Father in His Destiny as a Therapist of Christianity." *Quadrant* 18, no. 1 (Spring 1985): 23–33.

Stephansky, Paul E. "The Empiricist as Rebel: Jung, Freud, and the Burdens of Discipleship." *Journal of the History of the Behavioral Sciences* 12 (1976): 216–39.

Storr, Anthony. "Individuation and the Creative Process." *Journal of Analytical Psychology* 28, no. 4 (1983): 329–43.

Ulanov, Ann Belford. "A Shared Space." *Quadrant* 18, no. 1 (Spring 1985): 65–80.

Van Der Leeuw, P. J. "The Impact of the Freud-Jung Correspondence on the History of Ideas." *International Review of Psycho-analysis* 4 (1977): 349–62.

Wallace, Edwin R. "A Commentary on the Freud-Jung Letters." *Psychoanalytic Review* 67, no. 1 (Spring 1980): 111–37.

———. "Freud's Father Conflict: The History of a Dynamic." *Psychiatry* 41 (Feb. 1978): 33–55.

———. "Freud's Mysticism and Its Psychodynamic Determinants." *Bulletin of the Menninger Clinic* 42 (1978): 203–22.

Walters, Orville S. "Metaphysics, Religion, and Psychotherapy," *Journal of Counseling Psychology* 5, no. 4 (Winter 1958): 243–52.

Whan, Michael. "Chiron's Wound: Some Reflections on the Wounded Healer." *Chiron* (1987): 197–208.

White, Victor, A. Plaut, and F. Spiegelberg. "Critical Notices." Review of *Psychology and Religion: West and East*, by C. G. Jung. *Journal of Analytical Psychology* 4, no. 1 (Jan. 1959): 68–78.

Wilmer, Harry A. "Jung: Father and Son." *Quadrant* 18, no. 1 (Spring 1985): 35–40.

Winnicott, D. W. Review of *Memories, Dreams, Reflections*, by C. G. Jung. *International Journal of Psychoanalysis* 45 (1964): 450–55.

Woodman, Ross. "Finding the Hidden Freud." *Newsweek*, Nov. 30, 1981, 64–73.

———. "Literature and the Unconscious: Coleridge and Jung." *Journal of Analytical Psychology* 25, no. 4 (Oct. 1980): 363–75.

Wolff, Toni, 27, 73, 82, 83, 89
  omission of, from *Memories*, 5,
    85, 86
  usefulness for Jung, 87
  companion of Jung during
    creative illness, 74
women
  Jung's attitude toward, 81–82,
    91

omission of, from *Memories*,
  4, 6
wounded healer, 160
  Chiron as, 177
  Jung as, 2, 15, 75

Yahweh, 49, 94, 130–33

Zarathustra. See Nietzsche